D1617184

THE DOMESTIC ANALOGY AND WORLD ORDER PROPOSALS

Cambridge Studies in International Relations is a joint initiative of Cambridge University Press and the British International Studies Association (BISA). The series will include a wide range of material, from undergraduate textbooks and surveys to research-based monographs and collaborative volumes. The aim of the series is to publish the best new scholarship in International Studies from Europe, North America and the rest of the world.

CAMBRIDGE STUDIES IN INTERNATIONAL RELATIONS

THE DOMESTIC ANALOGY AND WORLD ORDER PROPOSALS

HIDEMI SUGANAMI
Lecturer in International Relations
University of Keele

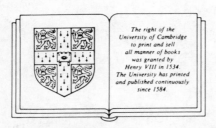

The right of the
University of Cambridge
to print and sell
all manner of books
was granted by
Henry VIII in 1534.
The University has printed
and published continuously
since 1584.

CAMBRIDGE UNIVERSITY PRESS
Cambridge
New York   Port Chester   Melbourne   Sydney

Published by the Press Syndicate of the University of Cambridge
The Pitt Building, Trumpington Street, Cambridge CB2 1RP
40 West 20th Street, New York, NY 10011, USA
10 Stamford Road, Oakleigh, Melbourne 3166, Australia

First published 1989

Photoset and printed in Great Britain by
Redwood Burn Limited, Trowbridge, Wiltshire

British Library cataloguing in publication data

Suganami, Hidemi
The domestic analogy and world order
proposals – (Cambridge studies in
international relations; 6)
1. Foreign relations. Theories
I. Title
327.1'01

Library of Congress cataloguing in publication data

Suganami, Hidemi.
The domestic analogy and world order proposals.

(Cambridge studies in international relations; 6)
Based on the author's thesis, submitted to the
University of London, 1985.
Bibliography.
Includes index.
1. International organization.   2. International
relations.   I. Title.   II. Series.
JX1954.S85   1989   341.2   89–883

ISBN 0 521 34341 0

CONTENTS

ACKNOWLEDGEMENTS

This book is based on my doctoral thesis submitted to the University of London in 1985. In the course of writing the thesis and transforming it into the present volume, I have incurred many debts.

The thesis was supervised by Professor Alan James at the LSE and, after his departure to Keele, by Mr Michael Donelan. Dr John Vincent of Nuffield College, Oxford, Dr Andrew Linklater of Monash, Mr Christopher Brewin of Keele and Ms Jane Davis of Aberystwyth were all generous in taking time to comment on my earlier drafts. Mr Murray Forsyth of Leicester and Dr Paul Taylor of the LSE, who jointly examined my thesis, gave me constructive criticisms and considerable support for its publication. Keele University granted me on four occasions a term's leave of absence which enabled me to continue my research. I am grateful to them all for having made it possible for me to initiate and carry out my study, and at long last to present its outcome in the form of this book.

In the second and third years of my study as a research student at the LSE I was fortunate enough to receive a Leverhulme Studentship and a Noel Buxton Studentship in International Relations. And in the autumn of 1987, I was awarded a Social Sciences Small Grant by the Nuffield Foundation. I am grateful to the trustees of the funds for their generous support. I would also like to thank Ms Pauline Weston of the Politics Department, Keele, for having typed the entire manuscript with speed and efficiency.

My greatest debt, however, is to my family in Japan, without whose understanding, encouragement and utterly unselfish support neither the thesis nor the present volume could have been written. It is to them that I dedicate this little book with gratitude.

INTRODUCTION

How beneficial is it from the viewpoint of world order to transfer to the domain of international relations those legal and political principles which sustain order within states? This has been one of the central questions in the study of international relations, and the term 'domestic analogy' has been used to refer to the argument which endorses such transfer. The 'domestic analogy' is presumptive reasoning which holds that there are certain similarities between domestic and international phenomena; that, in particular, the conditions of order within states are similar to those of order between them; and that therefore those institutions which sustain order domestically should be reproduced at the international level.

However, despite the apparent division, outlined in chapter 1, among writers on international relations between those who favour this analogy and those who are critical of it, no clear analysis has yet been made as to precisely what types of proposal should be treated as exemplifying reliance on this analogy. One of the central aims of this book is to clarify the range and types of proposal which this analogy entails, and chapter 2 makes a preliminary attempt at this task.

A substantial portion of this book (chapters 3–8) is devoted to the examination of the role which the domestic analogy has played in ideas about world order since the end of the Napoleonic Wars to the present. Particular attention is paid to the influence of changing circumstances in the domestic and international spheres upon the manner in which and the extent to which the domestic analogy has been employed.

The merits of the five main types of approach to world order which emerge from our analysis in chapters 3–8 are discussed in chapter 9. Each of the five types embodies a distinctive attitude towards the domestic analogy. The discussion shows that there are weaknesses in the approaches based on the domestic analogy, but that ideas critical of the analogy are not entirely flawless, and that some degree of concession to the analogy is beneficial.

Chapters 3–8 examine the role of the domestic analogy in six

1

historical periods. The following remarks by Morgenthau most suc-
cinctly account for the periodization in terms of which the materials are
arranged in chapters 3–5:

> While domestic liberalism converted public opinion in the eighteenth
> century and conquered the political institutions of the Western world
> during the nineteenth, it was not before the end of the Napoleonic
> Wars that important sectors of public opinion demanded the appli-
> cation of liberal principles to international affairs. And it was not
> before the turn of the century that the Hague Peace Conferences
> made the first systematic attempt at establishing the reign of liber-
> alism in the international field. Yet only the end of the first World War
> saw, in the League of Nations, the triumph of liberalism on the
> international scene.   (1946, 41)

If for 'liberalism' in the above passage we substitute its important
manifestations such as 'constitutionalism' or 'the idea of the rule of
law', the relevance of Morgenthau's remarks to the present study will
become clearer. Although the application of 'domestic liberalism' to
international relations is not the only way in which the domestic
analogy has been used, Morgenthau's periodization is useful for this
study. This is because liberalism has been a major force in the field of
activity which concerns this book although with the failure of the
League of Nations and the decline in the credibility of nineteenth-
century liberalism within the sphere of domestic politics, some important writers of the mid-twentieth century began to criticize the application of *laissez-faire* ideology to international relations.

Thus, in line with Morgenthau's periodization, we shall discuss in
chapter 3 the use of the domestic analogy in proposals for world order
formulated between the end of the Napoleonic Wars and the first
Hague Conference at the end of the century. This was the period in
which liberalism made advances within the domestic sphere while the
international system, despite a number of *ad hoc* conferences under the
Concert of Europe, remained relatively unorganized in terms of its
formal structure. Chapter 4 will examine the writings of the Hague
Conferences period, in which, internationally also, there began a rapid
development in the attempt to enhance the rule of law. But the optimism of the Hague Conferences period was soon to be shattered by the
outbreak of the Great War. The impact of this war upon the attitudes
towards the domestic analogy, and the use of this analogy by those
who were influential in the creation of the League of Nations will be
examined in chapter 5.

The League of Nations, however, soon began to show its inadequacies, while, within the domestic sphere, old liberalism had lost

much of its credibility. Chapter 6 will therefore examine attitudes towards the domestic analogy in the face of the failure of the League, and explore what ideas were developed against the new international and domestic backgrounds. Chapter 7 will then go on to assess which particular lines of thought identified in chapter 6 contributed most to the shaping of the new world organization, the United Nations, and examine the part the domestic analogy played in its establishment. Chapter 8 concludes the historical section by surveying the continuing role of the domestic analogy in contemporary international thought.

Chapters 3–8 may be considered as an attempt to write a history of ideas. In exploring the history of ideas in a relatively well-defined practice or discipline, such as physics, chemistry, mathematics, philosophy or theology, it is reasonable to confine one's attention to the ideas of the leading practitioners in the field. It is, moreover, relatively uncontroversial who these are. But in the area of activity which concerns this study, it is more difficult to agree on who the 'leading practitioners' might be, since it is not very much of an exaggeration to say that almost everyone has some ideas about how the world should be organized.

What this study aims at is to examine in some detail the attitudes towards the domestic analogy shown by a number of well-known writers on international law and relations in different historical periods. These writers have been chosen chiefly from those treated in major secondary works on peace projects. These include: Hinsley, *Power and the pursuit of peace* (1967); Schiffer, *The legal community of mankind* (1954); Beales, *The history of peace* (1931); Hemleben, *Plans for world peace through six centuries* (1943); Renouvin, *L'Idée de fédération Européenne dans la pensée politique du XIXe siècle* (1949); Phillimore, *Schemes for maintaining general peace* (1920); and Latané, *Development of the League of Nations idea* (1932). The writers from the more recent periods discussed in this study are chosen from among those familiar to the students of International Law and Relations particularly in the English-speaking world.

The publicists whose proposals are examined in this study are those from the above, and other related sources, and they have been chosen because their attitudes towards the domestic analogy illustrate strikingly the effects of the domestic and international circumstances in which proposals are formulated. However, to contrast with these writers, and to redress the balance, those whose views of world order and attitudes towards the domestic analogy are relatively unaffected by the historical changes in the domestic and international spheres are also included in our survey. The views of the authors examined in this

3

book may or may not be typical of each historical period in the purely statistical sense: it is the distinctive features of their views that attract our attention. It may be added here that none of the secondary sources listed above, with the exception of Beales 1931, examines proposals after the creation of the League of Nations, and even Beales does not treat fully ideas after 1919. By contrast, the present study attempts to bring the survey and analysis of world order proposals up to date.

Of the several secondary works listed above, Hinsley 1967 and Schiffer 1954 are by far the most important in terms of their range and depth of analysis. The other items, with the important exception of Renouvin 1949, which unfortunately is only a short essay, are mainly descriptive in character. While these serve as a useful source of reference they lack the historical and analytical depth of the works by Hinsley and Schiffer. Moreover, neither Hinsley 1967 nor Schiffer 1954 is without certain shortcomings which the present study endeavours to overcome.

The two chapters of Hinsley 1967, dealing with nineteenth-century proposals, which provide the basis of investigation for chapters 3–5 below, contain a number of serious factual inaccuracies. Hinsley relies heavily on secondary works, and does not appear to have studied his sources closely in writing these chapters. Care is taken in what follows to present all the proposals to be examined accurately without relying on secondary works. Moreover, Hinsley's argument that 'every scheme for the elimination of war that men have advocated since 1917 has been nothing but a copy or an elaboration of some seventeenth-century programme' (1967, 3) misleads one to assume that twentieth-century proposals have for the most part been written on the basis of the knowledge of earlier schemes, and underestimates the extent to which those proposals have been formulated with the awareness of the new historical context in the domestic and international spheres.

Schiffer 1954, while relatively accurate in exposition, overstresses the influence of natural-law thinking upon world order ideas. The gist of his argument is as follows.

Ordinarily, the existence and the binding force of legal rules presuppose the state. But the natural-law doctrine that there is law independent of any connection with a state made it possible to hold the view that the relations of states are governed by law despite the absence of universal state-like organization above the states. This idea was inherited by certain positivist writers despite their explicit rejection of the natural-law doctrine. The essence of the modern patterns of thought concerning world organization is that international law and order can be maintained by a League-type institution, that is, by an association of sovereign states which is not itself a state. Such a pattern of thought could not have arisen unless it had been assumed that there existed or could exist a legal order binding upon independent states. Such an assumption has its historical origin in natural-law doctrine, and, when combined with the idea of progress, contributed to the emergence of the League of Nations (Schiffer 1954, 8–9, 29, 107–8).

It is true, as Schiffer points out, that natural-law theorists advanced the idea that, despite the absence of a state-like organization above them, the relations of sovereigns or sovereign states were governed by a set of normative principles. It may also be true, although Schiffer does not show this historical link, that the natural-law theorists' ideas initially helped sovereigns and their officials to accept in practice the notion that their mutual conduct was governed by the law of nations. It is also true, although Schiffer does not make this point precisely enough, that unless such a notion had been accepted by the sovereign states themselves, it would not have been possible for anyone to argue that a League-type world organization could maintain law and order in international society. Unless international law were assumed by states to be binding upon them, no League-type organization could come into existence, for such a body would have to be constituted by a treaty, and this would presuppose the principle of *pacta sunt servanda* embedded in the law of nations. Moreover, unless states believed that they were bound by international law, there could not be any international law to be maintained by a League-type organization. To this extent, therefore, we may agree with Schiffer in seeing the link between the doctrine of natural law and the modern approach to world organization as represented by the League of Nations.

Moreover, certain similarities are found between the prescriptions of the natural-law writers and those of the advocates of a League-type organization. First, neither of them considers the establishment of a world state as a necessary condition for world peace. Second, the advocates of the League-type organization favour the prohibition of the use of force by states or at least the circumscription of the conditions under which states can legitimately resort to force. This corresponds to the *bellum justum* principle of the natural-law writers. However, not all natural-law writers fully supported the *bellum justum* principle. Vattel, in particular, in effect abandoned it (Forsyth, Keens-Soper and Savigear 1970, 121–5). Moreover, none of the classical natural-law writers, not even Grotius, argued that states have an *obligation* to aid the victim of aggression ([1646] 1925, bk 1, chap. 5, secs. 1–2;

bk 2, chap. 25, secs. 6 and 7). It is precisely the absence of such an obligation in international society that many advocates of a League-type world organization were most concerned to rectify.

However, in arguing for such a transformation of international society, what many of the planners of world organization have in mind is the way in which domestic society is organized. Indeed, compared with the near universal and conscious acceptance of the assumption by the advocates of a League-type institution that what is needed in the international sphere is the borrowing of some basic organizing principles from the domestic sphere, the case where they actually think of themselves as relying on the tradition of natural law appears extremely rare.

The natural-law theory, as Schiffer contends, may have made the modern idea of world organization *possible*. But, as the present study will show, what actually *shaped* the idea of world organization, which when the conditions were ripe led to the establishment of the League of Nations and the United Nations in this century, was the assumption that international society should become more closely analogous in its structure to domestic society. In what ways and to what extent international society should become more like domestic society was a question to which there were many different answers depending on how the 'domestic analogy' was used. And this in turn, as will be shown, often depended on the changing international and domestic circumstances under which proposals were formulated. Thus, to complement Schiffer's argument this book contends that it is because those who advanced world order proposals in the periods of our concern lived in separate states, and were invariably familiar with domestic institutions, that they conceived of a world organization in the ways they did.

A line of argument similar to this contention is advanced by Bull 1966b. However, in this article Bull contrasts Grotius ([1646] 1925) and Oppenheim (1905–6) as representing opposing attitudes towards the domestic analogy. Grotius, Bull maintains, makes important concessions to this analogy while Oppenheim's system is free of it (1966b, 65). The juxtaposition of these two writers is not entirely satisfactory since one is concerned primarily, though not exclusively, to reveal natural-law prescriptions while the other is concerned with the exposition of positive law (Grotius [1646] 1925, Prolegomena, esp. secs. 39–40; Oppenheim 1905–6, vol. 1, chap. 1, 1, sec. 1). Had the Grotian natural-law prescriptions been transformed into the positive law of nations, then it would have made better sense to compare that system with Oppenheim's, and to suggest that the Grotian system was more analogous than Oppenheim's to a domestic model. However, as they stood, the two systems were incommensurate. More importantly, as will be shown later in more detail, it is doubtful whether the thought process of such early writers as Grotius involved analogical reasoning. At the same time, as will be noted, Oppenheim in his own proposals for world order did make concessions to the domestic analogy, which Bull has failed to note. Thus, Bull 1966b is also inadequate from the viewpoint of an accurate presentation of the history of ideas regarding the domestic analogy.

The ideas and proposals that will be discussed in the following chapters are chiefly from English-speaking writers on international law and relations, although when helpful German- and, exceptionally, French-speaking writers have been consulted. Thinkers from the English-speaking world have contributed much to the growth of international institutions, as well as to the development of International Law and International Relations as academic subjects. Therefore, it is reasonable for us to focus our attention chiefly on these writers. Some prominent publicists on international law and relations in the English-speaking world, however, are Germanic in origin, and the study of their writings in some cases inescapably directs us to the works of other writers from the German-speaking world. This explains partly why a number of German writers, not very well known in the English-speaking world, are included in the following discussion.

The publicists whose ideas will be examined in the following chapters are not confined to academic writers. Particularly in dealing with the impact of the Great War and the birth of the League of Nations, it is necessary to study the ideas of those who were close to the process of its creation, and these include statesmen and government officials of the period. This step is indispensable, despite the emphasis this book places on academic writers, so as to reveal the extent to which the domestic analogy guided the creation of the League. This in turn is a necessary step in the development of this book as will be revealed in chapter 6 which examines the effect of the failure of the League on attitudes towards the domestic analogy. As it happens, some of the statesmen and government officials influential in the formation of the League were also academics or intellectuals, for example, President Wilson and General Smuts. The episode of the creation of the United Nations will be discussed in chapter 7 in relation to the main patterns of thought which arose in response to the failure of the League. Again, the ideas of those politicians and officials who directly influenced the eventual outcome will be investigated.

One of the reasons why the writers dealt with in this book are mainly academics or intellectuals is that their ideas are relatively easy to identify through their publications. Moreover, their professional skill often enables them to express their views in a clear and coherent manner. Furthermore, unlike government officials, their views may be less directly influenced by the concern for a particular country's national interests. In other words, we may expect to find more genuine instances of 'proposals for world order' in their writings.

Naturally, there are some academics and intellectuals who advance an argument whose nationalistic bias is easy to detect. Moreover, the concern for a particular social value, such as 'world order', may be an unconscious reflection of the position of the country to which a given author belongs. These are important points to bear in mind, but will not foredoom an attempt to explore ideas about world order held by the main type of thinkers included in this book. What is important is not to lose sight of the possible national and ideological biases of their proposals. Indeed, part of the aims of the discussion which follows is to reveal these very biases of the major writers on world order.

In sum, the main objectives of this book are threefold. First, to analyse what the domestic analogy is, and to clarify the range and types of proposal which arguments involving this analogy may entail. Second, to explain how changing domestic and international conditions have influenced the extent to which and the ways in which well-known planners of world organization from the early part of the nineteenth century to the present have resorted to the domestic analogy, and how some writers on international law and relations have attempted to remove this analogy from their ideas and proposals. And third, to classify the proposals discussed into major types in the light of their attitudes towards the domestic analogy, and to evaluate the merits of the main approaches which underlie these proposals. We shall begin, however, by taking a brief look at the 'domestic analogy debate' in the next chapter.

1 THE DOMESTIC ANALOGY DEBATE: A PRELIMINARY OUTLINE

According to Hans Morgenthau, 'the application of domestic legal experience to international law is really the main stock in trade of modern international thought' (1946, 113). More recently, Charles Beitz made a similar point when he remarked that 'most writers in the modern tradition of political theory, and many contemporary students of international politics, have conceived of international relations on the analogy of the [Hobbesian] state of nature,' and that 'perceptions of international relations have been more thoroughly influenced by the analogy of states and persons than by any other device' (1979, 179, 69). What the two writers are pointing to is the prevalent influence upon international thought of what some theorists of international relations call the 'domestic analogy'.

This analogy, however, has had its critics. Indeed, among many professional writers on International Relations, reliance on the domestic analogy appears no longer to be considered as a very respectable thing. This analogy is associated with 'all that was wrong' about the theory and practice of international relations before E. H. Carr (1939) wrote a telling critique of the League of Nations approach to the problem of world order. Moreover, those, such as C. A. W. Manning, who endeavoured to win for International Relations the status of an academic discipline saw in the modern states system unique qualities which, in their judgement, could best be appreciated if the habit of thought cultivated for the understanding of domestic social phenomena could be discarded (Suganami 1983). At the least there appeared something less than fully satisfactory in the use of analogy in a scientific pursuit which, within the limits of possibility, International Relations has aspired to be since its existence was recognized as a separate branch of academic enquiry (Bull 1966a, 45).

Within the discipline of International Relations, doubts about the domestic analogy, or about certain forms of this analogy, became more frequently expressed from about the 1930s. It may, however, be noted that a tendency to regard inter-state relations as fully comprehensible

9

only through the rejection of this analogy had existed among some political philosophers and legal theorists long before International Relations came to be treated as a special branch of academic enquiry.

Against the apparent intellectual legitimacy of the belief in the defectiveness of the domestic analogy, particularly among the contemporary academic specialists of International Relations, there lingers the notion that perhaps some form of domestic analogy is acceptable after all. To take one example, Andrew Linklater stated recently that 'a progressive development of international relations necessitates the transference of understandings of social relations from their original domestic setting to the international arena' (1982, 193). However, Moorhead Wright, in his review of Linklater's book, criticized him for a heavy reliance on the 'problematic analogy between domestic and international society' (1984, 235).

Clearly, the validity or otherwise of the domestic analogy has been a contentious issue in the study of international relations, and the debate continues today. It is the aim of this chapter to outline this debate. We shall first glance at those who have made critical remarks about the domestic analogy, and move on to those who appear to have supported it. This may seem to reverse the proper order of presentation, but it is not in fact unnatural since in the contemporary study of international relations the debate about the domestic analogy has been stimulated by those who consider it as problematic rather than by its supporters.

Critics

While the mode of reasoning here labelled the 'domestic analogy' has had a broad range of supporters and critics, the label itself is relatively uncommon. The term 'domestic analogy' has a somewhat pejorative connotation in that an analogical mode of reasoning is thought not to have the validity of logical deduction or the firmness of scientific induction. It is not surprising, therefore, to find one of the early instances of the use of the label in the writings of C. A. W. Manning, a critic of the domestic analogy.

Manning has some claim to be one of the founders of International Relations as an academic discipline in Britain, and perhaps, more broadly, in the English-speaking world (James 1973, Preface). It does not appear to be a pure coincidence that a scholar who devoted much of his life to the establishment of International Relations as a unique subject, dependent on, but separate from, Politics in particular, should also have been a critic of the domestic analogy. If international phenomena could be understood sufficiently well through the application of the existing ideas about domestic phenomena, then the claim for International Relations to be a separate subject would be undermined.

Manning's reference to the term 'domestic analogy' appears in the lecture entitled, 'The future of the collective system', which he delivered in 1935 at the Geneva Institute of International Relations. Having stated that a problem of promoting international order through international law and organization is a problem *sui generis*, 'one where analogies drawn from domestic experience may admit, at best, of only the most hesitant application' (1936, 165) he remarked:

> And now let us finally ask what will be the true, the only possible, foundation for any effectively functioning collective system? For once, I'll accept the domestic analogy. What, ultimately, is the basis of orderly coexistence within the local community? Nobody has put it more simply than Professor MacIver. You'll remember his phrase – 'the will *for* the State' – that is, the sufficiently prevalent disposition, if not to approve, then anyway to tolerate, the retention of those social arrangements that form the constitutional régime. Correspondingly, if the Collective System is ever to have the strength of the domestic order, it will be upon the foundation of an adequate 'will *for* the Collective System'. (1936, 174; emphasis Manning's)

Here the term 'domestic analogy' is used in a rather open-ended way to mean analogy drawn from domestic experience, from within the state.

A more specific definition of the term is given by Hedley Bull, upon whom Manning's thought exerted considerable influence (Bull 1966a, 35 n. 1; 1977, ix). Bull's ideas about international relations are widely known, and it may not be an exaggeration to say that he is one of the best-known critics of the domestic analogy in the English-speaking world today. According to him, the 'domestic analogy' is

> the argument from the experience of individual men in domestic society to the experience of states, according to which the need of individual men to stand in awe of a common power in order to live in peace is a ground for holding that states must do the same. The conditions of an orderly social life, on this view, are the same among states as they are within them: they require that the institutions of domestic society be reproduced on a universal scale. (1966a, 35)

In his many writings, Bull exhibits his long-standing concern to comprehend what he regards as the *sui generis* problem of international order with as little concession as possible to the domestic analogy (1966a, 1966b, 1971, 1977). Bull's acknowledged position on the question of the domestic analogy among contemporary writers is seen, for instance, in Ian Clark's work, where Bull's explanation of this analogy

11

cited above is reproduced and some of his critical remarks about idealism in general, and the domestic analogy in particular, are also quoted (1980, 26–7, 33, 49, 56). Bull's ideas about the domestic analogy are also referred to by Michael Walzer (1978, 58, 339 n. 9) and by Richard Falk (1968, 60 n. 27). David Fromkin praises Bull for many services he has performed and treats the domestic analogy disdainfully as 'false', though Bull's name is not mentioned in that context (1981, 45 n. 3, chap. 4).

The tendency to regard inter-state relations as fully comprehensible only by way of the rejection of the domestic analogy, however, had existed long before Manning or Bull. The idea that relations between states are not fully analogous to those between individuals is found in an embryonic form already in Hobbes.

As is well known, Hobbes used international relations as an example to illustrate his contention that the state of nature would be the state of war. However, it seems that he needed to explain why the state of nature among states (the international state of nature) had not led to the creation of a 'greater Leviathan' when, according to him, the state of nature among individuals (the pure state of nature) would result in the emergence of the state. He argued, therefore, that the state of nature among states was less intolerable to men than the pure state of nature. He wrote:

> But though there had never been any time, wherein particular men were in a condition of war one against another; yet in all times, kings, and persons of sovereign authority, because of their independency, are in continual jealousies, and in the state and posture of gladiators; having their weapons pointing, and their eyes fixed on one another; that is, their forts, garrisons, and guns upon the frontiers of their kingdoms; and continual spies upon their neighbours; which is a posture of war. *But because they uphold thereby, the industry of their subjects; there does not follow from it, that misery, which accompanies the liberty of particular men.*   ([1651] 1962, 144–5; emphasis added)

It is instructive to note here that Frederick Schuman, who was critical of the states system, when quoting the above and the subsequent paragraphs from Hobbes, deleted the italicized sentence, replacing it with a few dots (1969, 265). Those, like Schuman, who see in the fragmentation of the world into sovereign states the main cause of the unmitigated power struggle between peoples tend to identify the international state of nature with the pure state of nature without incorporating Hobbes' own qualification in this respect.

But the Hobbesian qualification, embryonic in his writing, became developed into the argument in the theory of international relations that the conditions of social order among states are not similar to the conditions of order among individuals. This line of thought was adopted and expanded by Spinoza, Pufendorf, Wolff and Vattel, some of whom clearly influenced Bull's conception of international law and relations (Spinoza [1677] 1958, 285; Pufendorf [1688] 1935, 163; Wolff [1764] 1934, Preface; Vattel [1758] 1916, Preface; Bull 1966b).

In addition, among some international lawyers, particularly of the late nineteenth and the early twentieth century, there was a tendency to regard international law as *sui generis*, although not all those who adhered to this view rejected the domestic analogy entirely (Lauterpacht 1933, chap. 20). In fact, the view of international society held by Manning, Bull and others who share their position, is in some respects similar to the doctrine of the specific character of international law advanced by such international lawyers. Thus Georg Jellinek, who was influential among the German adherents of this doctrine, characterized both international law and the community of states as 'anarchisch' (1922, 379), a description later to be popularized by Hedley Bull's *The anarchical society*.

Here we may outline Bull's argument to reveal the underlying rationale of the position against the domestic analogy. The starting point of Bull's analysis is that security against violence, observance of agreements and stability of property are the three primary goals of society (1977, 4–5). This is so, according to him, not only with any existing society, but also with the postulated world society of mankind.[1] A state is required to protect these goals, although, as Bull notes, primitive stateless societies are in their own ways also capable of maintaining order in the sense of the tolerable degree of satisfaction of these primary goals (1977, 53–65). But, as the classical writers suggested, when states have come into existence there is no overwhelming necessity for them to leave the international state of nature (Forsyth, Keens-Soper and Savigear 1970, 97). This is because, Bull argues, 'anarchy among states is tolerable to a degree to which among individuals it is not' (1966a, 45).

There are four grounds for this assertion. First, unlike the individual in the Hobbesian state of nature, the state does not find its energies so absorbed in the pursuit of security that the life of its members is that of mere brutes. The same sovereigns that find themselves in a state of nature in relation to one another have provided, within their territories, the conditions in which the refinements of life can flourish. Second, states in the international state of nature are free from all kinds of vulnerability to which individuals in the pure state of nature are subject. Third, to the extent that states are vulnerable to external

13

attacks, they are not equally so: the vulnerability of a great power is qualitatively different from that of a small state. This can be contrasted with the Hobbesian state of nature, where men are so little different in their individual physical abilities that even the weakest could have a fair chance of killing the strongest. Fourth, compared with individual human beings, states are much more economically self-sufficient. Thus states can survive without a high degree of economic co-operation much more successfully than can individuals among themselves (1966a, 45–8).

When Bull maintains that anarchy among states is tolerable to a degree to which among individuals it is not, it is a little unclear which two things he is comparing. Bull's first point, noted above, is that the international state of nature is not so intolerable to individuals as, to them, is the pure state of nature. Yet in his other three points, he is comparing the conditions of 'life' of the personified states in the international state of nature with the conditions of life of individual persons in the pure state of nature. Since such a term as 'vulnerability' or 'economic self-sufficiency' means different things when applied to individual persons and to personified states, it is doubtful whether there is much sense in comparing the two cases. Bull's point, therefore, may not be that states in the international state of nature are less vulnerable or more economically self-sufficient than are individuals in the pure state of nature, but rather that categories like 'vulnerability' and 'economic self-sufficiency' which we may use to characterize the life of individual persons do not apply in the same sense to personified states.

At any rate, on the four grounds noted above, Bull argues against the idea that what Hobbes suggested men in the state of nature would do, should be done in the international state of nature. As will be explained more fully later, a social contract among sovereign states to leave the international state of nature can be of two types, corresponding to what we shall call throughout this book the 'cosmopolitanist' and 'internationalist' forms of domestic analogy. The domestic analogy in the 'cosmopolitanist' form leads to an argument for a world state, and its 'internationalist' form produces an argument that certain basic principles of domestic society should be transferred to the international sphere without thereby altering the fundamental structure of international relations as a system of sovereign states. Bull is opposed to both, arguing against the substitution of a world state for the present sovereign states system, and, within the present system, against those elements of international law relating to the control of force in particular which have been introduced to the system in the twentieth century

14

under the influence of the ('internationalist') domestic analogy. In contrast, Bull advances an elaborate argument to the effect that states can maintain ordered relationships among themselves through the operation of what he calls the 'institutions of international society', namely, the balance of power, international law, diplomacy, war and the special role played by the Great Powers through their co-operation (1977, 65–74, pt 2). According to him, a world government may undermine individual liberty, and is no guarantee of peace and security where mutually hostile communities have to coexist; and the international law of the twentieth century, as embodied in the Covenant of the League of Nations, the Kellogg–Briand Pact and the Charter of the United Nations, is not only ineffective in the control of force, but also positively harmful to the maintenance of international order since it interferes with the operation of other institutions of international society, the balance of power and war in particular (1966a, 48–50; 1966b, 69–73; 1977, 142–5, 252–4, 283–8).

Bull acknowledges that the goals of economic and social justice, and of the efficient control of the global environment are hard to attain within the framework of the sovereign states system. However, in his judgement, even with respect to these goals, the states system is an acceptable mode of organizing the world. According to him, peace and security between separate national communities are a prerequisite for any move towards economic and social justice, or towards an improved control of the global environment, and the states system is a suitable means for obtaining these preliminary goals. Moreover, in his view, the states system does in fact make some, not inconsiderable, contribution and might even be expected in future to increase its contribution towards the goals of justice and efficient environmental control. At any rate, there is no assurance that a world government as such can render to mankind significant assistance in its pursuit of these goals since economic and social injustices and environmental problems have much deeper causes than the political organization of the world (1977, chap. 4, 288–95).

To the extent that we can treat Bull's argument as revealing the implicit assumptions and attitudes of those who oppose the domestic analogy, we can see that their position stems from a number of interrelated factors. Among them are: confidence in the sovereign states system to cope with multifarious problems facing mankind; a conservative inclination to prefer small adjustments within the system to its radical structural alterations; a clear differentiation between intrasocietal and inter-societal human relationships, and a tendency to see the state as a different kind of person from the individual; a relatively

15

low estimation of the degree to which the moral standards of human relationships at the international level can be brought up to those of the domestic sphere; a belief in the priority of security, order and peace to economic justice and social welfare; and the mistrust of legalism.

Supporters

Against the critics of the domestic analogy, going back as far as Hobbes and other classical writers and coming down through certain international lawyers to Manning, Bull and a number of other contemporary writers on international law and relations, there is the opposite tendency, to uphold the domestic analogy, which has been shared by a vast number of writers through the generations. The period of the First World War, leading to the creation of the League of Nations, teems with arguments based on this analogy as will be shown later. But even before the Great War, many thinkers had advanced arguments based upon it.

For example, James Lorimer, an Edinburgh Professor of Public Law and the Law of Nature and Nations, who put forward one of the most detailed proposals in Britain in his time for an international government, stated that the ultimate problem of international jurisprudence was to find international equivalents for the factors known to national law as legislation, adjudication and execution (1884, 2:186).

Lorimer conceded that the future ingenuity of man might discover 'a self-adjusting balance of power, a self-modifying European concert, or some other hitherto unthought-of expedient, which, in the hands of diplomacy, [would] act as a cheaper guarantee against anarchy' than could international institutions built on the analogy of municipal law (1884, 2:190). However, he maintained that, in the domestic sphere, the harmonious action of the three factors, legislation, adjudication and execution, had been found universally to be inseparable from the existence of the body politic (1884, 2:186–7). He argued that in the international sphere all the methods which had been suggested as being capable of creating and preserving order, but did not involve the establishment of an international government, for example, the balance of power or free trade, could be shown to be unsatisfactory (1884, 2:197–216). Thus, in Lorimer's view, an international government, embracing the functions of legislation, adjudication and execution was indispensable.

Lassa Oppenheim, who wrote a generation after Lorimer, is thought by some to belong to the other camp, the critics of the domestic analogy

16

(Bull 1966b, 52, 65). Indeed, he was opposed to an unlimited use of the analogy and, especially before the First World War, he was against the idea of introducing organized sanctions to international law (Oppenheim [1911] 1921, 21–2; 1905–6, 2:55–6). Nevertheless, he associated himself with the supporters of the domestic analogy when he stated in his well-known textbook that the progress of international law depended to a great extent upon 'whether the legal school of International Jurists prevail[ed] over the diplomatic school' (1912, 1:82). The legal school, according to Oppenheim, desired international law to develop more or less on the lines of domestic law,

> aiming at the codification of firm, decisive, and unequivocal rules of International Law, and working for the establishment of international Courts for the purpose of the administration of international justice. The diplomatic school, on the other hand, consider[ed] International Law to be, and prefer[red] it to remain, rather a body of elastic principles than of firm and precise rules. (1912, 1:82)

According to him, the diplomatic school opposed the establishment of international courts 'because it consider[ed] diplomatic settlement of international disputes, and failing this arbitration, preferable to international administration of justice by international Courts composed of permanently appointed judges' (1912, 1:82).

Among the better-known international lawyers of this century, one of the most determined critics of the tenets of the diplomatic school was Hersch Lauterpacht, a Cambridge professor and judge at the International Court of Justice. Lauterpacht expressed his ideas on the problem of world order through a number of scholarly writings. In one of his earlier works (1927), he revealed the extent to which the concepts, rules and institutions of contemporary international law were derived by analogy from domestic private law sources. However, the correspondence between private law and international law broke down in one important respect. Within a domestic system the use of force is generally prohibited, while in the international system the freedom of states to resort to force had traditionally been regarded as being outside the concern of positive law. Consequently, the acquisition of territory by conquest and, more broadly, the imposition of treaties under duress were permitted by the traditional system of public international law, while private law does not recognize such a mode of acquiring property or making contracts (Lauterpacht 1927, 105–6, 161–7).

Lauterpacht held that this lack of correspondence should not be regarded as an inevitable feature of the law of nations. He

17

characterized this dissimilarity as a 'missing link' of the two systems of law and remarked:

> The development of international law towards a true system of law is to a considerable degree co-extensive with the restoration of the missing link of analogy of contracts and treaties, *i.e.* of the freedom of will as a requirement for the validity of treaties, and with the relegation of force to the category of sanctions. The Covenant of the League of Nations, which, in its Article 10, safeguards the political independence and territorial integrity of the Members of the League from acts of external aggression, may be regarded as containing, *in gremio*, the elements of this development. (1927, 166–7)

It was probable, he speculated, that a body of rules might evolve which would closely correspond to public law within the municipal sphere, for instance, constitutional and administrative law (1927, 82 n. 2). However, such a development was hindered, he thought, by the influential doctrine of the specific character of international law (1933, chap. 20). In the field of adjudication, this doctrine manifested itself as that of the inherent limitations in the judicial process in international law, for the refutation of which he wrote another major work.

Lauterpacht's view that international law should not be treated as a type of law intrinsically different from municipal law was clearly stated in the following passage in that work:

> The more international law approaches the standards of municipal law, the more it approximates to those standards of morals and order which are the ultimate foundation of all law ... It is better that international law should be regarded as incomplete, and in a state of transition to the finite and attainable ideal of a society of States under the binding rule of law, as generally recognized and practised by civilized communities within their borders, than that, as the result of the well-meant desire to raise its formal authority *qua* law, it should be treated as the perfect and immutable species of a comprehensively diluted *genus proximum*. (1933, 432)

It is with this line of thought and possibly with this particular passage in mind that Manning, a critic of the domestic analogy and one-time colleague of Lauterpacht at the London School of Economics, was later to remark:

> It is more ... realistic to see international law as law of a different species, than as merely a more primitive form of what is destined some day to have the nature of a universal system of non-primitive municipal law. (1972b, 319).

The line of thought followed by Lauterpacht appears now to be somewhat out of fashion, and even in its heyday there were some who never fully subscribed to it, or were critical of it. The idea that the domestic analogy is misleading has become so well-established, it seems, that even those, like Richard Falk, who are progressivist in their outlook, warn against the reliance on this analogy (1970, viii-ix).

This does not mean that the domestic analogy has disappeared from contemporary international thought. We have already noted Andrew Linklater's remark, which appeared in 1982, regarding the transference of the understandings of social relations from their original domestic setting to the international sphere. A book published a few years before by Carey Joynt and Percy Corbett also endorses the domestic analogy as being essentially correct (1978, 48). However unfashionable in comparison to the first half of this century, there are still many advocates of international federalism and of world peace through law, as chapter 8 will reveal. Moreover, the domestic analogy can be said to form part of the assumptions of any contemporary writer on international affairs who attributes the instability of the international system primarily to its decentralized structure. Kenneth Waltz is one such writer, as can be seen in two of his major works (1959; 1979).

Just as the critics of the domestic analogy can claim, so to speak, a distinguished pedigree in the classical tradition of political and international thought, so can the supporters of this analogy. This, of course, does not mean that a pattern of thought with a distinguished ancestry is inherently superior. But it does suggest that the validity or otherwise of the domestic analogy has been one of the central concerns in the history of international thought.

When early instances of the domestic analogy are sought in the classical literature on international theory, it is sometimes suggested that they are to be found in the early writings on international law. Indeed it is well known that natural-law writers of the early modern period freely borrowed principles and concepts from municipal-law sources, the Roman *ius gentium* in particular, and applied them to their new subject matter (Lauterpacht 1927). In the words of T. E. Holland, the law of nations 'is an application to political communities of those legal ideas which were originally applied to the relations of individuals' (1898, 152).

It is questionable, however, that very early writers considered their legal reasoning as being specifically analogical when they asserted that certain principles governed the relations of sovereigns. These principles, in their view, were axiomatic and governed human conduct universally. It was because of this axiomatic universal validity that, in their view, natural law governed international relations. Thus, according to Joynt and Corbett, 'For the earliest writers, the law of nations . . .

was world law equally binding upon governments and individuals. The sovereign and the common man were alike members of a world community and, in their different stations, subjects of its law' (1978, 35).

In the natural-law tradition, the transfer of principles from the municipal to the international sphere was largely in the area of private law, although an element of public law was also transposed to the international sphere. Thus, as Michael Donelan points out, in the natural-law tradition, war was often conceptualized as a process whereby sovereigns were to act as *judges* (1983, 233–7). The idea that sovereigns should act as judges, or as if they were judges, however, differs from a proposal for establishing an international court in which there *are* judges. Although some natural-law writers commended arbitration and conferences (Grotius [1646] 1925, 185, 560–3), it was not their primary concern to advocate the reorganization of international society by transferring domestic constitutional institutions, such as the court of justice.

The writings of those who considered it as their primary task to propose a plan for the reorganization of international society may be said to form a separate genre from the works on natural law. Hinsley's *Power and the pursuit of peace* (1967) and a number of works concerned to exhume the precursors of the League of Nations idea, such as York, *Leagues of nations, ancient, mediaeval, and modern* (1919) and Hemleben, *Plans for world peace through six centuries* (1943), record many such plans. Among these, for instance, is Saint-Pierre's project which, according to Murray Forsyth's study, was inspired by the domestic analogy. In Forsyth's judgement, Saint-Pierre believed that 'the kind of arguments that Hobbes had used to demonstrate the necessity for men to unite into states, could be transposed one stage further to demonstrate the necessity for states themselves to form a universal union' (1981, 87). Furthermore, according to Forsyth, it is clear from Saint-Pierre's writings that 'the Swiss Confederation, the United Provinces of the Netherlands, and above all the Germanic Empire, provided the guidelines for the kind of organization that he wished to see established at the European level' (1981, 87).[2]

The observation that Saint-Pierre wrote his project under the influence of Hobbes is of great importance. It suggests that the domestic analogy entered the theoretical discourse on international relations when sovereigns or sovereign states came to be regarded as coexisting in the pre-societal state of nature. There is a clear tension between such a view of international relations and the older view that 'the sovereign and the common man were alike members of a world community and, in their different stations, subjects of its law'. The use of the domestic analogy indicated both the decline in the assumption of the universal moral community as a foundation of international theory and the felt need to reconstruct the international system so as to enhance co-operation between states or to realize the potential unity of mankind.

Statements along the lines of the domestic analogy are also found in Kant, who built on the works of Saint-Pierre and Rousseau. Kant wrote:

> What avails it to labour at the arrangement of a Commonwealth as a Civil Constitution regulated by law among individual men? The same unsociableness which forced men to it, becomes again the cause of each Commonwealth assuming the attitude of uncontrolled freedom in its external relations, that is, as one State in relation to other States; and consequently, any one State must expect from any other the same sort of evils as oppressed individual men and compelled them to enter into a Civil Union regulated by law.
>
> (Forsyth, Keens-Soper and Savigear 1970, 183)

In a later work, Kant also wrote:

> Inasmuch as the state of nature among nations, just like that among individual men, is a condition that should be abandoned in favour of entering a lawful condition, all the rights of Nations and all the external property of Nations that can be acquired or preserved through war are merely provisional before this change takes place; only through the establishment of a universal union of states (in analogy to the union that makes people into a state) can these rights become peremptory and a true state of peace be achieved.
>
> (Forsyth, Keens-Soper and Savigear 1970, 253)

Kant added the qualification that the universal union of states could not in fact take the form of a world state, but should be a 'permanent congress of states' (Forsyth, Keens-Soper and Savigear 1970, 253–4).[3] According to Forsyth, Kant gradually shifted his view on the extent to which justice could be realized within the existing framework of international relations, and, by the time the above passage was written, he had come to favour a less radical change than in his earlier days when he preferred a somewhat closer union of states (Forsyth 1981, 103). Nevertheless it remains the case that the basic structure of Kant's argument was along the lines of the domestic analogy: states must unite into an international body just as it was necessary for individuals to unite under separate states.[4]

Throughout the nineteenth century after the Napoleonic Wars many proposals for European or international organization were put forward. As early as 1814, at the time of the Congress of Vienna,

Saint-Simon in France advanced a proposal for the reorganization of European society. Towards the middle of the century, in the United States, William Ladd, the founder of the American Peace Society, formulated his plan for a Congress and a Court of Nations. Towards the end of the century, there was a project by James Lorimer mentioned earlier, and a counter-proposal advanced in Germany by J. C. Bluntschli. Proposals by these writers are examined in chapter 3.

Those who appear to support the domestic analogy are not uniform in their fundamental assumptions. For example, Saint-Pierre argued along utilitarian lines whereas Kant, by contrast, held it to be a moral imperative to overcome the unlawful conditions of the existing states system. Yet there are certain common elements in the beliefs and attitudes of those who appear to support the domestic analogy. Among them are: a general dissatisfaction with the ways in which the international system is organized, and, in some cases, an acutely critical attitude towards the sovereign states system as such; a belief in the possibility, or even the actuality, of the historical progress of mankind towards more harmonious relationships; the tendency to regard war as an unacceptable institution; the desire to transform the present conditions of international life in which power dominates into a more rational system based on free consent, and to expand the realm of the rule of law from within the state to external relations of states.

Qualifications

Thus we now have a rough picture of the debate about the domestic analogy. On the one hand, the opponents of the domestic analogy appear to include: Hobbes, Spinoza, Pufendorf, Wolff and Vattel; certain international lawyers of the late nineteenth and the early twentieth century who stressed the specific character of international law; Manning, Bull, and those who follow, or agree with, their basic tenets about the uniqueness of international society. On the other hand, the supporters of the domestic analogy seem to include: Saint-Pierre and Kant; Saint-Simon, Ladd, Lorimer and Bluntschli; Oppenheim, Lauterpacht, and those contemporary writers who follow their paths either in advancing a proposal or in diagnosing the conditions of international life.

It may be objected here that it is an anachronism to depict these individuals as having a *debate* about the domestic analogy. Apart from some exceptional instances where a debate appears actually to have taken place between a set of contemporary thinkers, the idea of a 'debate' is metaphorical. What can in fact be said to have existed are contending intellectual dispositions in the long line of speculation about the system of states.

In understanding these intellectual dispositions, however, we must also bear in mind the fact that a writer's own pronouncement on the validity or otherwise of the domestic analogy is not necessarily a reliable indicator of his actual position on the subject. This is mainly due to the fact that the concept of 'domestic analogy' has not been delineated with sufficient precision in the 'debate' about it. This may be because a paradigmatic instance of the domestic analogy is easy to see: the international police idea, for example. It may also be because the term 'domestic analogy' or its equivalents has been used more as a weapon of debate than as a tool of analysis. Under these circumstances cases are conceivable where one writer, who claims to favour the domestic analogy, and another writer, who claims to be opposed to it, turn out upon closer examination to be making a similar degree of concession to it. Those who in principle endorse the domestic analogy may in fact resort to it in such diverse ways that there may be a good deal of disagreement among them. Moreover, those who at first appear to be using the domestic analogy may turn out to be advancing a type of argument which is logically distinct from this analogy, and conversely, those who appear not to be using the analogy may turn out to have resorted to it in some way.

Since this book attempts to make sense of, and to scrutinize, commonly held ideas about how the world should be organized specifically from the viewpoint of their reliance on, or independence of, the domestic analogy, our first task must be to examine the range and types of this analogy. What types of proposals should be regarded as being based on this analogy? What kinds of argument will count as instances of the domestic analogy? These are the questions to be discussed in the next chapter. Only with some clear ideas about these questions can we hope to discuss how the domestic analogy has been used, or rejected, in proposals for world order.

2 THE RANGE AND TYPES OF THE DOMESTIC ANALOGY

It is important to point out at the outset that in the following pages the word 'analogy' is used in the sense of 'analogical reasoning.' The *Oxford English Dictionary* defines this sense of the word as: 'The process of reasoning from parallel cases; presumptive reasoning based upon the assumption that if things have some similar attributes, their other attributes will be similar'.

The term 'analogy' has a number of other related usages: to make the point that a treaty is like a contract, it is sometimes said (1) that there is an 'analogy' between treaty and contract, or, exceptionally, and perhaps incorrectly, (2) that the 'domestic analogy' of treaty is contract. In (1), the word 'analogy' means 'correspondence', 'affinity' or 'similarity', and in (2) it really means an 'analogue', 'counterpart' or 'comparable object'. This book, however, is concerned with 'analogy' only in the sense of 'analogical reasoning.' The term 'analogy' will be used in this sense alone throughout the following discussion except when it has been used otherwise in a passage to be quoted from other works.

The 'domestic analogy', then, may broadly be defined as presumptive reasoning (or a line of argument embodying such reasoning) about international relations based on the assumption that since domestic and international phenomena are similar in a number of respects, a given proposition which holds true domestically, but whose validity is as yet uncertain internationally, will also hold true internationally. A line of argument involving the domestic analogy therefore assumes explicitly or implicitly that there are some similarities between domestic and international phenomena, that there already exist some propositions which hold true domestically and internationally. It also asserts that a certain other proposition is valid with respect to the domestic sphere. And, without being able as yet to demonstrate the truth of the proposition with regard to the international sphere, it concludes, presumptively, that the proposition will hold true internationally also.

24

The exclusion of logical deduction

There is one particularly important point to notice with regard to the structure of argument constituting the 'domestic analogy'. It is the fact that the proposition which is said by the argument to be valid domestically, and hence, by analogy, internationally also, must *not* be of the kind which is true, or presented as true, independently of substantiation in the light of domestic phenomena. To put it another way, the proposition must be of the type whose validity requires substantiation with reference to domestic phenomena. This important observation draws attention to two types of argument which are not analogical arguments at all, and which accordingly are excluded from the category of the domestic analogy.

One is the case of logical deduction from a normative proposition asserted to be valid in any human context, domestic, international or otherwise. For example, it might be held that the precept that promises must be kept applies universally in any human context. If that is the starting point of one's argument, then the conclusion that treaties must be kept follows logically. The force of the argument does not depend on the credibility of analogical reasoning, but entirely on the validity of the normative stance taken at the outset because a treaty *is* a form of making promises.

The other type of argument also excluded from the category of analogical reasoning, and hence that of the domestic analogy, is a case of logical deduction from a statement which must necessarily be true regardless of its substantiation with reference to the domestic or international sphere. Perhaps the best illustration of this case is found in Manning, and his example is particularly noteworthy because he himself mistook his line of argument to be an instance of the domestic analogy (1936, 174).

As we noted in the previous chapter, Manning maintained that in order for a social system to function effectively, there would have to be a sufficiently prevalent disposition among its units at least to tolerate it. From this he concluded that in order for the 'Collective System' under the League of Nations to function effectively, there would have to be a sufficiently prevalent disposition among states at least to tolerate it.

However, given that any social system is at least partly human- . operated, Manning's initial premise cannot fail to be true. The crucial word, 'sufficiently', makes the statement true by definition, and accordingly any attempt at substantiation would be quite redundant. After all, if the disposition at least to tolerate the system were

25

insufficiently prevalent among its units, the system could not function effectively. And since the 'Collective System' is, just like any other social system, at least partly human-operated, it follows logically (and not by the force of any analogy) that its effective functioning cannot but require a sufficiently prevalent disposition among states at least to tolerate it.

In suggesting that he was, for once, accepting the domestic analogy in the above context, Manning appears to have assumed that a 'social system' meant a society of individuals and that therefore the 'Collective System', a system of states, was not actually a 'social system': it was *like* a 'social system'.[1] However, whether Manning was aware of it or not, his initial premise was structured so as to apply to any social, at least partly human-operated, system. Thus, there is no need to say that the term 'social system' in his initial premise should only mean a society of individuals. Indeed, to do so would be to draw an unnecessary demarcation line between 'social' and 'international'. It is on the basis of this demarcation, which was unnecessary in the context of his initial premise, that Manning appears erroneously to have conceived of his reasoning as being analogical. This may be an instance where his determination to see international phenomena as *sui generis* clouded his power of analysis.

The exclusion of two other types of argument

There are at least two other types of argument, which, unlike the cases of logical deduction, might satisfy a broad definition of the 'domestic analogy', but will not be included in our discussion. One is municipal law analogies within the sphere of legal reasoning.

D. W. Bowett, for example, has argued that the right of collective self-defence under Article 51 of the United Nations Charter cannot be exercised by a state which could not legally have exercised a right of individual self-defence in the same circumstance (1958, chap. 10). This interpretation, as Michael Akehurst points out, is based partly on analogies drawn from English law at the time Bowett was writing. At that time, English law did not allow one person to use force in defence of another unless there was a close relationship, for example a family relationship, between the two persons concerned (Akehurst 1984, 224).

Bowett's argument is advanced as an interpretation of existing international law. Although, admittedly, the boundary between what is to count as an interpretation of existing international law and what is in effect an argument about desirable international law may in some cases be obscure, municipal law analogies which occur within the framework of legal discourse, purporting to state what the law is on a given issue, will not form part of the concern of this book.

The other type of argument, also excluded from our purview, has to do with the definition of those words which occur both in the domestic and international contexts. Take the word 'law' for example. Many writers distil the definition of 'law' from what they see in municipal legal systems, and then go on to judge whether international law is really law or not by the domestically arrived-at criteria (Kelsen 1967, 3–173). In so doing they are deliberately or unwittingly carrying over to the international context the definition which is appropriate in the domestic context.

Interestingly, in some cases the claim that international law is not 'law' because it does not satisfy the domestically arrived-at criteria is mixed in with the logically separate claim that in order to serve effectively as a means of maintaining international order international law must develop along the lines of municipal law (Nardin 1983, 119–20). The latter is clearly an instance of the domestic analogy whereas the former might be called an international application of a domestic definition. This may in fact be a subspecies of the 'domestic analogy' as broadly defined. However, this type of reasoning about the meaning of words which have domestic and international uses will not be included in our discussion unless it has a direct bearing on ideas about world order.

So far we have supplied a broad definition of the 'domestic analogy', and distinguished it from two types of argument which are instances of local deduction. We have also pointed out that neither municipal-law analogies in legal argument nor what might be called an international application of domestic definitions will form part of our concern. We now move on to examine what types of proposal will count as embodying the domestic analogy. One effective way of conducting this examination is to scrutinize Bull's seemingly innocuous formula that according to the domestic analogy 'the institutions of domestic society be reproduced on a universal scale' (1966a, 35). This formula is chosen for our discussion because it epitomizes the type of domestic analogy which is central to our enquiry, and yet it is so general as to leave many ambiguities. We shall first delineate the types of purpose which proposals based on the domestic analogy may aim to achieve. This will be followed by an investigation into the means suggested by this analogy.

Purposes

Bull has explained the domestic analogy as the argument which holds the conditions of an orderly social life to be the same among states as they are within them. However, 'order' is not the sole purpose of those proposals whose reliance on (or independence of) the domestic analogy we may discuss. Although Bull himself distinguishes not only between 'order' and 'justice', but also between 'order' and 'peace', it would be unreasonable if he were to insist that only those proposals which were concerned with 'order' could be of interest in discussing the domestic analogy.[2] Thus we shall include in our purview analogical arguments concerning the conditions not only of order, narrowly defined, but also of other related social goals, such as peace, security, welfare and justice in international society. This last phrase, 'in international society' points to the fact that in order to count as an instance of the domestic analogy a proposal must aim at the realization of a social goal or goals which can appropriately be characterized as 'international'. The idea of an international goal, or purpose, however, needs to be looked at carefully.

Typically, a proposal based on the domestic analogy will suggest, for example, that just as order among individuals within a state requires a national police force, so order in international society requires an analogous institution, an international police force. There will be little hesitation in characterizing such a proposal as one dependent on the domestic analogy. What can be said, however, if a proposal for an international institution, which is in some way inspired by a domestic model, aims chiefly at the simultaneous attainment of a certain goal *within* each member-state?

For example, it may be proposed that the problem of unemployment cannot be solved without an international authority which can co-ordinate the economic policies of separate states. An institution proposed on such an assumption may have been inspired by a domestic model, for example, an economic planning agency, but will be designed chiefly for the purpose of creating jobs for the citizens of separate states. This kind of goal may not be characterized as 'international', unlike the purpose, for example, of an international police force, which is the maintenance of order *between* states, and which may therefore be said to be 'international'. The subjects of economic and social welfare which an international agency of the kind under consideration aims to enhance are not states coexisting in international society, but men and women located in separate states. The purpose of

28

such an agency may therefore be better characterized as 'cross-national'.

Despite such a consideration, a proposal for an international economic planning agency for the solution of the unemployment problem is in fact similar to a proposal for an international police force: they both stress the need to upgrade the level of management from the domestic to the international, and to seek a solution in international institutional co-operation in the place of self-help by each state. Moreover, the difference between the two types of proposal in regard to the location of their respective problems (in the one case, 'between' states and in the other, 'within' each state) is more apparent than real. What is apparently a domestic issue (an issue 'within' each state), such as the problem of unemployment, can in fact be regarded as an international issue (an issue 'between' states) to the extent that its full solution cannot be obtained without recourse to *international* co-operation.

It may be noted that whereas the international police idea is based on analogical reasoning involving the personification of states, the economic agency idea does not rely on the notion that states are like natural persons. Yet the latter idea does involve the notion that just as certain economic problems within a state require domestic economic planning, so other economic problems, which are experienced within each state, but are international in terms of the location of their cause, require international economic planning. This would seem to satisfy the broad definition of the 'domestic analogy' we adopted at the beginning of this chapter. Therefore, in the following pages both types of proposal will be included in our survey, although the difference between the two types will be noted when we encounter actual examples.

Means

From the investigation into purposes, we may turn to the means: what means are suggested by those proposals which can be regarded as involving the domestic analogy? According to Bull, the means offered are the 'reproduction of the institutions of domestic society on a universal scale'. What is meant by 'institutions' here?

1 Institutions

Perhaps it is natural to assume that by 'institutions' Bull has in mind legal institutions of a state. But the term 'institutions' has a somewhat broader connotation than legal arrangements or devices, and includes rules, practices and conventional techniques of a society which are not expressed in the form of law. Bull himself includes under the category of 'institutions' conventional rules and practices which are non-legal (1977, pt 2).

A point made by Inis Claude (1962, 255–71) is relevant here. He is critical of the domestic analogy exercised in a legalistic fashion, particularly where the argument is based on the criminal-law model. But he is not opposed to borrowing political techniques for the management of power from within the sphere of domestic politics to apply to the international domain. Thus, in his view, what we can fruitfully learn from our domestic experience is not how a government deals with individual robbers, but how, through 'sensitive and skillful operation of the mechanisms of political adjustment' (1962, 271), it deals with the problem of maintaining order among conflicting groups.

'Sensitive and skillful operation', on the part of a government, 'of the mechanisms of political adjustment' is a rather vague formulation. None the less, it seems doubtful that one can be said to be resorting to the *domestic* analogy unless the guiding principles of such an operation, whose application to the international sphere one is proposing, belong primarily to the realm of domestic politics. By this we mean that the principles' effectiveness in bringing about the desired ends must have some support based on observations about domestic phenomena, but that their applicability to the international sphere must as yet be lacking in substantiation. This point may be clarified by the following example.

One of the most essential techniques of the non-legal kind for the management of power is, in some writers' view, the balance of power. This is treated by some writers not only as the most fundamental, but also as a distinctive, institution of international society (Bull 1966a, 48). However, there are also some, like J. Allen Smith, who see the balance of power idea in international relations as 'merely an application of the check and balance theory of the state to international politics' (Morgenthau 1973, 170 n.5). Thus, according to one view, an argument in favour of the balance of power as a means of creating and maintaining international order will not count as an instance of the domestic analogy while, according to another view, it will.

As we noted above, however, a proposal can only be regarded as an instance of the domestic analogy if the institution in question belongs primarily to the domestic sphere. The balance of power does not satisfy this condition since it is a device or technique found both in the domestic and international spheres. Moreover, the balance of power is a practice which statesmen had operated in inter-state relations long before the idea began to be formulated in theoretical terms (Wight 1973, 86). Thus, while some theorists may have argued, along with J. Allen Smith, that the balance of power in international relations is an application of a domestic political theory and practice, this does not provide a sufficient ground for saying that a proposal for the mainten-ance of international order through the balance of power is essentially an instance of the domestic analogy. If the argument which supports the proposal is explicitly based on a domestic model, however, it will be difficult to deny that in that particular instance its author is resorting to the domestic analogy, although it is unnecessary for him to have done so.

Let us return to the Bull formula of the domestic analogy, as there are a number of other points which require clarification. In Bull's view, the 'domestic analogy' holds that 'the institutions of domestic society be reproduced on a universal scale'. It has been noted that here Bull probably has in mind the legal institutions of domestic society. In this context, however, he could not have in mind *all* the legal institutions of domestic society. However much we may be used to thinking of states as though they were persons, not all legal institutions relating to natural persons are relevant to entities which are persons only by imputation (Dickinson 1916–17).

Thus Bull may be saying that, according to the 'domestic analogy', most of the important legal institutions of domestic society, which can meaningfully be applied to international relations, should be repro-duced on a universal scale. According to this criterion, there might be little doubt that James Lorimer, for example, was resorting to the domestic analogy since he advocated the creation of an international government consisting of a legislature, judicature and executive.

One important question arises here, however. If, for example, one advocates the need for an international legislature and judicature, but argues against the necessity for an international executive organ, can one still be said to be using the domestic analogy? The answer must be in the negative, if we understand the 'domestic analogy' to be an argument in favour of creating most of the important institutions of domestic society which can meaningfully be applied to international relations, for clearly an executive organ is one of such institutions.

In fact, some writers stress the absence of an executive organ from their proposals as one of their distinctive features. Oppenheim, for example, was emphatic that his proposed international organization was *un*state-like precisely because of this feature ([1911] 1921, 16, 21–2). Bull, as we saw, has remarked that according to the domestic analogy 'the need of individual men to live in awe of a common power

31

in order to live in peace is a ground for holding that states must do the same' (1966a, 35). The Hobbesian phrase 'in awe of a common power' suggests that, like Oppenheim, Bull may be of the opinion that a proposal which does not involve the creation of an international executive authority does not count as an instance of the domestic analogy.

However, there is an important distinction to be drawn between the assertion that one's proposed international organization is *un*state-like, and the assertion that there is no element of the domestic analogy in one's proposal. In the first place, however *un*state-like, the proposed body may have some residual affinity with the state. After all, no organization is perfectly state-like unless it actually is a state. Secondly, regardless of the degree of affinity which may exist between the organizational structure of the state and that of the proposed body, one's argument in support of the proposed body may be based explicitly on analogical reasoning derived from domestic experience.

Thus, the absence of a particular domestic-type institution from a proposed entity does not by itself show that the proposal is free of the domestic analogy. Oppenheim's own project gives a good illustration here, because, despite his claim that his proposed body was *un*state-like, he explicitly based his argument for the establishment of an international court and courts of appeal upon the experience of the judicial system in the domestic sphere ([1911] 1921, 14, 51–2).

This leads to the conclusion that even if one's proposal is far more modest than, for instance, James Lorimer's, and even if it only suggests, for example, that arbitration should become an international practice in the place of war, the proposal may be said to involve the domestic analogy. This is because an international system equipped with an arbitration treaty is more analogous to the domestic system than is an international system not so equipped. Moreover, however negligible the affinity between the proposed body and a domestic system, the proposal may nevertheless be based explicitly on the domestic analogy. Thus, for example, although the proposal advanced in the middle of the nineteenth century by an American peace advocate, William Jay was, as a practical first step, simply to insert an arbitration clause in the next treaty between the United States and France, he must none the less be said to have resorted to the domestic analogy since he wrote as follows in support of his plan:

> Individuals possess the same natural right of self-defence, as nations, but the organization of civil society renders its exercise, except in very extreme cases, unnecessary, and therefore criminal ... Instead ... of

resorting to force, he [a citizen] appeals to the laws. His complaint is heard by an impartial tribunal, his wrongs are redressed, he is secured from farther injury, and the peace of society is preserved.

No tribunal, it is true, exists for the decision of national controversies; but it does not, therefore, follow that none can be established . . . It is obvious that war might instantly be banished from Europe, would its nations regard themselves as members of one great society, and, by mutual consent, erect a court for the trial and decision of their respective differences. ([1842] 1919, 52–3)

The same type of question as arose in relation to the balance of power earlier may arise in the case of arbitration. Is 'arbitration' primarily a domestic institution? The problem here is that the practice of arbitration could be traced back to ancient Greece. It may be argued that arbitration is not primarily a domestic institution on the grounds that the ancient Greeks resorted to it in resolving disputes between their city-states.[3]

This appears to be a rather strained argument, however. Arbitration has not always been a well-established institution of international relations. Thus there does not seem to be a strong enough reason to insist that an argument in favour of arbitration in the international sphere does not count as an instance of the domestic analogy, unless, of course, the argument specifically uses as models examples from the international sphere, such as the practice of arbitration between Greek city-states.

It ought perhaps to be stressed here that for a proposal to count as an instance of the domestic analogy it is sufficient that the institution concerned is found primarily in domestic society, that the institution's effectiveness in bringing about the desired ends has some substantiation from within the domestic sphere, but is as yet lacking in international substantiation. To put it more fully, the institution need not be an *essential* institution of domestic society in the sense of being a defining condition of a state. There are a number of institutions found primarily, or even exclusively, within the domestic sphere which are not integral to the concept of state. The arbitral tribunal, as opposed to a judicial authority, may itself be among them. The institution of the courts of appeal is another. A parliament is not integral to the concept of state, and even the police is a relatively modern invention (Morgenthau 1964, 211ff.). It would be absurd to insist that a proposal for the reproduction of any of these institutions in international society was not an instance of the domestic analogy because they were not essential to the concept of state.

2 Domestic society

This leads to another problem which arises from the Bull formula. He refers to the 'institutions of domestic society', but what precisely is *domestic* society? The term 'domestic' indicates that the society, the transfer of whose institutions into the international sphere is in question, should itself be a state. Hence Bull's own remark that according to the domestic analogy the conditions of social order are the same 'among states as they are within them'.

But what is *the state*? Some difficulty can arise here because it is usual to consider 'unitary states' and 'federations' as 'states', but to exclude 'confederations' from the category of 'states'. The German terms 'Bundesstaat' and 'Staatenbund' express this point well. A federation (Bundesstaat) is a state (*Staat*), but a confederation (Staatenbund) is a union of states (*Staaten*). If someone who proposes a scheme for world order argues that the institutions of a certain confederation be transferred to international society, in other words, if his model is a confederation and hence not a state, he may well claim that no *domestic* analogy is involved in his scheme. In an intellectual environment where the domestic analogy is treated with suspicion, a claim not to be using the domestic analogy, because the model employed is confederal, is one which an advocate of such a scheme may well advance.

However, a confederal model, while it is, strictly speaking, not a domestic model, is not a genuine 'international' model either. A confederation embodies institutions which are either borrowed from, or similar to those of, the domestic sphere. Thus, a confederal model is, so to speak, a second-order domestic model. Because of this it would seem more advisable to include in our purview those cases where confederal models are used than to exclude them from it entirely. Here it may be noted that Oppenheim, for example, included in his scope of 'state-like' entities not only unitary and federal states, but also confederations ([1911] 1921, 16).

The ambiguity arising from the case where the model used is confederal is not of marginal significance. It directs our attention to the degree of artificiality involved in separating institutions into those of the domestic sphere and those of the international sphere. The division between the two types of institution is somewhat obscured by the presence of confederations in the middle. Another factor which can obscure the division is the historical development of international institutions.

We may suppose that since the time Saint-Simon put forward his proposal ([1814] 1952) for the reorganization of European society at the end of the Napoleonic Wars, the principles which govern inter-state relations have become somewhat more analogous to those pertaining to the domestic sphere. Disregarding for the moment the effectiveness of those institutions which have been transferred from the domestic to the international sphere since the time of Saint-Simon, and especially since the end of the First World War, we may say that institutional grafting has already taken place to some extent. This means that those who formulate a scheme for the reorganization of international society, unlike in earlier times, may no longer have to depend on the domestic analogy explicitly. This point can be illustrated by comparing the arguments of William Jay, noted earlier, and those of the Bryce group for the establishment of a League of Nations.

As we saw, writing in the middle of the nineteenth century, Jay, in a relatively unambitious proposal for the eventual creation of an international tribunal, had argued explicitly on the basis of domestic experience. But, by the time the First World War was fought, international society had seen some degree of institutionalization. Thus, rather than turning to strictly domestic experience, the Bryce group, in the period of the Great War, could propose the establishment of a League of Nations on the basis of existing international institutions, such as the 'Bryan Treaties' and the Hague system of arbitration, although, admittedly, 'teeth' were to be added to them. The Bryce group argued that they were building upon existing facts and tendencies of international life, and claimed that they were not advocating a revolutionary change, but an orderly development. This claim had some plausibility because the suggested change was small enough to enable the plan to be explained more economically as a generalization and systematization of existing international institutions than in terms of any domestic model (Bryce *et al.* 1917, 14–15).

This does not mean that the Bryce group proposal was not in the end based on the domestic analogy. What this example shows is that a dividing line between the institutions of domestic society and those of international society is historically variable. This point will be discussed further in relation to the Bryce group proposal itself in chapter 5.

3 *Reproduction*

Finally, Bull's view that according to the 'domestic analogy' the institutions of domestic society be 'reproduced on a universal scale' requires attention. 'Reproduction', in this context, can take one of two basic forms, one retaining the sovereignty of the states involved, the other removing their sovereignty altogether.

If it is proposed that the sovereign states system should remain intact, but that the relations between legally independent political communities should now be governed by a legal system containing a set of principles more analogous to those of municipal law than at present embodied in international law, then the proposed reproduction of the domestic institution is of the first form. By contrast, if the suggestion is that the new entity should be organized in such a way that it will itself count as a sovereign state, then the proposed reproduction is of the second kind. The first form of reproduction is less far-reaching than the second since in the second case the existing sovereign states will transform into provinces of a unitary state or member-states of a federal union.

Paradoxically perhaps, there may be a case for saying that of the two basic types only the first form of reproduction should count as an instance of the domestic analogy. This rests on the following consideration. To the extent that the domestic analogy is interpreted as an argument which holds the conditions of order (or other related social goals) to be the same either within or among sovereign states, in each case requiring the same type of institution, the argument can be understood to hold that the type of institution in question must govern sovereign states *as such*, that is, without affecting their constitutional independence.[4] Therefore, on this view the second basic form of reproduction under consideration, inasmuch as it advocates the replacement of the sovereign states system by a universal sovereign state, cannot count as an instance of the domestic analogy. Thus, for example, when Frederick Schuman argued that reforms within the framework of the sovereign states system were unsatisfactory, and that peace required the replacement of the sovereign states by a world state, his advocacy, on this view, was not an instance of the domestic analogy – it was something beyond (1945; 1954, 419–20).

However, this view of the domestic analogy may be considered as a little too narrow. The difference between the two basic forms of reproduction may be seen as a matter of degree inasmuch as the two types of body resulting from them, seen from the viewpoint of formal structure, are different only in terms of the degree of centralization. Moreover, if the 'domestic analogy' is seen to lead to an argument that domestic-type institutions be employed to govern the relations of those communities *at present* divided into sovereign units, it can be made to encompass both types of proposal.

It is interesting to note here that Bull himself seems to have no hesitation in considering as an instance of the domestic analogy an argument in favour of the replacement of the sovereign states system by a single universal state (1966b, 53, 65). In fact, it even appears that the first form of reproduction discussed above, in Bull's view, is not actually an argument based on the domestic analogy, but one which makes 'concessions to it' (1966b, 65). In the following discussion both forms of reproduction noted here will be included under the rubric of the domestic analogy. A distinction will be made between them, however, by calling the type of domestic analogy embodying the first form of reproduction 'internationalist', and the other mode of domestic analogy 'cosmopolitanist'. The existence of the two types of domestic analogy is consonant with the fact that, unlike the social contract among individuals to move out of the state of nature, the corresponding social contract among states can either leave each state's personality (or sovereignty) intact, or remove it altogether.

A summary and further preliminary observations

The foregoing discussion reveals that the domestic analogy has a very wide range of instances. It will be useful to summarize the main points made so far.

The domestic analogy is an analogy drawn from observations about domestic phenomena, and it must be distinguished from logical deduction from those propositions which are true, or purported to be true, independently of substantiation in the light of domestic experience. Proposals based on the domestic analogy may aim to achieve not only order in international relations, but also such other related social goals as peace, security, welfare and justice.

The domestic analogy typically involves the personification of states, but as we saw in the case of a proposal for an international economic planning agency for the solution of the unemployment problem within each state, a scheme which does not rely on the idea that states are like natural persons may still count as an instance of the domestic analogy.

A proposal based on this analogy will suggest that the institutions of domestic society, that is, those which are found primarily in the domestic sphere, but are not necessarily legal in character, should be transferred to the international sphere. For a proposal to count as an instance of this analogy, the institutions to be transferred to the international sphere need not be essential institutions of domestic society in the sense of being part of the defining conditions of the state. The institutions to be transferred may encompass many of the important institutions of domestic society which can meaningfully be transferred to the international sphere, but the domestic analogy may lead to a much less extensive scheme. A body proposed on the basis of the domestic analogy can therefore take a wide variety of forms. We have also argued that those proposals which advocate the creation of a single state, unitary or federal, in the place of the existing sovereign states will count as an instance of the domestic analogy.

A claim not to be using the domestic analogy because the model employed is confederal or because the proposed institution is no more than a slightly modified version of what already exists in the international sphere creates some difficulty. A confederal model, however, is not a genuine international model, and can be interpreted as a second-order domestic model. Whether or not the domestic analogy is being used where the proposed organization is merely a slightly modified version of what already exists in the international sphere is a question which should best be examined when we face a concrete example.

In the following pages, proposals to be examined are referred to as 'world order proposals,' or treated as falling into that category. This should not be taken to mean that we are excluding proposals for peace, security, welfare or justice. As it will be tedious to have to spell out each time that we are talking about proposals for order or other related social goals such as peace, security, welfare or justice, we will use the term 'world order' as a convenient shorthand for all.

Nor shall we exclude from our discussion those proposals which do not encompass the whole world. Historically, schemes designed to cover all the nations of the world are relatively rare. A large proportion of them are concerned with major countries of the world, chiefly European nations and the United States. In some cases, proposals were formulated for a small number of states with a clear expectation that the number would gradually increase. In other cases, authors appear to have thought that if order could be achieved between the major countries of the world, the problem of 'world' order would largely be solved. In other cases, especially in an earlier period, some European writers may have been sufficiently Eurocentric not to be concerned with problems outside Europe: to them Europe was the world. In any case, it is only in the recent period that proposals to encompass the whole world began to be advanced, and hence the necessity to distinguish between schemes for 'regional' organization and those for 'global' organization began to be felt. Although from today's standpoint this distinction is significant, its utility as a tool of analysis is limited when we consider proposals from an earlier period. In the following discussion, therefore, unless there is a special reason for the purpose of exposition to characterize a proposal as one for 'regional' order as opposed to 'world' order, it will be treated as belonging to the general category of 'proposals for world order'.

It should be added here that, in the following, 'world' order and 'international' order are used interchangeably unless otherwise specified. It may be possible to draw a distinction between the two along the lines suggested, for example, by Hedley Bull. According to him, the units which enjoy 'international' order are sovereign states while the units of 'world' order are individuals (1977, 20–2). However, most authors discussed in the following use terms such as 'international peace and order', 'world peace', 'peace and welfare of nations', 'liberty and happiness in Europe' and so on without abiding by any clear common linguistic convention. Moreover, some proposals aim at the attainment of social goals 'among' sovereign states and 'within' them at the same time, and, as we pointed out, we are including in our discussion those proposals which aim primarily at the cross-national enhancement of goals 'within' separate states. Furthermore, even where a proposal is intended specifically for an 'international' goal, such as the maintenance of order in the external relations of sovereign states, its author is at least implicitly committed to the view that the proposed international institution, in conjunction with certain domestic institutions, would ensure the achievement of 'world' order in Bull's sense of the term. Therefore, as part of the characterization of the proposals in the following, we shall treat the terms 'world' and 'international' as though they were interchangeable. However, 'world state' (and 'world government') will be distinguished from 'international government': unlike the former, the latter does not replace the system of sovereign states, but operates within that framework.

Enough has been said by way of preliminary remarks. We shall move on to examine the extent to which and the ways in which the domestic analogy has been used in proposals for world order from the early part of the nineteenth century to the present.

3 SOME NINETEENTH-CENTURY EXAMPLES

This chapter is concerned with the use of the domestic analogy in the period after the Napoleonic Wars and before the first Hague Peace Conference at the end of the century. Four writers, Saint-Simon, William Ladd, James Lorimer and J. C. Bluntschli have been selected for discussion chiefly because their proposals give a valuable insight into the use of the domestic analogy in international thought. Apart from partly confirming Morgenthau's general statement, noted in the Introduction, that during the nineteenth century important sectors of public opinion demanded the application of liberal principles to international affairs, these four writers also reveal in a striking manner the extent to which one's choice of a particular domestic model is influenced by one's immediate domestic political experience. Moreover, the four authors share a number of characteristics which it is interesting to compare with those of other groups of thinkers from other historical periods.

The similarity of methods used by these authors, however, is not the sole ground for our special attention. What is also important is the divergence in the legal character of the bodies they proposed. Saint-Simon's project appears to involve the federal integration of Europe; Ladd's scheme envisages a rather loose association of states; and Lorimer's and Bluntschli's solutions, despite their disagreements, were confederal. Thus, Hinsley (1967, chaps. 6, 7) has treated these writers among others as representing the three distinct approaches of the nineteenth century to the problem of peace, each dictated by a combination of his specific historical tradition and circumstances. Their approaches, from the viewpoint of the legal character of the bodies proposed, are indeed mutually exclusive, and conjointly close to being exhaustive of the general categories. It is a common pattern in their use of the domestic analogy against the background of the wide divergence in their respective proposals that attracts our attention to the writings of these publicists.

40

Saint-Simon's grand design

Claude-Henri de Rouvroy, Comte de Saint-Simon (1760–1825), an eccentric French aristocrat descended from Charlemagne, considered it as his mission to contribute to the reform of society both within and across the borders of states. He fought in the American War of Independence on the side of the colonies, and relinquished his title, though he regarded the French Revolution as a mainly destructive process and did not take an active part in it. His chosen weapon of reform was the dissemination of his ideas about how best to organize a society (E. Wilson 1960, 82ff.). Among the many essays he published on this subject was *De la réorganisation de la société Européenne* which he wrote in collaboration with Augustin Thierry in the autumn of 1814. Having lived through the great upheaval of the revolution and wars, he was deeply concerned with the problem of how to re-establish a stable order not only in France but also in Europe as a whole. But such a goal, in Saint-Simon's view, could not be achieved by a congress then assembled in Vienna. This was because, he wrote, 'none of the members of the congress [would] have the function of considering questions from a general point of view; none of them [would] be even authorized to do so' ([1814] 1952, 34). The problem, he thought, required a much more radical solution.

Saint-Simon's own plan was based on the view that the peace and prosperity of Europe, or the liberty of the Europeans, could not be attained without the establishment of a common government for Europe, which was in the same relation to the different peoples as national governments were to individuals. Moreover, he insisted, the best possible constitution that the contemporary state of human knowledge could reveal should be applied to all the national governments as well as to the common government ([1814] 1952, 31–2, 39).

Saint-Simon was somewhat of an intellectual megalomaniac and, whatever his subject-matter, he insisted on building his monument on what he regarded as first principles, thereby giving his work the appearance of grandness but adding also cumbersome theoretical decor. This was certainly the case with his European reorganization plan of 1814, which, to make matters worse, was written in a hurry. Moreover, Saint-Simon's mind lacked discipline, though it was highly perceptive. Contradictions are not infrequent in his works, and his own explanations are not a sure guide to what his thought actually amounted to. His own theoretical explanation of the principles of the best possible constitution is not an exception in this regard. It is so confused and misleading that it need not detain us here. Suffice it to note that, in his judgement, these principles were embodied in the English constitution, and that therefore all the national governments as well as the common government of Europe should be modelled on that constitution ([1814] 1952, 41–5). On the basis of these preliminary considerations, Saint-Simon proposed the establishment of a European Parliament consisting of a King of Europe and Houses of Peers and of Commons ([1814] 1952, 46ff.).

The work of 1814, however, was incomplete. Saint-Simon postponed the discussion of the choice of the King of Europe to a sequel ([1814] 1952, 48), but this appears not to have materialized. Nor did he, in his 1814 essay, discuss the constitutional position of the King outside the Parliament, except to say that the King should be hereditary and should be the first to take up office in order to enable, under his initiative, an orderly formation of the two Houses ([1814] 1952, 48). Moreover, while the European Parliament was also to function as a judiciary, Saint-Simon failed to make explicit how international disputes were to be adjudicated ([1814] 1952, 48). Furthermore, he failed to clarify the jurisdictional relationships between the proposed common government and the national governments of Europe ([1814] 1952, 38, 46).

Despite these flaws, the outline of the proposed European Parliament was clear enough, an outline which, according to Saint-Simon's own account, was drawn from the English model. There were, however, at least two points at which his European Parliament deviated significantly from the actual English constitution.

First, Saint-Simon's three legislative authorities, the King, Peers and Commons, were to be equal in their power, each having the right of initiating, and vetoing, any legislative measures ([1814] 1952, 41). This was not the case with the actual English constitution (Halévy 1937, 1: 31–2 n. 2; Blackstone 1773, bk 1, 261, 154; de Smith 1973, 58). Second, Saint-Simon introduced an original provision as regards the election of the members of the European House of Commons. This was original in that the proposed method of election was neither in line with the actual English constitution nor based on what Saint-Simon claimed was the case with that constitution. He wrote:

> For every million persons in Europe who know how to read and write there should sit as their representatives in the House of Commons of the great parliament, a man of business, a scientist, an administrator and a lawyer. Thus, assuming that there are sixty million men in Europe who know how to read and write, the House will be composed of 240 members. The election of members will be made by the

professional body to which they belong. They will be elected for ten years. Every member of the House must possess 25,000 francs income at least, from landed property. ([1814] 1952, 47)

Saint-Simon's own justification for devising such a method of election to the European House of Commons was as follows. He argued that institutions moulded men, and hoped that the European Parliament, once established, would foster 'a patriotism beyond the limits of one's fatherland' or the 'habit of considering the interests of Europe instead of national interests' ([1814] 1952, 46–7). However, Saint-Simon contended that an institution could not take root if men were not adapted to it beforehand, for, in his view, it was also the case that men made institutions. Thus, in order for the European Parliament to function well, it was necessary that its members be motivated by European patriotism. It was patriotism that enabled a national government to have a 'corporate will', and the same would be the case with the European government, he argued. Saint-Simon then remarked that European patriotism was to be found only in a certain class of people, and maintained that men of business, scientists, magistrates and administrators belonged to that class because of their wider contacts, emancipation from purely local customs and their occupations, which were cosmopolitan in aim rather than national ([1814] 1952, 46–7).

Thus, according to Saint-Simon's own account, the special provision noted above was necessary for the election of the European House of Commons for otherwise it would not function as one body. However, it seems wrong to suppose that Saint-Simon's sole purpose in proposing such a form of election was to foster unity in the European House of Commons. This point can be explained on the basis of the following three considerations, and these in turn will reveal what Saint-Simon really had in mind when he argued that an English-type constitution should be applied to the European government.

First, the type of persons to be elected to the European House of Commons were those who could be regarded as the leading members of the bourgeoisie (Cobban 1970, 7–21). Although Saint-Simon himself did not explain the composition of the House in these terms, it would be quite reasonable to suppose that he was aware of this distinctive feature of the House he was proposing.

Second, this House was to coexist, on an equal footing, with the other authorities, the King of Europe, and the European House of Peers. The peers were to be nominated by the King without limitation of numbers, and every peer was to possess at least 500,000 francs income from landed property. Peerage was to be hereditary (Saint-Simon [1814] 1952, 48). Thus, the European House of Peers can be considered as representing the views and interests of the European aristocracy as a whole.

Third, Saint-Simon must be regarded as having overstated his case when he argued that *whatever* common interests existed in the European community could be traced to the sciences, arts, law, commerce, administration and industry ([1814] 1952, 47). The interests of these professions, which, in Saint-Simon's view, transcended national parochialism, were to make the European House of Commons function as an effective organ. But his proposal undoubtedly presupposed the transnational solidarity not only of the social stratum to be represented in the House of Commons, but also of the aristocratic class of Europe who were to provide the House of Peers. Otherwise, his European Parliament could not consistently be held to be workable, for one of its branches, lacking in solidarity, would have to be admitted to be as incapable of reaching any decision as he considered diplomatic conferences inevitably to be ([1814] 1952, 34–5). It must be remembered here that Saint-Simon's European Parliament was to enact laws through the concurrence of decisions among its three branches. If any one of them could not reach a decision, then the whole system would be immobilized. Therefore, in order to be consistent, Saint-Simon could not have thought that the *only* social stratum which had transnational solidarity consisted of scientists, artists, lawyers, businessmen and so on.

This last point somewhat weakens the supposition that Saint-Simon's *sole* aim in proposing his original method of European Commons elections was to foster unity in the House. If unity had been the sole purpose, he could equally well have suggested that the European Parliament be unicameral, consisting of the peers of Europe, for implicitly he was committed to the idea that they too had transnational solidarity.

Combined with this point are the first two considerations noted above, that the House of Commons was to represent the European bourgeoisie, and that the House of Peers, which was to stand on an equal footing with the House of Commons and the King of Europe, was to represent European aristocracy. These suggest that what Saint-Simon had in mind was the creation of a stable social order in Europe through the balancing of social classes across borders. In short, the theory of domestic politics which he was trying to apply to Europe as a whole was that of the mixed constitution.

This theory, like the theory of the separation of powers popularized by Montesquieu, used to be associated with the English constitution, although the former had a far longer history than the latter in Western political thought (Sabine 1963, 558ff.). The basic tenet of the theory of the mixed constitution was that a good constitution combined and balanced the elements of monarchy, aristocracy and democracy in such a way that the state was governed conjointly by the king, nobles and people. Bolingbroke, for example, explained the English constitution in the light of this theory when he stated: 'It is by this mixture of monarchical, aristocratical and democratical power, blended together in one system, and by these three estates balancing one another, that our free constitution of government hath been preserved so long inviolate' (Sabine 1963, 560; see also Shackleton 1949).

Saint-Simon did not explicitly advance the theory of the mixed state. Nor did he explain the excellence of the English constitution in the light of that theory, although he betrayed its influence upon him when he characterized the function of the English House of Lords essentially as a balancer of monarchic and democratic forces ([1814] 1952, 43). Working backwards from his project itself, however, it is possible to conjecture that Saint-Simon was in fact trying to create a mixed constitution at the European level, and to balance the interests of the king-to-be, the aristocratic class and the rising professional classes of Europe by a new institutional arrangement. There are indeed a few remarks scattered in the latter part of his essay ([1814] 1952, 55–7) which partly confirm that he favoured the idea of a mixed constitution. Thus, he expressed his dislike of the despotism both of a single man and of the people: the former would lead to tyranny, the latter to democratic anarchy. Therefore, he argued, 'the moderate part of the nation' ([1814] 1952, 56) was needed to restore social order.

It is pertinent to note here the particular political circumstances of France at the time Saint-Simon drafted his proposal. Napoleon had abdicated in April 1814, and was at that time in Elba. Louis XVIII, who had been in exile in England, was restored to the throne in the following month, and in June that year he bestowed on his subjects the *Charte Constitutionnelle*. This Charter was based on a compromise between the principles of the *Ancien Régime* and those of the Revolution. Thus, although a great deal of power was left in the hands of the King, the Charter did introduce a parliamentary system along the lines of the English constitution. The Parliament was bicameral, the Chamber of Peers recruiting its members largely from the Imperial Senate, and the Chamber of Deputies from the Legislative Body, of Napoleon's days. Like the English House of Commons, the Chamber of Deputies was to be subject to election on the basis of property qualifications (Bury 1950, 1–9; Lough and Lough 1978, 44–6).

This Charter was undoubtedly an attempt to maintain a balance among the restored Bourbon dynasty, the aristocracy and the middle classes, and shows some striking resemblances to Saint-Simon's project for a common government of Europe (compare Saint-Simon [1814] 1952 and Bury 1950, Appendix III). It is safe to assume that he was familiar with this Charter. Thus it would not be wild to conjecture that his immediate model was in fact the French Charter itself, although this in turn was modelled on the English constitution.

It must also be noted here that Saint-Simon was convinced that England, France and Germany all faced an internal crisis, which could lead to a revolution in each country ([1814] 1952, bk 3, chaps. 4–12). This could be obviated, he thought, if these countries were to unite under the constitution he was proposing. Apparently, it was not sufficient, in his view, that each country be equipped with a good, English-type, constitution; unless a common government was also established, international conflict and intrigues would continue, which would in turn destabilize the internal order of those countries ([1814] 1952, 61, 63, 66).

This then was Saint-Simon's grand design, however incomplete, for the creation of a stable social order both within and between the nations of Europe. What he applied to the international level in his 1814 proposal was a theory of domestic politics which was implicit in the model or models he employed. He did not identify this theory by name, but it was one which undoubtedly appealed to him as a means of re-establishing order in Europe in the aftermath of the French Revolution and the Napoleonic Wars.

Because he did not clarify the jurisdictional relationships between the proposed common government and the national governments, it is not possible to determine unequivocally the legal status of the proposed union. However, his European Parliament was not like the legislative body of a confederation, despite his reference to the proposed union by that term ([1814] 1952, 49). Unlike many other proposals for an international assembly designed basically to be regular meetings of government representatives acting in accordance with a set of common procedural rules, Saint-Simon's proposal involved a full-scale merger of the existing sovereign states into one single polity at least insofar as his legislature was concerned. The function of the proposed Parliament was consequently very broad, and included even the codification of national and individual ethics ([1814] 1952, 49, 62).

Given the structure and function of the proposed common Parliament, his European Confederation may fall into the category of a federal or even a unitary state.

As we noted, Saint-Simon's 1814 plan, which presupposed the transnational solidarity of the aristocracy as well as that of the professional classes, would not have made sense if he had been right in his assertion that *whatever* common interests existed in Europe could be traced to the sciences, arts, law, commerce, administration and industry. None the less, the stress he placed on the transnational solidarity of interests on the part of the professional classes reveals the direction in which Saint-Simon, once freed from his infatuation with the English-type constitution, was to develop his new idea for the reorganization of Europe in the coming age. This was the doctrine of industrialism.[1]

In this doctrine, the transnational unity of the interests of the 'industrial' class becomes the basis of the new social order in Europe, instead of the earlier notion of the transnational balancing of the interests of different classes. According to the new doctrine, the purpose of a society is the efficient production of useful things on the basis of advancing scientific knowledge. The 'industrialists' are those who engage themselves in production, as opposed to those who are the idle parasites of a society: the former includes managers and workers alike, and embraces also those owners who actively participate in the productive processes of their society, as opposed to those who merely sit idly on their property. In Saint-Simon's scheme scientists and artists, who contribute positively to a society's goal, are placed on the same footing as the producers of goods. The gist of his doctrine, which was put forward in a number of pamphlets, is that the decision-making function of a society should be transferred from the political institutions of the state to an administrative body consisting of the able members of the industrial class. Saint-Simon noted, however, that no individual country could proceed to the establishment of an industrial–administrative system, unless similar movements took place in other countries; industrialism could only be achieved at the European level. At the same time, he believed that there was no conflict of interests between the industrialists of different countries; national bellicosity was the remnant of the feudal system in which the idle aristocratic class influenced the foreign policy of the state.

What form of institutional framework is needed at the international level when a plurality of European states have developed the industrial–administrative system within? Saint-Simon did not answer this important question. Nor did he explain how his earlier plan for a European union was to be modified in order to harmonize with his new doctrine.

Emile Durkheim has suggested that Saint-Simon never in fact abandoned the fundamental position expressed in the 1814 proposal that the national governments and the common European government must be homogeneous, and that they must therefore be based on the same institutional principle. Thus, in Durkheim's view, Saint-Simon would have argued that the common parliament of Europe should be recruited in accordance with the rules set out for the national councils, and that it should administer the common affairs of Europe in the spirit of industrialism, thereby placing the constitution of the European Confederation in harmony with the national governments (Durkheim 1959, 1977–8). Some form of general parliament along the lines suggested by Durkheim might well be what Saint-Simon had in mind as an overall arrangement for Europe, since diplomatic conferences would have been unacceptable to him. But in the absence of his own proposal we are unable to say how he would have used the domestic analogy in his new phase of planning.

Saint-Simon's 1814 proposal appears to involve a federal merger of European states. What he wished to do was to extend the existing domestic institutions to cover the whole of Europe rather than to apply the principles of domestic society to the relations of European sovereign states as such. Although Saint-Simon's concern did not cover the entire globe, the domestic analogy he used can be said to be in its 'cosmopolitanist' as opposed to its 'internationalist' form. His choice of the domestic model, in the case of his 1814 proposal, was a reflection of one of the most important domestic political issues of contemporary France: the creation of stable social order in the period after Napoleon. The place of the domestic analogy, however, remains uncertain in Saint-Simon's later doctrine of industrialism.

Ladd's Congress and Court of Nations

Saint-Simon was a prolific writer and was a powerful source of inspiration for many of the prominent thinkers of the nineteenth century in the field of social theory. He also stimulated writings on the unification of Europe, particularly in France (Renouvin 1949, 6–7; Ionescu 1976, Introduction). In the Anglo-Saxon world, however, the exploration of the road to peace in the aftermath of the Napoleonic Wars had a different source of inspiration: Christian pacifism. This soon became an organized movement also on the European continent (Renouvin 1949, 5; Hinsley 1967, chap. 6).

Early pacifist thinkers of the nineteenth century were, however, concerned primarily with the conversion of individuals to the doctrine of non-violence (Worcester 1822; Dodge [1815] 1905). If such an approach could be termed 'first image' pacifism, after Kenneth Waltz's well-known classification, 'third image' pacifism, seeking a solution at the international level while also adhering to the doctrine of non-violence, was soon to develop (Renouvin 1949, 5–6; Waltz 1959). The proposal advanced towards the middle of the century by William Ladd (1778–1841), who had in 1828 founded the American Peace Society, was an early example of this approach, and was among the more influential ones in the nineteenth-century peace movement (Beales 1931). His proposal is still noted through its republication by the Carnegie Endowment for International Peace (Ladd [1840] 1916), and through Georg Schwarzenberger's detailed study (1936a). We shall now turn to his work to see how this Harvard-educated Christian minister and peace advocate used the domestic analogy, and how his choice of the domestic model reflected the American theory and institutions of domestic politics of his time.

Ladd was familiar with the works of natural-law writers on the law of nations, such as Grotius and Vattel. However, while appreciating the beneficial influences these writers had exerted on mankind, he noted that there were many serious disagreements over details among them, and thought that it would be better if periodic meetings of ambassadors could be arranged to settle disputed principles of international law, and to conclude treaties to promote the peace and welfare of nations ([1840] 1916, chaps. 3–6). This was his idea of a Congress of Nations, which was later to be realized, in a somewhat more unstructured way, in the form of the Hague Peace Conferences.

According to Ladd, the distinctive characteristic of his project was that, in addition to a Congress, which he regarded as a legislature, there was to be established, as a separate body, a Court of Nations, a judiciary: the executive functions were to be left entirely to the strength of world public opinion, which he trusted ([1840] 1916, xlix-1).

Ladd's argument for the establishment of a Court of Nations was based explicitly on the domestic analogy ([1840] 1916, 5). Moreover, he relied, unexpectedly perhaps, on the argument from domestic experience even in his attempt to show the redundancy of an executive organ at the international level. His point was that, even in the domestic sphere, the effectiveness of law did not depend on 'the sword of the magistrate'. In his judgement, 'fear of disgrace' was the most important source of the effectiveness of law, and therefore a Court of Nations could function without the support of an executive. 'If it were disgraceful to go to war when there is a regular way of obtaining satisfaction without,' he wrote, 'wars would be as rare as duels in New England, where they are disgraceful' ([1840] 1916, 77–8).

Despite his explicit reliance on the domestic analogy, however, Ladd's Congress and Court of Nations were dissimilar to their domestic counterparts in certain important respects. Without a doubt, his Congress could be said to resemble a domestic legislature to the extent that it was designed as a permanent organ whose members were to hold a periodic session to enact laws in accordance with a set of established procedural rules, and that, therefore, one session was to have structural continuity with another. However, his Congress differed from a domestic legislature in that the unanimous consent of the nations represented at the Congress, as well as ratification by their governments, were to be required for any legislative enactment. Furthermore, it differed even from a federal-type legislature in that the Congress was to have nothing to do with the 'internal' affairs of nations. Likewise, his Court of Nations, while resembling a domestic judicature to some extent, fundamentally differed from it in that his Court was not equipped with the power of compulsory jurisdiction, though, in this respect, Ladd compared his Court to a chamber of commerce to show that a domestic counterpart could be found ([1840] 1916, 9, 10, 34).

It is in line with the relatively unambitious nature of Ladd's proposed international organization that he did not argue for a ban on the use of force by states. Thus, one of the major functions of the Congress of Nations was to be the settlement of disputed principles of international law chiefly in the area of the laws of war ([1840] 1916, chaps. 3–5). However, it was in keeping with his progressivism that Congress was to consider whether a nation, unless attacked, had a right to declare war against another or to make reprisals until it had resorted to all other means of obtaining justice ([1840] 1916, 13). If, after the establishment of the Congress, its members were to decide to renounce such a right, then the international organization, based on Ladd's proposal, would become more analogous to domestic society, where there is also a general ban on the use of force. However, as it stood, the similarity between his proposed organization and an ordinary domestic society was very limited.

It might be supposed that, in advancing this relatively unambitious proposal, Ladd perhaps used a confederal model, and that the deviations of his proposed organs from their counterparts in the domestic sphere resulted from this. Indeed, he maintained, in support of his plan, that the 'civil part' of the Helvetic Union, which was a confederation, was the 'nearest working model' of his Court and Congress ([1840] 1916, 44).

Ladd's knowledge of the Helvetic Union, however, was rather limited. He did not show in any detail the similarities between his Court and what he called 'the court of judges or arbitrators' ([1840] 1916, 44) of the Helvetic Union. The truth was that the sources of information he relied upon did not provide him with sufficient knowledge on the subject. Moreover, what little information he managed to obtain regarding the 'court' of the Helvetic Union was misleading. It was not entirely his fault to have believed that his proposed Court resembled the 'court' of the Helvetic Union, but a brief survey of those few basic treaties constituting the Union, mentioned in Ladd's sources, shows that there never was a judicial or arbitral 'court' specifically designed to deal with inter-cantonal disputes in the period of Swiss history with which his sources were concerned.[2]

Ladd managed to obtain a little more substantial information regarding the Diet of the Helvetic Union, and his description of it shows that he was aware of some important similarities that actually existed between the Swiss Diet and his proposed Congress: neither of them was concerned with the 'internal' affairs of the member states, and both of them worked essentially as a regularized form of the conference of ambassadors.[3]

Thus, taken as a whole, Ladd's knowledge of the Swiss Confederation might have helped him to form his conception of the Congress and Court of Nations, but it is not likely to have been the original source of his inspiration. It appears that Ladd's ideas were in fact more closely linked with his experience at home. Here we are in the realm of speculation, but not in an entirely unfounded one.

There are some remarks which Ladd made in his essay which tend to confirm the view that his actual model was American. Thus, in order to form a Congress, ambassadors were to be sent to 'a convention', which would then adopt rules and regulations necessary for the Congress – a procedure reminiscent of the birth of the American Constitution. The permanency of his Court was compared by him to that of the American Supreme Court, and the periodic nature of the sessions of his Congress to the case of the Congress or Senate of the United States. Ladd also compared the ability of the American Supreme Court to settle inter-state boundary disputes with what a Court of Nations, when established, could achieve ([1840] 1916, 8, 9, 35). Moreover, in omitting an executive organ from his scheme, Ladd might have taken note of the fact that in inter-state disputes the 1787 federal Constitution does not provide for the execution of Supreme Court decisions by force (Schuman 1945, 17–19). Ladd's proposed Congress, however, might have been modelled on the Congress of the United States under the Articles of Confederation of 1777 (Newton 1923, 70–7).

The idea that Ladd's proposal was inspired by the experience of the United States is supported by J. B. Scott in his preface to Georg Schwarzenberger's *William Ladd*. According to Scott, Ladd was 'well-nigh contemporary with the young republic' (Schwarzenberger 1936a, xiv), as the Articles of Confederation (1777) came into force when Ladd was three (1781), and the new Constitution of the United States was drawn up when he was nine (1787). Scott suggests that Ladd was permeated with the constitutional ideas of the United States and was fully informed of its institutions (Schwarzenberger 1936a, xiv).

Central to the constitutional ideas of America was the notion of the separation of powers. The 1776 Declaration of Independence itself, while not using the term 'separation of powers' explicitly, accused George III of his tyrannical deeds, among the most serious of which was stated to be his refusal to acknowledge the independence of the legislative and judiciary powers from his authority over the colonies. He abolished, according to the Declaration, 'the free system of English laws in a neighbouring province, establishing therein an arbitrary government' (Newton 1923, 68–9).

Moreover, apart from its enshrinement in the Constitution of the United States of 1787 itself, the principle of the separation of powers was accepted by the various state constitutions. One notable example, the Massachusetts Constitution of 1780, stated: 'In the government of this commonwealth, the legislative department shall never exercise the executive and judicial powers, or either of them: the executive shall never exercise the legislative and judicial powers, or either of them: the judicial shall never exercise the legislative and executive powers or either of them' (Pritchett 1977, 3). This constitution, which built on the constitutions of certain other states, was itself soon to be copied by the second constitution (1784) of New Hampshire, where Ladd was born (Ladd [1840] 1916, iv; W. P. Adams 1973, 269).

It seems almost without doubt then that Ladd's taken-for-granted attitude towards the idea of the separation of powers, which shaped the framework of his plan, derived from his close familiarity with the constitutional history of the United States. The idea was in the air. It is true that Ladd did not stress, along with the doctrine of the separation of powers, that it was the liberty of nations that was at stake in separating the Court from the Congress. However, he did remark that one of the main weaknesses of the regional confederations in the past had been the union of the three powers in one body, and that this had caused 'intrigue, ambition, and many other baleful passions and practices' ([1840] 1916, 86). The sufficiency of Ladd's historical knowledge may be doubted in such a statement, but it does indicate his implicit acceptance of the liberal doctrine.

The foregoing discussion suggests that Ladd's reference to the constitution of the Helvetic Union, his knowledge of which was limited, was chiefly for the purpose of making his plan appear more relevant to international problems. Other things being equal, a union whose constituents are more diverse is naturally more valuable as a model for an international organization, for the latter will have to overcome wide national differences. Ladd therefore may have thought the Swiss example to be more impressive than the American model. He stressed differences 'in language, religion, laws, forms of government, manners and customs', which existed among the members of the Helvetic Union, and argued that no 'good reason [could] be given why a plan, which [had] worked so well on a small scale, [might] not be extended, so as to embrace all Christian and civilized nations' ([1840] 1916, 44). Whatever his actual model, however, it seems clear that Ladd's proposal reflected one of the most important doctrines of domestic politics in the United States of his time.

It should be noted that, unlike Saint-Simon's 'European Confederation', Ladd's proposed international body was not itself a state. This was due to the fact that, unlike Saint-Simon, Ladd used the domestic analogy in its 'internationalist', as opposed to 'cosmopolitanist', form. Ladd's units of international organization were sovereign states. Another point to note is that, in reproducing some of the domestic institutions at the international level, Ladd seems to have been clear that the principles underlying these institutions need to be modified substantially. However, this appears, in the case of Ladd, to have resulted from his consideration of practicability rather than from the view that the inherent nature of international law made it impossible for it to become analogous to a municipal legal system beyond a certain point.[4] This view, or the doctrine of the specific character of international law, will be discussed in the next chapter. There is no trace in Ladd's writing of his adherence to such a doctrine.

Lorimer and Bluntschli: intermediate approaches

Saint-Simon's European reorganization plan and Ladd's Congress and Court of Nations stood at the opposite ends of a spectrum.

The former emphatically dismissed the method of diplomatic conference, and envisaged a merger of Europe into a single polity. The latter, being more optimistic about the ability of states to behave reasonably towards one another, and being more practically minded, held that only two institutions would be sufficient for the creation of international order: a regularized form of diplomatic conference to determine the law, and a machinery to settle international disputes on an entirely voluntary basis.

Between the two approaches of Saint-Simon and Ladd, there was a third: one which envisaged an international government less centralized than Saint-Simon's ideal, but more closely organized than Ladd's proposed institutions. This intermediate vision was held, among others, by James Lorimer (1818–90), whose position on the domestic analogy was noted briefly in chapter 1.

Lorimer was appointed in 1862 to the Edinburgh Chair of Public Law and of the Law of Nature and Nations. He published his project for European organization in 'The ultimate problem of international jurisprudence', written as the final part of his *The institutes of the law of nations* (1884). This was in substance the same as his earlier essay, 'Le problème final du droit international' (1877), but contained some further explanations, in view of its critical reception by the members of the Institut de Droit International, of which Lorimer was himself an active member and in whose journal his essay had appeared.

Among Lorimer's critics was Johann Caspar Bluntschli (1808–81), a distinguished Swiss jurist who had emigrated to Germany and was at the University of Heidelberg as a Professor of International Law and Political Science, having held a similar position earlier at the University of Munich (H. B. Adams 1884). In reply to Lorimer's 'Le problème final', Bluntschli published in 1878 in a popular journal, *Die Gegenwart*, an essay entitled, 'Die Organisation des Europäischen Statenvereines'.[5] However, Bluntschli's own plan, while somewhat less centralized than Lorimer's, was also of the intermediate kind, not involving the unification of Europe under one sovereignty, but envisaging nevertheless a far-reaching alteration in the international legal framework of Europe. The works of these two writers will be examined below to see what their domestic models were, and how, despite their disagreements, their use of the domestic analogy reflected the domestic political concerns of the period in Great Britain and the newly unified Germany.

According to Bluntschli's criticism, it was Lorimer's mistake to have gone too far in his attempt to apply domestic political institutions to the international sphere. Bluntschli accused him of attempting to create a

European federal republic on the principle of a representative government and the separation of powers borrowed from Anglo-American
constitutional doctrine and practice (1879–81, 2: 293-4). To this Lorimer
replied that his proposed international body was not a federal republic,
and that the closest existing parallel to the functions which it would be
called upon to discharge would be found 'in those assigned to the
"Delegations" by the constitution of the Austro-Hungarian empire –
the international executive corresponding to the central Ministry of
War' (1884, 2:275–6). Neither side was entirely right in this exchange.

The correspondence, in structural terms, between the 'Delegations'
system and the Ministry of War of the Austro-Hungarian Empire, on
the one hand, and Lorimer's proposed international legislature and
executive bodies, on the other, were negligible. Moreover, the functions of Lorimer's proposed bodies were more extensive than those of
their supposed counterparts of the empire. It is therefore somewhat
doubtful that Lorimer had modelled his project on the Austro-Hungarian Constitution.[6] A closer examination reveals similarities, and in
some cases almost verbal correspondence, between the articles of
Lorimer's project and certain legal provisions of England, the United
States, and the Swiss Confederation. Thus, Lorimer's judiciary was
similar in a number of ways to the English system, and his bicameral
legislature was close to the English Parliament, though some of the
procedural rules proposed resembled the American model. Lorimer's
executive branch, however, showed similarities with that of the Swiss
Confederation under the Constitution of 1874.[7] Bluntschli, therefore,
was correct to point out the similarities between Lorimer's proposal
and the Anglo-American principles. It is curious that Bluntschli, himself a Swiss, did not mention the Swiss Confederation as one of
Lorimer's likely models.

On the other hand, Lorimer was right to insist that his proposed
international body was not itself a state. The main reason for this is that
his legislature was designed to enact *international* law, and not laws
directly binding on the citizens of a member state (Lorimer 1884, 2:279,
283). Thus although Lorimer's international government came close to
being a federal government, it appears in fact to have lacked one of the
distinctive characteristics of a federation. Therefore, Bluntschli's assertion that Lorimer's project entailed the creation of a European
federal republic cannot be accepted.

By contrast with Lorimer's far-reaching scheme, Bluntschli claimed
that his own project was based on the 'indispensable principle' of 'the
careful preservation of the independence and freedom of the associated states', particularly those of the Great Powers (1879–81, 2:299). As

an application of this principle, questions concerning the existence, independence and freedom of states, or matters of 'high politics', were to be treated as 'non-justiciable'. Thus, in Bluntschli's view, it was only for the solution of relatively unimportant matters, such as commerce, communication, transport, hygiene, weights and measures, extradition and so on, that an arbitration clause might be adopted, permanent international tribunals set up, and an international court of justice established (1879–81, 2:307–8).

Also as an application of the above principle, the 'College of the six Great Powers' was proposed in the place of Lorimer's highly centralized international executive, of which Bluntschli was very critical (1879–81, 2:297, 309). Thus, according to Bluntschli, any enforcement measures were to be conditional, among other things, upon the unanimous consent of the six Great Powers: Germany, France, Great Britain, Italy, Austria-Hungary and Russia. Lorimer's highly centralized international executive was based on the assumption that proportional disarmament had been undertaken as a preliminary step, but Bluntschli rejected such an assumption as unrealistic: according to him, disarmament would come about gradually only after Europe had been reorganized along the lines of his proposal (Bluntschli 1879–81, 2:298, 309–10; Lorimer 1884, 2:245ff., 279).

Despite these differences between the two writers, there were also some basic agreements. Both writers stressed the inevitability of change in international relations, and considered a mechanism for peaceful change as indispensable. Moreover, they both recognized the fact of inequality in the power of states, and believed it necessary for the new organization of Europe, in order to be effective, to take this into consideration. But, most important, Bluntschli praised Lorimer for having realized the necessity of popular representation in the running of international affairs, and consequently, for having incorporated this idea in the proposed European organization (Bluntschli 1879–81, 2:292–3, 300; Lorimer 1884, 2:193–4, 218ff.). The difference between the two writers on this point was a matter of degree. This can be appreciated when we compare the structure of legislatures proposed by the two writers respectively, and to this we now turn.

Lorimer's international legislature was bicameral, consisting of the Senate and the Chamber of Deputies. Popular representation in the running of international affairs, he thought, could be achieved if a direct link could be established between the national legislatures and the proposed international legislature. Thus, the senators were to be chosen by the crown or other chief authority, acting along with the upper house, of each state; or, in states where there was no upper house, by the central authority of the state. In a parallel fashion, the deputies were to be chosen by the lower house of each state where there was a lower house; in states where there was but one house, by that house; and in states where there was no representative government, they were to be nominated by the crown or other central authorities of the state (Lorimer 1884, 2:279–80, 240ff.).

Lorimer expected the Senate to consist of those who had already attained to high position and fortune, but there was no such expectation as regards the Chamber of Deputies (1884, 2:280). Lorimer seems to have held that the national will could be best represented in an international legislature if the will of the upper class was represented separately from, but on the same footing as, that of the rest of the society. In this respect, Lorimer appears to have intended to transfer the basic structure of the English Houses of Parliament to the international sphere. It seems very likely, moreover, that Lorimer's concern to introduce the principle of popular representation into his proposed international government was prompted by the gradual democratization which had been taking place in the government of Britain throughout the nineteenth century.[8]

Bluntschli's proposed legislature was also bicameral. But, unlike Lorimer, who applied the principle of popular representation to both chambers of the proposed international legislature, Bluntschli combined this principle with the traditional principle of international practice: the diplomatic representation of the will of the sovereign (executive) authority.

Bluntschli's bicameral legislature was therefore a hybrid between Lorimer's international legislature and Ladd's Congress of Nations. On the one hand, there was to be a House of Representatives or Senate, whose members were to be selected by national legislatures, and who were, therefore, to be expected to represent the peoples of Europe. On the other hand, there was to be the Council of Confederation (Bundesrath), which was to be in essence a regularized form of a conference of ambassadors sent and instructed by the government (the executive authority) of each member state (Bluntschli 1879–81, 2:302ff.). In presenting such a form of legislature, Bluntschli appears to have used the German Imperial Constitution of 1871 as his model. This can be surmised from the following points of correspondence between the two institutions.

As in Bluntschli's project, the German Imperial legislature was bicameral, consisting of the Reichstag and the Bundesrath. The members of the German Reichstag represented the German people as a whole: like Bluntschli's senators, who were to represent the peoples of

Europe, they were not bound by instructions from their national governments. On the other hand, like Bluntschli's Bundesrath, the German Bundesrath consisted of diplomatic agents, appointed by, and voting under instructions from, their respective governments (Newton 1923, 239–62; Bryce 1928, 480).

Moreover, as in Bluntschli's proposal, the majority of votes in both chambers was necessary and sufficient for any legislative enactment of the German Empire, although, unlike the legislature of Germany, the law to be enacted by Bluntschli's legislature was to have the character of international law.[9] It may also be noted here that according to the German Imperial Constitution, an inter-state constitutional dispute, for which no competent judicial authority was found in either of the contestants was to be 'amicably arranged' by the Bundesrath or settled through Imperial legislation. This provision is reminiscent of Bluntschli's suggestion that the question of 'high politics' within the proposed European Confederation, being non-justiciable, should be entrusted to the Bundesrath, and that recourse might be had to legislative solutions.[10]

Unfortunately for our argument, Bluntschli himself remarked that the German Empire was unsuitable as a model for the European organization. However, the source of his objection was that European nations could not, in his view, allow one single state to become the leading partner of their confederation, as Prussia was of the German Empire (1879–81, 2:299). A union of states, such as the German Empire, where one member had a dominant constitutional position, Bluntschli called a Bundesreich, and distinguished it from an ordinary confederation of states or Staatenbund (1878, 90–2). A Bundesreich-type structure, he thought, was unsuitable for Europe. Nevertheless, in his proposed European Confederation, Bluntschli did give a constitutionally dominant position, not to any single state, but to the six Great Powers conjointly (1879–81, 2:300ff.). It appears therefore that, despite his express denial of so doing, Bluntschli did in fact model his European legislature on that of contemporary Germany, and that, in so doing, he substituted the principle of hexarchy for that of Prussian supremacy.

It must be noted here that Bluntschli had been called to the University of Heidelberg in 1861, five years before the outbreak of the Austro-Prussian War. He was made a Privy Councillor by the Grand Duke of Baden, where liberal and democratic attitudes were more strongly rooted in comparison to many other parts of Germany characterized by autocracy. Bluntschli himself was a liberal parliamentarian, and was instrumental in the constitutional reform of Baden in 1864. He represented Baden in the Tariff Parliament of 1867, and did much to prepare the way for the union of North and South Germany. He was therefore very closely involved in the development of German constitutional history in the latter part of the nineteenth century (H. B. Adams 1884, 14ff.; Snell 1976, chap. 7). Given this background, Bluntschli's remark that the proposed unification of Europe could not be more difficult than had been the unification of Germany is specially noteworthy (1879–81, 2:312). It would not be surprising if he was thinking that the new Imperial Constitution could offer some useful ideas for the reorganization of Europe.

Thus, despite their disagreements at the surface level, Lorimer and Bluntschli seem to have employed the same method in working out a major part of their respective proposals. This was to transpose certain basic constitutional principles of their respective countries to the international sphere. This is particularly true of the proposed legislatures. In applying these principles to the international system, neither of them advocated the replacement of the sovereign states system by a single sovereign state, although in some respects Lorimer's proposed international body was close to being a federation.

It is particularly interesting to observe that both these writers appear to have been significantly affected by what was at that time regarded as among the most vital issues of domestic politics in their own countries. Their use of the domestic analogy was therefore affected by their interest in the rising power of the representative legislature *vis-à-vis* the executive authority. What they advocated was an extension of this tendency or idea to the international sphere, rather more fully in the case of Lorimer than Bluntschli. Reflecting the limitations on the representative character of the English Parliament, Lorimer's proposed Senate was to consist of those who had already attained to high positions and fortune. Reflecting the special circumstances of Germany, which had been unified after a long period of confederal division, Bluntschli's proposed legislature was to combine the principle of democratic legislature with that of diplomatic conference. Here then, after Saint-Simon and Ladd, we have two more cases which illustrate the extent to which one's choice of a domestic model is influenced by one's immediate domestic political experience.

An overview

The domestic analogy employed by Saint-Simon, leading to his idea of a European federation, was of cosmopolitanist form, whereas, by contrast, Ladd resorted to the internationalist form of the analogy. Lorimer and Bluntschli, advocating an intermediate solution, used the domestic analogy which went beyond its standard internationalist form, but which fell short of the cosmopolitanist form. The distinctive feature of the domestic analogy employed by Lorimer and Bluntschli consists in their suggestion that the principle of popular representation, accepted as legitimate within democratic states, should replace or at least balance the traditional principle of representation by diplomats in the management of international affairs. Murray Forsyth has remarked that confederations tend to be 'anti-democratic' since their law-making congresses are not closely controlled by the national parliaments (1981, 186). The projects by Lorimer and Bluntschli, which can both be characterized as confederal, attempt to overcome this, and might therefore be labelled 'democratic confederal'.

Despite these differences, the four writers also had a number of intellectual dispositions in common. Among these were their belief in the progress of human civilization, and their confidence in certain existing forms of government.

The belief in progress was clearly expressed by Saint-Simon and William Ladd.[11] Even Lorimer, who did not believe his project to be realizable in his own generation, was confident that proportional disarmament, which was to be the preliminary condition for the establishment of his proposed international government, would sooner or later be undertaken, and that the boundless progress of human civilization ensured the eventual formation of the proposed government itself (1884, 2:193–7, 248). Bluntschli, who had in fact written that he did not know if or when his project could be put into practice, nevertheless stated that his proposed European Confederation would be easier to form than was the German Empire, whose establishment he had himself witnessed (1879–81, 2:312).

One of the factors which had led these writers to hold a progressivist view of history was their judgement that the political conditions of some states had shown marked improvements in the recent past. The domestic experience of these writers was not like that of the earlier writers, Rousseau, for example (see Forsyth, Keens-Soper and Savigear 1970, 131–66). France was now equipped with the best, 'English-type', constitution, said Saint-Simon ([1814] 1952, 50). In civilized nations, force was no longer regarded as an honourable means for obtaining justice, wrote Ladd ([1840] 1916, 84–5). Satisfaction with certain existing domestic legal systems is implicit in Lorimer's claim that universal experience proved domestic social order to depend on the harmony of legislation, adjudication and execution (1884, 2:186-7). Bluntschli, too, appears to have been satisfied with certain political developments in Germany (H. B. Adams 1884, 15, 18; Snell 1976, 174–6).

It is little wonder then that these nineteenth-century writers believed that there was something to be learned from their domestic experience. Whether they were right in applying it to the international sphere in the way they did is open to question. But it is clear that they were all favourably impressed by the advances made in the domestic sphere of some states, saw this as a mark of human progress, and thus thought it right to apply the relevant principles of domestic organization to the comparatively underdeveloped area of international relations.

It is important to note that the international system of the period, in which these writers produced their plans, was largely lacking in formal international organizations. International administrative institutions began to emerge in the final quarter of the nineteenth century. But these institutions do not appear to have attracted the attention of peace advocates till later. There was of course the diplomatic practice of *ad hoc* conferences, the Concert of Europe. But Saint-Simon, seeing no merits in diplomatic conferences as such, would have been dismissive of it. Ladd briefly referred to the Holy Alliance, but his knowledge of it was thin. He was more concerned to praise its supposed Christian basis than to use it as a model for his Congress of Nations ([1840] 1916, 45–7). Lorimer was very critical of the Concert, and only Bluntschli saw it somewhat more positively as an embryonic international organization (Holbraad 1970, 65–70, 187). The relative lack of formal organization at the international level may explain why these writers relied rather conspicuously on concrete domestic models. There was little in the international system itself which they could point to as a foundation for future progress towards peace, while there were certain domestic institutions which in their view were successful, and which therefore appealed to them as good models.

The situation was markedly different for the writers at the beginning of the twentieth century. While the earlier writers' attempts to transfer all at once to the international sphere those domestic institutions which they considered as necessary for the achievement of world peace had proved futile, international law nevertheless began to show signs of step-by-step progress at the turn of the century. The most remarkable among them were the Peace Conferences at The Hague. These appeared to many writers on world order to signify the arrival of a new era in the history of international relations. In the next chapter, we shall examine the views of those who wrote against this new background.

4 CONTENDING DOCTRINES OF THE HAGUE PEACE CONFERENCES PERIOD

The aim of this chapter is to examine the effects of the development of international law, and relative peace, at the turn of the century upon the use of the domestic analogy in proposals for world order. In the first part of this chapter, we shall examine the ideas of Walther Schücking, a Marburg Professor of International Law, and those of his Cambridge counterpart, Lassa Oppenheim. These writers' views illustrate in a striking manner the impact of the contemporary international and domestic situations on the use of the domestic analogy.

Later in this chapter, we shall study writers on international law who appear to have belonged to Oppenheim's 'diplomatic school'. These were Oppenheim's contemporaries, and wrote from the same historical background of progress in international law. Yet, as we noted, this school was said by Oppenheim to be opposed to the development of international law along the lines of municipal law.

As it turns out, apart from one possible exception, none of the authors whom Oppenheim may have considered as belonging to this school was well known or influential. None the less, we shall discuss the views of those authors so as not to lose sight of the fact that the development of international law at the turn of the century did not necessarily produce a uniform response among international lawyers in favour of a further approximation of international law to municipal law than it had already accomplished by that stage. Indeed it appears to have been partly as a reaction to the strong current of progressivism among international lawyers, and to the rapid progress of international law at that time, that the writers of the diplomatic school produced their conservative views.

Schücking's gradualism

The Hague Peace Conferences of 1899 and 1907 produced a large number of conventions and declarations, and established a Permanent Court of Arbitration (Scott 1909). The Geneva Convention of 1906 amplified that of 1864, and eliminated certain obscurities in the laws of war (Hall 1909, v). A Naval Conference met in London in 1908 and 1909, and drew up laws of naval warfare with the view to providing the International Prize Court, proposed at the second Hague Conference, with necessary legal criteria.[1] The Hague Court of Arbitration was used on several occasions, and more than one hundred arbitration treaties were negotiated in the first decade of the twentieth century (Lawrence 1910, iv). Textbooks of international law were revised and updated to incorporate such rapid developments, and the authors expressed hopes for its further improvements (Hall 1895; 1904; 1909; Lawrence 1895; 1899; 1900; 1910; 1913).

One of the major effects of these developments was the growth of gradualism based on optimistic, progressivist assumptions. Instead of debating on the impracticable ideal, the writers of this period began to concentrate on the theme of the gradual modification of the existing system. The optimistic yet gradualist interpretation of the development of international law at this time was vividly expressed in relation to the Hague Conferences by J. B. Scott. According to him, they were 'the first truly international assemblies meeting in time of peace for the purpose of preserving peace, not of concluding a war then in progress': they marked, in his view, an epoch in the history of nations for they 'showed on a large scale that international cooperation [w]as possible, and they created institutions – imperfect it may be, as is the work of human hands, – which, when improved in the light of experience, will both by themselves and by the force of their example promote the administration of justice and the betterment of mankind' (Scott 1920, v–vi).

It is not suggested here that gradualism was totally absent from nineteenth-century proposals. Such a categorical statement is not likely to be true in the study of human thought. Thus, we noted earlier that William Jay's proposal advanced in the middle of the nineteenth century was characterized by gradualism. There was an element of gradualism also in William Ladd's proposal. However, at the turn of the century, gradualism appears to have become much more pronounced among those who planned for peace.

One of the most systematic proposals on peace through law made along the lines of gradualist progressivism is found in the work of Walther Schücking (1875–1935), a Professor of International Law at the University of Marburg, active Social Democrat and judge at the Permanent Court of International Justice. His book ([1912] 1918) contained a complete programme for a step-by-step development of international law, from the immediate future, in which a third Hague Conference was expected, into the more distant. Such an approach to peace-planning was based on a prevailing belief in the unilinear progress of mankind towards the goal of peace.

In Schücking's view, mankind was not starting from nought in this process, as it had in earlier times. As he saw it, the organization of the world had already reached the stage of a loose confederation through the institution of the Hague Conferences and the laws that were emanating from it.[2] He thought there was a 'well-known inherent law of things that a development once begun increases its pace as it proceeds' ([1912] 1918, 282). A further institutional development of this existing confederation into a more fully equipped international government, and, if necessary, into a world federation was, in his opinion, the line of future progress. A more detailed presentation of his proposal reveals how he used the domestic analogy in each stage of his argument.

Among the tasks of the immediate future in Schücking's programme were the conversion of the Hague Conference into a formal legislative organ of the international community and the development of an international judiciary. In order to heighten the sense of solidarity among the participants of the future Hague Conferences, and to formalize the hitherto *de facto* world confederation, the name 'Union des Etats de la Haye' was to be given to it, and its constitution drawn up ([1912] 1918, 153–277).

This constitution, as Schücking envisaged it, was to establish formally a union of sovereign states, which was to be looser than the German Confederation of 1815 ([1912] 1918, 247 n. 1). There are frequent references in his proposal to the constitutional instruments of this confederation (the German Act of Confederation of 1815, and the Vienna Final Act of 1820), as well as, in minor procedural matters, to the German Imperial Constitution of 1871 ([1912] 1918, 247ff.). It is beyond doubt that his close knowledge of German constitutional history helped him work out in detail his project for the 'Hague Union'.

At this stage in Schücking's programme, the proposed world confederation stood between the proposals of William Ladd and James Lorimer. It resembled Ladd's plan in that they both lacked an executive organ. Moreover, Schücking's legislative body was in essence a regularized form of diplomatic conference like Ladd's Congress of Nations. On the other hand, the highly developed judiciary which Schücking expected to see in the 'Union' was more like the judicial department of Lorimer's international government (see Lorimer 1884, 2:284–5).

Schücking did not stop here, however. There were more developments to be made in the next stage of the gradual perfection of the legal organization of mankind. Among the goals of the more distant future in Schücking's programme were the mutual recognition by the member states of their independence and territorial integrity, the renunciation of war, compulsory adjudication of all disputes without reservation, and the creation of an international executive organ ([1912] 1918, 278ff.). As for the last of these, Schücking incorporated a plan put forward by his contemporary, Cornelius van Vollenhoven (1874–1933) of Leyden, but considered all these goals to be inter-related, and in his view, the time was not ripe for their realization.[3] In addition, Schücking considered as necessary the gradual development and systematization, under the Hague constitution, of international administrative unions, and the creation of a World Parliament to work as a second legislative chamber side by side with the periodic Hague Conferences of government representatives ([1912] 1918, 304ff.).

This World Parliament was to be composed, as in the case of Blunt-schli's proposed European Senate, of delegations from the parliaments of the contracting parties. Here Schücking referred not only to the proposal of Bluntschli, whose legislature, we argued in the previous chapter, was derived from the model of the German Imperial legis-lature, but also to the latter legislative body itself, as well as to some German constitutional reform projects which had been advanced in the 1850s and 1860s. According to Schücking, these projects all clung to the idea of a confederation as the type of union desirable for Germany, but at the same time they envisaged the creation of a unified assembly as one of its constitutional organs. He wished to see the same principle applied eventually to the 'Hague Union' ([1912] 1918, 305ff.).

Schücking went even further. Just as the United States of America, Switzerland and Germany grew out of the stage of a confederation into that of a federation, it might, in his view, become necessary in the very distant future for the whole world to make their bond even closer. Eventually, therefore, the 'Hague Union' might develop itself, if such necessity should arise, into a world federal state ([1912] 1918, 313–14). Here Schücking's programme is completed.

The foregoing exposition reveals that in Schücking's view inter-national law could approximate the domestic legal system as much as necessary, and could even transform itself into a federal legal system. Schücking himself did not specify any clear threshold which, in its gradual approximation towards municipal law, international law would have to cross in order to serve effectively for peace, although there were some writers among his contemporaries who did. For instance, Vollenhoven, a Leyden Professor of International Law,

65

whose plan Schücking incorporated in his programme, insisted that the creation of an international executive was an indispensable condition of peace (Nijhoff 1915, 1–82). There were also some writers who thought the federal merger of the existing states to be an essential step towards world peace.[4] But these views were all accommodated within the gradualist framework of Schücking's programme. His was undoubtedly one of the most comprehensive of all contemporary projects on peace through law, ordering the rest, from the more modest to the radically ambitious, along the time scale of future human progress.

The view that there was no limit to the gradual approximation of international law to municipal law was not peculiar to Schücking. For example, T. J. Lawrence (1849–1919), a British textbook writer of the same period remarked confidently that an International Prize Court would come into existence in the immediate future, a High Court of Arbitral Justice would probably follow at no distant date, and, if sanctions were needed, something resembling an international police was within the limits of possibility (1910, iv).[5] The rapid development of international law which Lawrence was witnessing appeared to him to ensure the coming of an organized international society, equipped with legislative, executive and judicial organs (1910, v; see, for a similar view, La Fontaine 1911).

However, there were also some writers at the turn of the century, who, while concerned to develop international law gradually on the basis of its contemporary achievements further along the lines of municipal law, stressed that it was unnecessary for the former to approximate the latter beyond a certain limit. Among them was Lassa Oppenheim (1858–1919), one of the most eminent international lawyers of his generation, to whose ideas we shall now turn.

Oppenheim's limited use of the domestic analogy

As we saw in chapter 1, Oppenheim was of the opinion that the progress of international law depended to a great extent upon whether the 'legal school of International Jurists' prevailed over the 'diplomatic school'. The 'legal school', according to Oppenheim, desired international law to develop more or less along the lines of domestic law, while the 'diplomatic school' was critical of such a vision. He did not say which particular international lawyers of his day belonged to these schools, with the exception of John Westlake, of whom he said that he was a champion of the legal school (1914, x). It should be clear, however, that Oppenheim considered himself as a member of this school, for otherwise it would have been odd for him, as an international lawyer concerned for the future of international law, to say that this depended on the prevalence of this school over the other.

Like Schücking and Lawrence, Oppenheim was impressed by the contemporary development of international law. He took the view that international law had entered a 'new and pregnant epoch' where the beginning of the development was before their eyes, and that, in order to create a more peaceful world, any scheme of international organization must try to build gradually on the foundation laid at The Hague ([1911], 1921, vi, 5, 17).

Oppenheim's heightened confidence in the future of international law can be shown by comparing a passage from the first edition of his well-known textbook (1905–6) with a corresponding passage from its second edition (1912). In the former, he had stated that international law did not object to states waging war, but now in the latter, he qualified this by adding the phrase 'at present'. Likewise he now held it to be only 'at present' that eternal peace was an impossibility, whereas earlier he had stated this goal to be merely an unrealizable ideal: it now seemed to him that this ideal would 'slowly but gradually be realized' (1905–6, 2:56; 1912, 2:56). It would appear that the development of international law which had taken place in the intervening years, which had necessitated the revision of his book, had itself raised his confidence in the future contribution of international law to world peace.

It is very important to realize, however, that it was international law *qua* 'international' law that he, as a member of the legal school, desired to see perfected on the lines of domestic law. To put it more fully, there was for Oppenheim a definite line beyond which 'international' law could not go, without contradicting its essential nature, in the process of its assimilation to a domestic legal system. If international law were to be made to approximate a domestic legal system beyond this border-line, in Oppenheim's view, it would cease to be 'international' law, i.e., the law *between* sovereign states.

Therefore, while Oppenheim wished to see international law develop 'more or less on the lines of municipal law', he was equally opposed to those who desired to develop it beyond that borderline, and, who, in Oppenheim's conception, were consequently attempting to substitute a 'world state' for the sovereign states system governed by 'international' law. As we shall see presently in more detail, this borderline consisted, for Oppenheim, in the introduction of the idea of organized sanctions into international law, which, in his view, would fundamentally contradict the 'nature and definition' of that system of law.[6]

Naturally, the mere notion of what is to count as 'international law', whether it be a popular or scientific definition, cannot by itself dictate to mankind the limit beyond which its global legal system could or should not develop. One might accept Oppenheim's criteria as to what is to count as 'international law', and yet suggest that 'international law' thus defined, however closely it might be made to develop along the lines of domestic law, was not good enough as a means of organizing the world. To those who think it essential to bring the global legal system even nearer to a domestic model, the scholarly admonition that such a system would contradict the concept of international law would be irrelevant.

What underlay Oppenheim's position was not only his definition of international law, upon which his textbook as well as his proposal was built, but his confidence in the power of international law thus defined. International law, which, by his definition, was incompatible with the idea of organized sanctions, appeared to Oppenheim as a satisfactory means of organizing the world. The introduction of such an idea would be not only logically incompatible with the concept of international law as he defined it, but also unnecessary, in his opinion.

Oppenheim's belief in the redundancy of organized enforcement in the international sphere was explicitly grounded on his perception of the development of law within the domestic sphere. He wrote:

> In the internal life of states it is necessary for courts to possess executive power because the conditions of human nature demand it. Just as there will always be individual offenders, so there will always be individuals who will only yield to compulsion. But states are a different kind of person from individual men; their present-day constitution on the generally prevalent type has made them, so to say, more moral than in the times of absolutism. The personal interests and ambitions of sovereigns, and their passion for an increase of their might, have finished playing their part in the life of peoples. The real and true interests of states and the welfare of the inhabitants of the state have taken the place thereof. Machiavellian principles are no longer prevalent everywhere. The mutual intercourse of states is carried on in reliance on the sacredness of treaties. Peaceable adjustment of states disputes is in the interests of the states themselves, for war is nowadays an immense moral and economic evil even for the victor state. ([1911] 1921, 54)

While Oppenheim was therefore of the opinion that organized sanctions would be both unnecessary and contrary to the definition of international law, he held it to be both necessary and consistent with its definition to form an international court of justice, consisting of permanently elected judges, and deciding the cases of international disputes laid before them in terms of strictly legal criteria.

In his proposal of 1911 he did not argue that this court should be endowed with the power of compulsory jurisdiction, although he was confident that this aim would be achieved in the third, or some later, Hague Conference ([1911] 1921, 52–3). In his view, the obligation to submit to the court all or certain types of international disputes would be unnecessary, for once the court had been established, states would, in his judgement, voluntarily submit to it a whole range of cases. The type of cases submitted would, in his view, at first be those of smaller importance, but he was confident that as the court's reputation became well-established, more important cases would come to be submitted. What was lacking was the machinery: once available, it would be used, and its role would expand ([1911] 1921, 53).[7]

In addition, Oppenheim, like Schücking, suggested the conversion of the Hague Conference into a permanent periodic assembly of government representatives for the codification of international law ([1911] 1921, 17; Latané 1932, 2:805). He also planned international courts of appeal, to be established at a later date, to stand above the international courts of justice, in order to make the voluntary accept-ance of the judgements more likely ([1911] 1921, 51–2).

All these proposed organs were, in Oppenheim's view, both necess-ary for, and consistent with the notion of, international law; anything beyond them both unnecessary and contrary to it.

At this stage, we may note that we have witnessed at least three different ways of using the domestic analogy, exemplified by Schück-ing, Oppenheim and Lorimer.

Lorimer recognized the principles of good government at work within the domestic sphere, but saw nothing in the international sphere to build on. He therefore advocated the direct transfer of those principles to the virgin soil of international relations. Schücking, on the other hand, noted within the international sphere a promising, embryonic institution in the form of the Hague Conferences. He there-fore argued that this could be developed gradually along the lines of municipal law to its logical end: the creation of a world federation. Oppenheim, too, saw both the principles of good government at work within the domestic sphere and embryonic institutions within the international system, and his approach was just as gradualist as Schücking's. But, unlike Lorimer and Schücking, he considered that the progress of government in the domestic sphere made it unnecessary for international law to develop beyond certain limits along the lines of municipal law.

Thus, in the case of Lorimer, we find the domestic analogy leading to an argument for outright transfer of some of the most important domestic institutions to the international sphere. In the case of Schücking, we see an extensive, but gradualist use of the domestic analogy. And, in Oppenheim, a gradualist, but limited use of this analogy.

The 'diplomatic school'

The development of international law at the turn of the century did not necessarily produce a uniform response among international lawyers in favour of a further approximation of international law to municipal law than it had already accomplished by that stage. There were those whom Oppenheim had called the 'diplomatic school'. In the remaining part of this chapter, we shall attempt to identify who belonged to this school and what its views were. What follows is somewhat conjectural as unfortunately Oppenheim himself did not disclose whom he counted as among this school.

According to the *Oxford English Dictionary*, a 'school' is a body or succession of persons who in some department of speculation or practice are disciples of the same master, or who are united by a general similarity of principles and methods, and hence, figuratively, a set of persons who agree in certain opinions. In describing the 'diplomatic school', Oppenheim did not suggest that it was headed by a particular 'master', nor did he state that the members of this school were 'united' in the sense of seeing themselves as united. We may thus suppose that when Oppenheim referred to the 'diplomatic school' he had in mind a set of international lawyers of his time who shared opinions on certain aspects of international law. Their ideas were similar, as Oppenheim stated, inasmuch as they were opposed to the creation of an international court of justice composed of permanently appointed judges, and they desired international law to remain a body of elastic principles rather than to work towards the codification of firm, decisive and unequivocal rules (1912, 1:82).

In fact it is not very easy to find an international lawyer among Oppenheim's contemporaries who satisfies his descriptions of the 'diplomatic school', although there may have been many politicians who, from the viewpoint of their respective national interests, were opposed to the establishment of an international court of justice or the codification of international law in some specific areas. However, an extensive survey of the relevant literature reveals that Otfried Nip-pold, born in Germany in 1864 but a naturalized Swiss, is most likely to have been among those whom Oppenheim had in mind as the members of this school. This suggestion is based on the following findings which it is necessary to present in full, since an accurate account of the school's belief could not be given unless we could be reasonably certain about who it comprised.

The opposition between the two schools appears to have occurred to Oppenheim some time between 1905 and 1911 or 1912. In 1905 the first edition of his textbook was published, but no reference was made to the two schools. In 1911 Oppenheim published *Die Zukunft des Völker-rechts*, in which he advocated the creation of an international court of justice. In this book, he briefly referred to those who were critical of the creation of such an institution, but he did not say who they were ([1911] 1921, 48–9). In 1912, the second edition of his textbook was published in which for the first time he referred to the two schools by their labels, and described the 'diplomatic school' in terms virtually identical to those which he had used in his 1911 work to characterize the opponents of an international court of justice (1912, 1:82).

In the work of 1911 Oppenheim had stated that it was among the old champions of arbitration that the most violent opposition was raised to the erection of a real court of justice ([1911] 1921, 48–9). Nippold fits into this category well as can be judged from his major work, published in 1907, in which he stressed the role of arbitration, but criticized the idea of adjudication (1907, 150–1). Furthermore, in 1908, Nippold published a two-volume work on the second Hague Conference, in which he repeated his opposition to the idea of an international court of justice (1908, 1:221ff.). The copy of the second volume available in the British Library of Political and Economic Science has an inscription on the title page, showing that it had been given personally to Oppen-heim by its author. Although the copy of the first volume, in which Nippold expressed his opposition to the idea of a court of justice, unfortunately has no indication that it had been given to, or read by, Oppenheim, it may well be that he had read both volumes. This could well have stimulated Oppenheim to characterize those who were opposed to the creation of an international court of justice in the way he did in his book of 1911, and, subsequently, to refer to the antag-onism between the two schools in the second edition of his textbook. The reference to the two schools reappears in all the subsequent editions (1955, 87–8, for example). On such indirect evidence, we may suppose that Oppenheim considered Nippold as a member of the 'diplomatic school', and shall examine the latter's view on the conditions of international order as an example of how that school treated the subject.

Curiously enough, the outline of Nippold's argument about the nature of international law turns out to be remarkably similar to that of Oppenheim. They both stressed the specific character of international law. There was, however, one important difference between the two writers. Oppenheim placed the borderline beyond which international law could not develop without contradicting its nature and definition at the level of creating a mechanism for organized sanctions. Nippold, by contrast, put this upper limit of international law at the lower level: the level at which states became subjected to an international court of justice composed of permanently appointed judges, and acting in accordance with its own procedural rules (Nippold 1907, 148–68).

Nippold's own plan, moreover, turns out to be a little more far-reaching than one might expect. He proposed a general treaty which obliged states to resort to one of the three peaceful methods: arbitration, mediation or inquiry by commission. Neutral states were to be legally obliged to remind the contestants of their legal duty to resort to one of these peaceful means (Nippold [1917] 1923, 13–26).

It will have to be accepted, of course, that the concession he made to the domestic analogy was small and more limited than the case of Oppenheim. Nippold's concession to it consisted in the fact that his proposal to impose a system of legal restrictions upon the freedom of states to resort to self-help was at least implicitly an attempt to emulate to some extent the achievements of a centralized legal order as shown within the borders of states.

The affinity between the two writers leads us to suspect that perhaps Nippold stood at the 'legalist' end of the spectrum among the 'diplomatists' (just as one might suspect that Oppenheim was at the 'diplomatist' end of the 'legalist' spectrum), and that some writers on international law at the time might have rejected the domestic analogy rather more fully than did Nippold. The writings of Karl von Stengel (1849–1930) and Thomas Baty (1869–1954) throw some light on this question, and we shall examine their ideas for world order in the following section.

Stengel and Baty

Karl von Stengel was a Professor of Law at Munich, and was appointed a member of the German delegation to the first Hague Peace Conference. Some of those who knew that he had written a book in praise of war and depreciating arbitration seem to have thought it odd that he should be among the delegation (Scott 1909, 1:146). Stengel's view of international law, however, was similar to that of Nippold (Stengel 1909, chap. 1). The main difference between them was that Stengel went further than Nippold in protecting the existing legal freedom of states to resort to force as a means of settling disputes.

In Stengel's view, an arbitral tribunal could have jurisdiction over a dispute insofar as the parties agreed to provide it with such jurisdiction. He held that a court of arbitration or justice equipped with compulsory jurisdiction was just as incompatible with the idea of international law as would be an international legislature capable of imposing laws upon states against their will. Should arbitration fail, he thought, states would have no other choice but to settle their differences by force in accordance with the laws of war (1909, 7–8, chap. 6).

Stengel's conservativism could be regarded as an instance of the rejection of the domestic analogy inasmuch as he was opposed to any attempt to move the then existing system of international law closer to a domestic model especially in the area of the settlement of disputes.[8] It is not known whether Oppenheim considered Stengel as a member of the 'diplomatic school', although Stengel's opposition to the aims of the 'legal school' had been noted, for example, by Walther Schücking ([1912] 1918, 93 n. 208). If we are right in our judgement that Nippold stood at the 'legalist' end of the spectrum among the 'diplomatists', it might be that Stengel was at the other extreme within the 'diplomatic school'.

However, in order to appreciate Stengel's view fully, it is vital to bear in mind that his position on international law was firmly rooted in German nationalism. In his view Germany, a late-comer to the international struggle, was encircled by hostile nations. They were, according to him, bound to start a war against Germany if, under the influence of misguided pacifism, it chose to reduce its armaments, trusting in the power of international arbitration. Thus, he concluded, pacifism would defeat its own aim, and militarism was what was needed in Germany at that time: only through the adoption of a militaristic policy now, he said, could Germany resort to a peaceable policy in a generation hence (1909, chap. 7).

Therefore, if we are to treat Stengel as exemplifying the attitude of the 'diplomatic school' towards the domestic analogy, we must not forget the fact that his view on this question was derived primarily from the viewpoint of protecting the position of one particular nation rather than from the viewpoint of world order as such. Although Stengel linked these two perspectives together, the overall bias of his book was clearly in the direction of German nationalism.

In contrast to the case of Stengel, there is no clear evidence to suggest that Thomas Baty's views on international law, in the area of our concern, were rooted in the interests of any one country as he perceived them to be, although it is of some interest to note that he was a legal adviser to the Foreign Ministry of another revisionist power, Japan in the inter-war years, and was a Shintoist (Baty 1959).

In the opinion of this little-known British practitioner and scholar, international law was a near perfect system as it stood. It was more perfect than domestic law because it worked well without a government. We saw that this belief was shared to some extent by Oppenheim, but Baty's admiration of international law was something of a different order. Baty wrote: 'It is the special glory of the Law of Nations that, so far, it has triumphantly overridden the policeman'; 'International law overrides the policeman, and can do very well without him. Equally is it able to do without a Legislature – and not only able, but exultant'; 'Nor does it call for an authoritarian Code'; 'the longer it does without [a legislature] the better'; 'It bows to no sovereign set of managers' (1930, 25–7).

Baty also argued that as a consequence of the anarchical structure of international society, its rules would have to be simple, certain and objective, while nevertheless elastic (1930, 27). Baty's emphasis on the elasticity of international law satisfies part of Oppenheim's criteria of the 'diplomatic school', although Baty's book appeared two decades after Oppenheim's reference to the two schools of thought. Baty's earlier work, *International law*, however, had been published in 1909, and this contained an interesting analysis of arbitration, and a somewhat unusual chapter on federation.

Baty's favoured solution in search of a substitute for war was a treaty for obligatory arbitration of all disputes without reservation. But unlike many elaborate proposals advanced by the peace advocates of his time, his plan consisted in a very simple declaration on the part of each contracting party to bind itself to discover a person in whom it would have confidence to come to a just decision in case of dispute with another unresolved by diplomacy (Baty 1909, 8–9). The actual choice of the arbitrator and the regulations of the procedure would have to be left, he thought, until each time the necessity for arbitration arose. This elasticity, in Baty's view, was the mark of arbitration, in contrast to adjudication, and was for this very reason particularly suited to the international environment. He rejected the 'fantastic projects for the composition of international courts' as being 'suitable material for undergraduates' essays in Political Science' and 'unnecessary to be recommended or adopted' (1909, 9).

Baty defended his preference for a simple and elastic treaty, consisting of a mere pledge to refer all disputed questions to arbitration by arguing that whether simple or complex, the substitute for war would have to be based on exactly the same foundation: the force of a world-wide opinion constraining the observance of treaties (1909, 10). He even maintained that the moral force of a simpler and freer treaty would be greater, for the more 'fair and liberal' an agreement, the more strongly would public opinion condemn its breach (1909, 10; see, for a similar view, Root 1908). He concluded: 'If the nations are still so prone to war that they will look without disapproval on one of their number making a peaceful settlement of a given dispute impossible, in defiance of her solemn engagement, it is evident that no scheme of obligatory arbitration, however detailed, is likely to succeed' (1909, 11). Furthermore, Baty went on to warn against the importation into the domain of international disputes 'the arts of the advocate' and the 'sordid and suspicious atmosphere of the law-court' (1909, 20–1). Excessive legalism, in his view, was harmful to the cause of arbitration.

Baty's position as regards the role of law for the achievement of international peace was thus in perfect accord with Oppenheim's description of the 'diplomatic school', and the possibility is not ruled out that he was among those whom Oppenheim had in mind. Baty's opposition to the establishment of an international court of justice was known to a German writer, Hans Wehberg ([1912] 1918, 241), and it would not be an unreasonable conjecture that Oppenheim, in England, was also aware of Baty's views.

Baty, however, went beyond the horizon of an ordinary international lawyer. He was convinced that the state was becoming obsolete and being overtaken by the social classes. This, in his view, might result in a completely different structure of the world. But once the old sovereign states system had been broken up, and a long period of uncertainty had passed, Baty assumed that local units, much smaller than the present nation-states, would gain ascendancy as the centres of true patriotism. What he envisaged as the model of a very distant future for the global organization of mankind was a 'federation' of these minute local units. However, this 'federation', in his view, should not be organized on the model of a domestic government: in particular, it was not to have a legislature or an executive, for, in his view, these organs were becoming the target of ever-growing criticism even within the domestic sphere. After all, it was the absence of those organs from the international sphere that had rejoiced Baty so much (Baty 1909, chaps. 7–8).

As we noted in chapter 2, an argument for the conclusion of an arbitration treaty between two states could be derived from the domestic analogy. *A fortiori*, Baty's proposed treaty, which, despite its flexibility, was general and was to cover all disputes unresolved by diplomacy, can be said to contain an attempt to move the world one step nearer to the conditions which obtain within the borders of states. But, on the other hand, Baty was emphatically opposed to pushing the world system closer to the domestic system than the point at which states pledged to use arbitration as a means of settling their disputes.

Moreover, in many of his remarks about international law and domestic systems, we can even detect the reverse of the domestic analogy: not that international law ought to emulate a domestic model, but that domestic law is inferior to international law, that even within the domestic sphere governmental machinery is under attack, and that the state will disappear as a unit of global organization in some distant future. Thus, in Baty, whether or not he was counted by Oppenheim as among the 'diplomatic school', we see the domestic analogy approach the vanishing point, be rejected in most parts and even reversed. The analogy was reversed in Baty's case in the sense that it was now international law which was to provide a model for municipal law, and not the other way round, even though with respect to arbitration he might be classed together with those who made concessions to the domestic analogy.

Because Oppenheim did not clarify who in his judgement belonged to the 'diplomatic school', it is difficult to know for certain who comprised it and what precisely its attitude was towards the domestic analogy. It would appear, however, that the 'diplomatic school' was a label which Oppenheim had imposed upon a number of international lawyers who were unwilling to see international law emulate a domestic model as far as he had himself desired. It is not surprising then that the difference between Oppenheim and Nippold, for example, was a matter of degree. It is nevertheless easy to appreciate Oppenheim's concern to draw a sharp demarcation line between himself and someone like Nippold, for the question which divided them was precisely that which carried particular significance in the aftermath of the second Hague Conference, the creation of an international court of justice.[9] Within the 'diplomatic school', the attitude towards the domestic analogy was not uniform. Nevertheless, we see in their prescriptions general scepticism towards reliance on the domestic analogy.

One observation needs to be added here. Just as gradualist progressivism, while particularly pronounced in the early twentieth century, was not absent from the nineteenth century, so the ideas advanced by the 'diplomatic school' were not confined to the Hague Conferences period. There were those who adhered to similar ideas before the first decade or so of the twentieth century. Thus, according to Lauterpacht, the idea that a permanent international court would be incompatible with the concept of the state (and hence with international law defined as law between states) had already been expressed by Bergbohm in 1877 (Lauterpacht 1933, 412). The views, rooted in German nationalism, advanced by Stengel were in many ways similar to those of Heinrich von Treitschke (Treitschke [1897–8] 1963, bk 5). Nevertheless, it remains the case that Nippold, Stengel and Baty all produced their works against what they perceived as the progressive potential of international law at that time, and also as a criticism of what they regarded as excessive concessions which a significant portion of international lawyers were making towards the domestic analogy.

It was characteristic of the optimism and self-confidence of the early twentieth century that the necessity for coercion in the international sphere was not very strongly felt among the writers on world order. Vollenhoven, who regarded the establishment of an international army and navy as a necessary condition of peace, appears in this respect to have been in the minority, as he was himself aware (Nijhoff 1915, 1–13). His plan for an international army and navy, as we saw, was incorporated in Schücking's long-term programme, but the latter was far from stressing the mechanism of coercion as a *sine qua non* of peace. Similarly, T. J. Lawrence, Schücking's contemporary, said of an international police force that it could be established in the distant future, if the necessity arose, given the trend of development in international law. His point was not that such an organ was an indispensable condition of peace, but rather that international law had reached the point of take-off for boundless progress (Lawrence 1910, Preface). Those who belonged to the 'diplomatic school' were, of course, utterly opposed to the idea of organized sanctions in international law, and so was Oppenheim who, as we noted, stood at the 'diplomatist' end of the 'legalist' spectrum.

Many thinkers on the future of international law and relations, who wrote in the aftermath of the second Hague Conference, did so with a third Conference in mind, which they expected in 1915 (Scott 1909, 2:289–91). What awaited them instead was the outbreak of the First World War a year earlier. This experience brought about a radical shift in the opinions of many of those who were concerned with the problems of world order. In the next chapter, we shall investigate the impact of the Great War upon the use of the domestic analogy, and examine how this analogy provided the basis of the League of Nations.

5 THE IMPACT OF THE GREAT WAR

The Great War of 1914–18 was undoubtedly among the most shattering experiences of the twentieth century. Its impact was particularly pronounced precisely because of the generally optimistic air that prevailed in the early part of the twentieth century among the thinkers on international law and international relations. George Keeton wrote:

> Whereas only a few years before many publicists thought that the Hague Peace Conferences had ushered in a new era in international relationships, during which mankind could look forward to long periods of unbroken peace and steady material progress, and while they were unanimous that the respect for international law was firmly based upon a public opinion whose censure would be sufficient to deter the potential lawbreaker, the war had made it necessary to abandon these doctrines, which were in fact no more than a late outcrop from a School of Jurisprudence whose underlying philosophy was the progressive evolution of the human race towards increased law-abidingness. (1939, 68)

And in a similar vein David Mitrany wrote:

> The generations of the Second World War can hardly realise what a shock that earlier event [the First World War] was – they had been prepared for violence and conflict by years of Hitler and Mussolini, of Bolshevik Revolution and the Spanish Civil War. For us 1914 followed a long period of stability and of liberal optimism, of expanding international trade and cultural intercourse, of pacifist movements and efforts – like the Hague Conferences at the turn of the century. (1975a, 4–5)

One of the consequences of this shattering experience was a tendency among the writers on world order to converge on one central theme: the introduction of the element of coercion into the international system. This point is illustrated particularly well by the change of attitude shown during the war by those who had previously been firmly opposed to the idea of organized sanctions in international law.

As we saw, Oppenheim was opposed to such an idea before the war, but now in his letter of February 1919 addressed to Theodore Marburg, one of the chief organizers of an American association called the League to Enforce Peace, he stated:

> As regards the question which you raise in your letter, namely 'whether it is necessary to provide for enforcing the judgment of the Court,' before the war I was of [the] opinion like you that, if we only got the International Court of Justice established, no enforcement of its verdicts would be necessary . . . However, the war has changed everything . . . In case, a party against which a verdict of the Court has been given disobeyed the verdict and resorted to hostilities, there is no doubt that the [proposed] League would have to take the side of the attacked party. (Latané 1932, 2:615)

In conformity with such a change of view, Oppenheim also wrote in the third edition of his textbook that the *right* of neutral states to intervene against belligerents violating the laws of war was insufficient, and that it should be made a *duty* of the League of Nations, which had by then come into existence, to exercise such intervention. Although this edition was produced by Roxburgh, the statement was Oppenheim's own (1920–1, 2:335).

The third edition also contained Oppenheim's criticism of the League of Nations. Among the defects of the League was, in his opinion, the fact that it was possible for a member either to withdraw, or to be expelled, from it. In his judgement, there ought not to be any such possibility, and the recalcitrant member should be coerced by force to submit to the decisions of the League, and fulfil its duties. Another important weakness of the League, in his view, was the absence of compulsory jurisdiction by the Permanent Court of International Justice (1920–1, 2:291ff.).

Even at this stage, Oppenheim refrained from joining those who criticized the League of Nations for not being a 'super-State'. By a 'super-State' he meant an international organization equipped with an 'international Government', an 'international Parliament with power to legislate by a majority' and 'an international Army and Navy to serve as a police force' (1920–1, 1:294). But the ground for dissociating himself from this type of criticism was simply that he did not consider any such advanced organization to be realizable. The kind of sharp doctrinal denunciation which one might have expected from pre-war Oppenheim was conspicuously missing. He simply stated that no state would at that time give its consent to the establishment of a League of Nations constituting a 'super-State' in this sense (1920–1, 1:294).

The example of Franz von Liszt is no less striking. The author of one of the best-known textbooks of international law in the German-speaking world, he had repeated in ten successive editions of his work the view that international law was based on consent between states and that the idea of coercion found no place in international law. But in the eleventh edition (1918) an important change of opinion is observable. International law was now said to be inferior in quality to domestic law in that it lacked organized sanctions: it was still at a primitive stage in the development of law, which domestic legal systems had long overcome. The incorporation of a coercive mechanism into the system of international law was now said to be the greatest problem for the future of the international legal order (Liszt 1915, 8–10; 1918, 8; Lauterpacht 1933, 432 n. 3).

Otfried Nippold, Oppenheim's likely 'diplomatist' critic, too, changed his mind through the experience of the war. This was disclosed in his *Die Gestaltung des Völkerrechts nach dem Weltkriege* (1917). Quoting a passage from his own work published in 1907, Nippold explained that before the war the idea of coercive measures was contrary to his conception of international law. There was no reason, in his pre-war view, why international law should require coercion. The fact that no state had yet unlawfully refused to accept an arbitral award appeared to him to prove that the advocates of international sanctions were unduly underestimating the lofty position of international law, lofty because its effectiveness rested entirely on the mutual confidence of civilized nations ([1917] 1923, 34–5).

But, he now stated, the war had been a severe lesson: many pre-war views had to go absolutely by the board, and views on international law were no exception. The call of the whole civilized world for more real sanctions for international law could not be ignored, he thought, for international law could no longer rest on its moral power alone ([1917] 1923, 35–6). In his book, he listed a number of writers from many parts of the world who joined in this call for a real guarantee in international law ([1917] 1923, 58ff.).

Thus the prevailing opinion of the international legal writers in the period of the Great War was that international law should become more analogous to municipal law by accommodating the idea of coercion. There were some, like Philip Marshall Brown, a Yale Professor of International Law, who still clung to the idea that international law was unique and that no coercion was necessary (Brown 1916).

Likewise, there were some who, from the pacifist or other viewpoint, rejected the idea of coercion (Latané 1932, 2:773–5). But they were less conspicuous. As some former champions of the doctrine of the specific character of international law revised their pre-war positions, the idea that some form of coercion was as necessary in international law as in domestic law gathered momentum as the central theme of those individuals and groups who actively participated in the debate about the postwar reconstruction of international society.

Those publicists, associations and statesmen, particularly those of Britain and the United States, whose proposals had a more direct influence on the eventual creation of the League of Nations, while tending to advocate less radical changes than academic writers, were also in agreement on one fundamental point: that international relations could no longer be organized in the nineteenth-century fashion, and that the freedom of states to resort to war would have to be legally restricted. The ideas formulated for this end included a cooling-off period, regular conferences, a security guarantee, the principle of the indivisiblity of peace, and an international court of justice. All these ideas contained an element of the domestic analogy, as the following examination will reveal.

A cooling-off period

The idea of a cooling-off period was contained in the Bryce group proposal, the Fabian Society programme, and was also implicit in the proposal advanced by the League to Enforce Peace (Bryce *et al.* 1917; Woolf [1916] 1971, 371ff.; Latané 1932, 2:790ff.). The last of these was headed by former President Taft, and it is indicative of the general climate of opinion of this association that he had written an article entitled 'United States Supreme Court the prototype of a world court' (1915).

Marburg, one of the chief organizers of the League to Enforce Peace, personally favoured the creation of an international army and navy to secure the submission of disputes and to enforce its decrees, and considered a 'super-State', 'dominating the various nations as the Federal Government dominates the individual States comprising the American Union', as the ideal solution to the problem of peace (Latané 1932, 2:767, 851). Marburg's correspondence and the summary of discussions at the early meetings of the association reveal that their idea of a League was closely guided by their understanding of the basis of order in the domestic sphere in general, and their knowledge of the American Constitution in particular (Latané 1932, 1:*passim*; 2:703ff.).

Dictated by the consideration of practicability, however, what emerged as the association's official proposal was along the lines of most other middle-of-the-road proposals of the period: compulsory submission of justiciable and non-justiciable disputes to a tribunal and a council of conciliation respectively (Latané 1932, 2:790ff.). Taft explained the idea behind the proposal as follows:

> We do not propose in our plan, to enforce compliance either with the Court's judgment or the Conciliation Commission's recommendation. We feel that we ought not to attempt too much. We believe that the forced submission, the truce taken to investigate and the judicial decision, or the conciliatory compromise recommended will form a material inducement to peace. It will cool the heat of passion and will give the men of peace in each nation time to still the jingoes.
> (Cited in Hemleben 1943, 152–3.)

It may be questioned here whether a proposal for the creation of an international institution embodying the idea of a cooling-off period can, by virtue of that fact, be regarded as involving the domestic analogy. The important point to note in considering this is that the idea that a moratorium on the use of force will tend to decrease tension between contestants is an empirical supposition. Those who favour the introduction of such an institution to the international sphere must therefore have some experience in mind in which 'delay' actually led to 'cooling off'. Admittedly, such an experience need not have taken place within the domestic sphere. However, if the supposition is based on the experience of inter-personal and/or inter-factional disputes within a state, then there is a case for saying that a proposal of this kind is an instance of the domestic analogy. The Bryce group proposal poses a rather complex question here, since the group borrowed the institution of a cooling-off period not directly from domestic sources, but from the so-called Bryan treaties which had by then come into existence (Bryce *et al.* 1917, 14–15; Carnegie Endowment for International Peace, Division of International Law, 1920).

As Bryan himself explained, however, his proposal for the compulsory investigation of all international disputes, accompanied by a moratorium on war, was an application to the international sphere of an idea which he had formulated for the solution of domestic (labour) disputes. According to his own account, he had for some time been advocating a plan for a compulsory investigation of all labour disputes when in 1905, during the Russo-Japanese War, it occurred to him that the same principle could be applied to the settlement of international disputes (Bryan and Bryan 1925, 384). It may thus be argued that there was an element of domestic analogy in Bryan's own thinking, and that therefore the Bryce group proposal, which reflected Bryan's ideas, involved the domestic analogy indirectly. Naturally, if the kind of arrangement contained in the Bryan treaties were well-established among several sets of states, an attempt to unite all these states under one system, incorporating the arrangement in question, and perhaps extending it to some other states, would probably not impress us as an instance of the domestic analogy. In reality, however, the Bryan treaties had been a relative innovation in the international sphere, and could hardly be classed as among the distinctive institutions of international society.

Moreover, the Bryce group's inclination not to bring in the domestic analogy in explaining their plan could be interpreted as being based on a tactical concern. Any impression that the structure of the proposed international body is in some way analogous to a domestic legal system could be exaggerated and used against it by conservative opponents. The argument that the new international body is 'like a state', and that therefore to become one of its members means the loss or infringement of 'sovereignty', is a weapon which those who endeavour to create such an institution will not wish their opponents to employ against them.[1] It was probably such a consideration that had led the Bryce group to refrain from explaining their proposal along the lines of the domestic analogy, although this analogy was perhaps in the back of their minds.[2]

The idea of a cooling-off period, contained in a number of influential proposals at the time, became incorporated in Article 12 of the Covenant of the League of Nations.

Regular conference

An element of the domestic analogy was present also in proposals for a regular conference. For example, a British Foreign Office Memorandum of November 1918 and General Smuts' plan were both inspired by the conference system of the British Empire. The Foreign Office Memorandum suggested that a standing conference, equipped with a permanent secretariat, should be established as a central organ of the League of Nations for a frank interchange of views between the governments. The foreign secretaries of the Great Powers were to meet annually, and those of all the signatories were to meet every four or five years (Zimmern 1939, 197–209).

Sir Alfred Zimmern devoted a chapter to the discussion of this memorandum in his well-known book (1939, chap. 7), and remarked that the memorandum's proposal for a regular conference was in-

spired by the model of the British War Council and Imperial Conference (1939, 191). Since the memorandum had in fact been written by
none other than Zimmern himself we can take his remark here as
authoritative (Public Record Office, FO 371/4353, 149–51). The proposal that the foreign ministers of the signatories should meet every
four or five years is said also by Zimmern to be 'like the British Imperial
Conference', and the memorandum itself remarks that 'as in the case of
Imperial Conference' a report of the proceedings of the conference,
with confidential matters omitted, should be issued subsequently
(Zimmern 1939, 192, 204).

The War Council, which Zimmern mentions as a chief source of
inspiration for the proposed system of a regular conference, had been
transformed in 1914 from the Committee of Imperial Defence. The
latter, established by Prime Minister Balfour in 1904, was a co-ordinating body for inter-departmental matters relative to defence, consisting
of the prime minister and any other persons he chose to invite to its
meetings, and was equipped with a permanent secretariat. In 1911, it
was enlarged to include the prime ministers of the self-governing
Dominions. During the Great War, this British institution served as a
model in the creation of the Supreme War Council of the Allied Powers
(Hankey 1921, 289–90, 292, 297; Palmer 1934, 106ff.).

General Smuts, whose plan attracted much attention on the eve of
the Paris Conference referred to the conference system as being 'in
vogue in the constitutional practice of the British Empire', and took
this, rather than a 'super-State', federation or confederation of states,
as the most suitable model for the League of Nations (1918, 32). What
he had in mind as the conference system of the British Empire included
the British Imperial Conference and presumably also the Committee of
Imperial Defence. What Smuts attempted was the further extension of
these institutions into a peace-time organization for international co-
operation on a wider scale. The idea of a regular conference equipped
with its own permanent secretariat became the basis of some of the
most fundamental articles of the Covenant.

It should be noted here that the idea of a regular conference was also
seen by some commentators on the League as an improvement on the
Concert of Europe. Indeed, some writers on international relations
treat the Concert system as an embryonic 'international government'
superseded by the League and the UN (Zimmern 1939, 190–3, 272–3;
Morgenthau 1973, 434ff.). However, the overall conception of the
League was more strongly propelled by the general desire to emulate
domestic institutions, as can be seen from the examples noted in this
chapter, than by a clearly felt need to base the new institution on the

nineteenth-century European practice. On the contrary, the bankruptcy of the nineteenth-century system is a very strong theme which runs through the writings of the Great War period. Edward Grey, the British Foreign Secretary at the outbreak of the Great War is well-known for his attempt to resurrect the Concert to prevent a general war in Europe, and for his support of the idea of a League as a new and much improved substitute for the Concert. But even he explained the League idea in terms of the domestic (criminal law) analogy (Grey of Fallodon 1928, 2:chap. 16; Bryce *et al.* 1917, 45–6; Trevelyan 1937, 107–8).

A security guarantee and the principle of the indivisibility of peace

Proposals for a security guarantee, and for adopting the principle of the indivisiblity of peace were also derived from domestic sources. Here it is necessary to explain the views advanced by President Wilson and Colonel House, his adviser.

The Great War, in House's opinion, resulted primarily from the lack of an organized system of international co-operation. Soon after the outbreak of the war, which signified to him the bankruptcy of the European diplomatic system, House felt the need to prevent the duplication of the mistake in the New World. He urged the president to take the initiative in developing a scheme for the preservation of peace in the western hemisphere. What House had in mind was a loose league of American states to guarantee security from aggression and to ban the private manufacture of weapons. Taken in conjunction with the Bryan treaties which had by then been concluded, House thought that the proposed scheme would be sufficient to preserve peace on the American continent, and that it would also serve as a model for the European nations when peace had been restored (Seymour 1926, 1:213–16).

According to Colonel House, Wilson, at House's suggestion, wrote down the basic principles of the proposed Pan-American Pact in two points: '1st. Mutual guaranties of political independence under republican form of government and mutual guaranties of territorial integrity. 2nd. Mutual agreement that the Government of each of the contracting parties acquire complete control within its jurisdiction of the manufacture and sale of munitions of war' (Seymour 1926, 1:216).

House himself did not explain how Wilson and he arrived at the precise wording of the first principle, but it is strongly reminiscent of a passage from the American Constitution (Article IV, Section 4): 'The United States shall guarantee to every State in this Union a republican form of government, and shall protect each of them against invasion.' R. S. Baker, President Wilson's biographer, has no doubt that the inspiration for this principle came straight from the American Constitution (Baker 1922, 1:219–21).

Here it is interesting to note that Wilson appears at least in principle to have favoured the idea of a United States of the World. According to Baker, as early as 1887 (that is, about the time of the Lorimer–Bluntschli debate) Wilson had believed that the rapid developments of modern politics would ultimately lead to a 'confederation' of nations; and in 1915 Wilson wrote to his college friend, Heath Dabney, that he was 'very much interested' in creating a world federation (Baker 1938, 6:204–5). According to the same source, in July 1917 Wilson commented on a former representative from Maryland, David J. Lewis' plan for 'adapting the federal Constitution of the United States to the purpose of international organization', and is reported to have remarked:

> I quite agree with your [Lewis'] purposes, but I fear that no accomplishment so great as our own Constitution can be hoped for. A most happy combination of historical conditions alone made that achievement possible. What I do hope to accomplish is to establish a structure containing the tendencies which will lead irresistibly to the great end we in common with all other rightly constituted persons desire. But there are going to be difficulties even with this modest programme. (Baker 1938, 7:155)

What is implicit in this statement is the idea that, despite its impracticability in the immediate future, the United States of the World on the model of the American Constitution was an essentially correct and desirable goal. What President Wilson had in mind as an immediate postwar goal was the creation of an association of nations which could serve as a realistic first step towards a more perfect union in the distant future.

The Wilsonian conception of postwar settlement, however, appears to have had at least one other source of inspiration. In May 1916, at the first Annual National Assemblage of the League to Enforce Peace, Wilson spoke favourably of the idea of a League. In his view, although the United States was not itself a party to the war, the American people were willing to become a partner in an association of nations for peace based on the principle of national self-determination and equality of nations if such an association was to be created after the war. According to him, the world is even now upon the eve of a great consummation, when some common force will be brought into existence which shall safeguard right as the first and most fundamental interest of all peoples and all governments, when coercion shall be summoned not to the service of political ambition or selfish hostility, but to the service of a common order, a common justice, and a common peace.

(League to Enforce Peace 1916, 163–4)

The expression 'common peace' was repeated in a similar context in Wilson's address to the United States Senate on 22 January 1917, and T. T. B. Ryder believes that this term was a translation of the Greek, *koine eirene* (1965, xi). According to Ryder's detailed study, this expression was used by the Greeks in the fourth century BC to refer to a special type of peace treaty. This type of treaty embraced all the Greek states, regardless of whether they had been belligerents in the war which was to be terminated by the treaty, guaranteed the independence of these states, and was intended to be perpetual in that, unlike other types of treaty, the duration of its validity was not specified (Ryder 1965, xvi, 1–2, 118–19). Wilson, as an academic, was well versed in the political history of ancient Greece, and it is conceivable that he saw his role as the president of a Great Power, on the analogy of the King's Peace of 387/386 BC, or of the Peace of 338/337 BC organized by Philip of Macedon (W. Wilson 1899, chap. 2; Ryder 1965, chaps. 2, 7).[3]

Wilson's earlier proposal for a Pan-American Pact noted above did not materialize, as Chile and Brazil, two of the three South American countries which House had approached, procrastinated until the United States entered the European war in the spring of 1917, when the whole scheme was pushed to one side in the face of the more urgent problems of the day (Seymour 1926, 1:226ff.). However, the idea of a security guarantee was incorporated in the plan for the League of Nations, which Wilson had requested House to draw up in the summer of 1918 (Seymour 1926, 4: chap. 1; Miller 1928, 2:10).[4] This idea later became the basis of the tenth article of the Covenant itself.

Colonel House's draft also included the idea that 'any war or threat of war is a matter of concern to the League of Nations, and to the Powers, members thereof', which became incorporated in the eleventh article of the Covenant (Miller 1928, 2:7). It appears that House owed this idea, which might be termed the principle of the indivisibility of peace, to former Secretary of State Elihu Root.

Root was among those whom House had invited to discuss how best peace could be preserved in the future. The following remarks in Root's letter to House are noteworthy for their explicit reliance on the domestic analogy, and merit full quotation:

The first requisite for any durable concert of peaceable nations to prevent war is a fundamental change in the principle to be applied to international breaches of the peace.

The view now assumed and generally applied is that the use of force by one nation towards another is a matter in which only the two nations concerned are primarily interested, and if any other nation claims a right to be heard on the subject it must show some specific interest of its own in the controversy ... The requisite change is an abandonment of this view, and a universal formal and irrevocable acceptance and declaration of the view that an international breach of the peace is a matter which concerns every member of the Community of Nations – a matter in which every nation has a direct interest, and to which every nation has a right to object.

These two views correspond to the two kinds of responsibility in municipal law which we call civil responsibility and criminal responsibility. If I make a contract with you and break it, it is no business of our neighbour. You can sue me or submit, and he has nothing to say about it. On the other hand, if I assault and batter you, every neighbour has an interest in having me arrested and punished, because his own safety requires that violence shall be restrained. At the basis of every community lies the idea of organisation to preserve the peace. Without that idea really active and controlling there can be no community of individuals or of nations. It is the gradual growth and substitution of this idea of community interest in preventing and punishing breaches of the peace which has done away with private war among civilized peoples.

(Zimmern 1939, 231–2; see also Seymour 1926, 4:10–17, 42–7)

Thus one of the main pillars of the League Covenant can be seen to have come, via House, from an American elder statesman who wished to see international society organized on the same basic principle as that which underlies the community of individuals.

An international court of justice

The House plan also contained an article providing for an international court, but President Wilson, when he revised the plan, omitted this article together with a number of others (Miller 1928, 1:16; 2:documents 2, 3). However, an argument in favour of a court of justice came from Robert Cecil, who had been appointed the head of the League of Nations section of the British Foreign Office. Cecil, in formulating his draft proposal, took the aforementioned Foreign Office Memorandum as his basis, and combined with it much of the British semi-official plan which had been prepared by Walter Phillimore's committee (Zimmern 1939, 195–6).[5] However, there were some new elements, one of which was the idea of a permanent court of justice. He explained the necessity for a League equipped with such an organ on the analogy of domestic experience, stating that just as the rule of law in England rapidly developed after the War of the Roses because there already existed courts of law, so must a true court be established in order for international law to become the normal procedure for settling disputes under the League (Miller 1928, 1:64).[6] The idea of a court of justice was incorporated in the Covenant, in accordance with the fourteenth article of which the Permanent Court of International Justice was established at The Hague in 1921.

The constitutional and criminal law analogies also underlay the scheme presented by the Phillimore Committee's French counterpart headed by Léon Bourgeois. He had been an ardent advocate of improved international organization since the time of the Hague Peace Conferences, had represented France there and was the president of the Association française pour la Société des Nations. In the League of Nations Commission of the Paris Conference, he fought for his convictions persistently, but in vain, against the opposition of Britain and the United States (Miller 1928, 1:*passim*; Latané 1932, 2:770ff.; Zimmern 1939, chap. 10).

Bourgeois' ideas were based on his belief that international peace, just as peace within the state, depended on a 'constitution' defining the 'law' and applying it. But 'law' already existed in the international sphere; what was needed in his judgement, therefore, was an additional institutional device to turn the international legal system into a true 'constitution'. This, according to Bourgeois, involved not the creation of a 'super-State', but the introduction of obligatory arbitration and organized sanctions to punish disobedience (1919, 64, 66ff.).

These ideas penetrated his committee's proposal, which envisaged the settlement of all legal disputes by an international tribunal, of all non-legal disputes by an international council composed of the heads of governments or their delegates, the enforcement of decisions reached by the tribunal or the international council and the formation of a standing international force at the disposal of the League (Miller 1928, 2:238ff.).

Although Phillimore commented on this proposal that it was sufficiently similar to that of his own committee to enable a meaningful exchange of ideas, it was virtually ignored by the British Foreign Office and President Wilson, and had little influence on the final outcome, the Covenant of the League of Nations (Miller 1928, 1:11; Walters 1952, 1:23).

The mandates system

To the above list of institutional devices invented as parts of the machinery to reduce the freedom of states to resort to war, we may add the mandates system. This was proposed by Zimmern's Foreign Office Memorandum, adopted and modified by General Smuts and President Wilson and was eventually incorporated in Article 22 of the Covenant (Smuts 1918, 7–30; Miller 1928, 2:87ff.; Zimmern 1939, 203–4).

The idea of a mandatory, acting on behalf of the League, as a guardian of those peoples and territories formerly governed by certain empires, combined the ideals of national self-determination and non-annexation of territories with the practical necessity to manage the postwar vacuum created by the demise of these empires. Indirectly, the system was aimed at the avoidance of friction among the victorious powers in the aftermath of the war.[7] Although neither Zimmern nor Smuts nor Wilson explained the mandates system in terms of a domestic model, it would appear undeniable that the very concept of a mandate derived from domestic sources.

In the international sphere there were some precedents, prior to the war, where the idea of a mandate, and the term itself, were used in regard to the government of certain territories in which the administration of a country was carried on by a person or a state responsible to another body (Bentwich 1930, 5–7). However, the legal conception of a mandate originates in Roman law, and forms part of the modern Civil Codes based on that law. The term may have seemed natural to General Smuts who was trained in Roman–Dutch law (Lauterpacht 1927, 191ff.; Bentwich 1930, 7). The essential idea of the League mandate, however, is said to be closer to the English conception of trust, that is, 'property held by one person on behalf of and for the benefit of another, for a particular purpose, and subject to a duty to render an account of the administration, when called upon, to a tribunal' (Bentwich 1930, 7). Moreover, the wording of the several paragraphs of Article 22 of the Covenant suggests very strongly that the idea of a mandate was based partly on that of the guardianship of minor persons.[8] Given that the term 'mandate' had at that time no well-established meaning in the practice of international relations while it was, together with 'trust' and 'guardianship', commonly used as a technical term in the domestic legal discourse, it would be reasonable to suggest that the mandates system was yet another instance of the domestic analogy (Lauterpacht 1927, 197).

A comparison with nineteenth-century proposals

It is clear from the foregoing discussion that the domestic analogy played a significant part in the minds of those academics, publicists and statesmen who planned for peace during the period of the Great War. Because the idea of a League of Nations was an outcome of communal thinking, and because its final structure was the product of diplomatic bargaining among the governments, it is not possible to state in any simple terms how the use of the domestic analogy influenced the shape of the new body. Its supporters saw it in different lights, gave it a different meaning and justified it in different terms. But it is difficult to deny that one of the main themes of this communal thinking was the idea which stressed the need to make international society more analogous to domestic society by transferring some of its legal institutions and principles to the international sphere.

It is interesting to note that, whereas the nineteenth-century writers discussed in chapter 3 were invariably concerned with the problem of international legislation and put forward projects for an international legislature in minute detail, the writers of the Great War period were less concerned with that aspect of international organization. In advancing their proposals for the reorganization of international society, the main concern of the thinkers of the Great War period was to devise a system of law whereby contestants would be forced to attempt to solve their disputes peacefully before resorting to war. The defence of the law was the major preoccupation.

Of course, it is not altogether true that the drafters of the Covenant ignored the aspect of international legislation entirely. Some of the major issues which the third Hague Conference was expected to deal with were to some extent covered by the League Covenant itself.

Thus, Article 14 provided for the submission by the Council to the League of plans for the establishment of a Permanent Court of International Justice, and this came into existence in 1921. The Council was also charged with the duty by the eighth article of the Covenant of formulating plans for the reduction of national armaments for the consideration and action of the governments. Furthermore, Article 19 provided that the Assembly might from time to time advise the reconsideration by the members of the League of treaties which had become inapplicable. However, in contrast to the nineteenth-century writers, it was not the chief concern of the drafters of the Covenant to create a central international body whose function it was to pass law at regular intervals like domestic legislatures.

Admittedly, the American League to Enforce Peace did propose a regular meeting of states to formulate and codify international law as part of their project (Latané 1932, 2:790ff.). But the Bryce group proposal did not insist on this point, nor did the Phillimore plan, which played an important role in the creation of the League of Nations (Bryce *et al.* 1917, 28; Miller 1928, 2:document 1; 1:chap. 1). General Smuts suggested that one of the functions of his proposed Council should be to formulate general measures of international law for the approval of the governments, but no similar provision is found in the House plan or in the Wilson drafts (Smuts 1918, 45–6; Miller 1928, 2:documents 2, 3, 7, 14).

David Hunter Miller, the American legal adviser, in commenting on Wilson's second draft, suggested that an article be added to provide for legislation in international law, but this was not incorporated in Wilson's subsequent drafts (Miller 1928, 2:92). Cecil's Draft Sketch of a League of Nations contained a suggestion that there might be a periodical congress of delegates sent by the parliaments of the states members of the League to take over the role of the Hague Conference, but this was excluded from his Draft Convention of 20 January 1919 (Miller 1928, 2:62, document 10). Neither the so-called Cecil–Miller draft nor the Hurst–Miller draft contained provisions for international legislation or codification as such (Miller 1928, 2:documents 12, 28).

Since all the proposals and drafts by those groups and individuals contained provisions for legal means of settling disputes and for sanctions against Covenant-breaking states, the general lack of interest among them in the problem of codification and legislation is striking, especially when compared with nineteenth-century writers. Given the historical background both in the domestic and in the international sphere, however, the difference in the focus of attention seems understandable. The nineteenth century was a period of relative peace in Europe, where, in the domestic realm, there was generally a marked interest and advance in the sphere of legislation and law-making machinery. At the same time, in the international sphere, there were many areas of uncertainty in the law. Thus, whatever else might have been needed, it seemed obvious to nineteenth-century writers that an international legislature of some kind would have to be created. By contrast, for writers of the Great War period, it was the absence of the machinery which could ensure the peaceful settlement of international disputes that had caused the catastrophe they were witnessing. In short, the general bias in the use of the domestic analogy in the period of the First World War was due to the predominant interpretation of the experience of the war itself.

6 THE EFFECT OF THE FAILURE OF THE LEAGUE ON ATTITUDES TOWARDS THE DOMESTIC ANALOGY

The League of Nations, which came into existence in January 1920, was an association of sovereign states, established 'to promote international co-operation and to achieve peace and security' (Preamble, The Covenant of the League of Nations). It acted also as an agency for the enforcement of certain provisions of the peace treaties and supplementary agreements (Rappard 1925; Schuman 1969, 213). Although the League, even in matters of peace and war, achieved some measure of success, especially in the first decade of its life-time, it could not withstand the worsening conditions of the 1930s. By 1940 only one Great Power was left in the League, Britain, and thirty-one smaller powers.

In the chapter entitled 'The lessons of the League' in his *A history of the United Nations*, Evan Luard remarks:

> All those involved in the deliberations [on how best to structure the world after the Second World War] had lived through the painful and disillusioning history of the League. All had shared, at least in some measure, the hope that that institution, revolutionary in its original conception, would be a means of abolishing war from the earth and substituting the saner procedures of international conciliation. Instead they had seen that brief and inglorious organisation prove totally ineffectual.
> (1982, 3)

We need not enter the debate here as to whether the League's history truly deserves to be labelled one of 'failure'. Suffice it to note, for our purpose, that its inability to cope effectively with the deteriorating international conditions in the 1930s has been treated by a significant set of writers on international relations as indicating its failure.

Since the League of Nations, as we saw in chapter 5, was a clear attempt at ordering the world along the lines of the domestic analogy, the failure of the League might be expected to have produced, or reinforced, the opposition to this analogy particularly among the more articulate portion of public opinion. It is our primary aim here to examine this hypothesis with reference to a number of well-known writers on international law and relations who witnessed the League's inadequacies and eventual collapse. In particular, we shall examine whether, according to these writers, the 'failure of the League' signified the 'fault of the domestic analogy', and if not, what criticisms were given to the particular forms of domestic analogy as embodied in the League Covenant.

The writers who considered the problem of world order against the background of the League's failure included the following four major types, though these are not exhaustive: those who clung to the notion that, despite its 'inglorious history', the League embodied an essentially correct answer to the problem of world order; those who saw the failure of the League as resulting not from its own structure but from the inherent instability of the international system as such; those who criticized the League for its dependence on outdated liberalism; those who saw in the League's inability to maintain world order the superiority of the pre-1914 system of international law in the area of the control of force. In the following sections, these four groups of thinkers are examined in turn.

The defenders of the League idea

Not all those who conceded the League's failure accepted the conclusion that it was based on an inherently wrong approach to the problem of world order. An example is found in the writings of Leonard Woolf. As a Fabian, Woolf was among those who actively supported the League of Nations idea during the First World War. He had tenaciously adhered to the view that the League embodied an essentially correct approach to the problem of world order in the face of its failure to preserve peace.

He maintained that the problem of international order was not *sui generis* (1940, 234). There was no reason why, in his view, the interests of nation-states were inherently incompatible (1940, 129ff.). Such an idea, to Woolf, was nothing but a 'realist' dogma, and he wrote, '*a priori* there seems to be no reason to believe that power has a different nature and reality in international society from what it has in national society or that it is not equally amenable to elimination and control in both' (1940, 46). To him, war was therefore not a fixed and immutable feature of international life. He stated. 'Whether we have war or whether we have peace depends not upon the inevitability of war, the utopianism of peace, or the "reality" of power, but upon the place which we assign to national power and force in our lives' (1940, 53).

Woolf was particularly anxious to show that E. H. Carr's attack on the League approach was mistaken. The idea of the League, Woolf insisted, was not formulated by an *a priori* reasoning, which Carr saw as a mark of utopianism, but was grounded in reason and experience – experience which mankind had gained in the domestic sphere through thousands of years with regard to the control of force. Because war was to him nothing but the use of force by a group of individuals against another, Woolf saw no reason why the same kind of method as employed in controlling the use of force by one individual against another, or one class of individuals against another within the domestic sphere could not be applied to the control of war (1940, 1ff., 57ff., 78ff., 105–6, 147ff.). The League of Nations did fail, Woolf conceded. But, to him, this no more proved that the League was based on an inherently wrong approach to the problem of world order than the failure of appeasement induced Carr, who gave a theoretical justification of it, to say that it was intrinsically utopian (Woolf 1940, 116 n. 10). The main cause of the League's failure, according to Woolf, was that there was not enough psychological motivation on the part of its members to uphold its principles (1940, 195–6, 201). But, he thought, another great war, which they were experiencing, might be enough to teach them a lesson (1940, 52, 206–7, 225–30).

There were, Woolf admitted, certain modifications to be made to the League system. In particular, he argued for a two-tier organization, consisting of the world peace system and regional collective security systems. The former was to be similar in its structure and functions to the League, except that the members were not to be obliged to come to the rescue of a victim of aggression unless the victim was a co-member of a regional collective security system (1940, 220ff.). But these were points of detail. In the main, he thought, the answer given in 1919 was still a valid one (1940, 235 n. 1).

Woolf, and a number of other thinkers who shared his view, did not argue for the merger of the existing sovereign states into a world federation (Woolf 1940, 191ff.; see also Lauterpacht 1937, 158; see, however, Manning 1937, 178–80). To them, the problem of world order could be handled within the framework of the sovereign states system if the system could be equipped with those institutions derived by analogy from the domestic sphere. There were, however, those who went further. To these thinkers, the sovereign states system was itself the cause of instability and war. Partial solutions, such as the collective security system, would not solve the problem. Therefore, what was needed was a world state. Among the writers who adhered to such a radical view were Georg Schwarzenberger, Frederick Schuman and Hans Morgenthau, whose ideas we shall set out below.

The critics of the states system

In his *William Ladd*, first published in 1935, Schwarzenberger did not in fact go very much further than suggesting the necessity for an international equity tribunal to operate alongside the Permanent Court of International Justice within the framework of the League of Nations (1936a, 64–76). In the following year, in *The League of Nations and world order*, he wrote a critique of the League, but he did not go so far as to suggest a world federation as the correct alternative (1936b, Conclusions). By 1941, however, when the first edition of his *Power politics* appeared, with a subtitle, *An introduction to the study of international relations and post-war planning*, he was no longer satisfied with the idea of a reformed League (1941, chap. 29). By now, a confederal approach was not radical enough for him (1941, chap. 24, 357ff.). 'Power politics, international anarchy and war are inseparable', and war's 'antidote is international government', he wrote (1941, 430, 399). He made it clear that by 'international government' he meant a 'super-State or world State', and for its constitution he considered federation as most suitable as it would balance the requirement of authority and liberty (1941, 401, 402–4).

However, in his judgement, an effective federation would be possible only among those states which shared the values of democracy and social justice (1941, chaps. 30–1, 427–8). An international community of such states was to be organized as a federation with a necessary minimum of supranational government (1941, 359, 403). The responsibility for moving the world in this direction lay, he concluded, with those advanced Christian national communities in which democracy and social justice had become a reality (1941, 418, 427–8, Conclusions).

Schwarzenberger's *International law and totalitarian lawlessness*, published in 1943, is also noteworthy. By this time, the disgust with the cynical disregard of international law on the part of Germany, Japan and Italy had led him to suggest that these states be banned from international society as 'outlaws'. Although in his legal reasoning he characterized 'outlawry in international law' as an act of reprisal by withdrawal of recognition against unlimited lawlessness comparable to that of pirate states, the source of his inspiration was found in the institution of outlawry in various municipal legal systems of the past (1943, chap. 4).

Frederick Schuman was also a federalist, as shown by the first edition of his *International politics* (1933). Later, in 1946, he was to publish an article, 'Toward the world state', and in 1954 he wrote a substantial book on the problem of world government under the title, *The commonwealth of man: an inquiry into power politics and world government*.

In his work of 1933, Schuman stressed the extent to which international politics was a competitive struggle for power (1933, viii, chap. 13–4, 730). War was an incident of this struggle, and could not be eliminated by attempts at disarmament, arbitration, adjudication, conciliation, collective security or the outlawry of war, pure and simple (1933, 642, 661ff.). Left to its own devices, the international system would face a catastrophe in the form of the collapse of the social and economic foundations of the Western culture as the result of self-seeking nationalism, imperialism and militarism of the nation-states (1933, 740). The future therefore depended on the political unification of the world, he maintained (1933, 828ff.).

Schuman acknowledged that a world state could not be established in any foreseeable future and stressed that political unity must therefore 'be achieved by institutionalized collaboration between States, by the gradual strengthening of the bonds of an "international government" resting upon States and gradually welding them together into a world-wide political community of interests' (1933, 830–1). He was, however, critical of those advocates of international government who emphasized the aspect of machinery and paid little attention to the more fundamental problem of national attitudes, interests and values (1933, 670). He was fully aware that 'the whole weight of the past, the whole force of habit and tradition [stood] in the way of the transformation' (1933, 853). Yet, he concluded:

> If those in authority fail to achieve a new orientation, they will not merely be endangering their own positions in western society, but they will be jeopardizing the very survival of western culture. This responsibility is overwhelming in its implications. These implications will be appreciated and will be acted upon within the next decade, or catastrophe will become inevitable.   (1933, 853)

It should be added here that in the postwar (Second World War) essay noted above, Schuman substituted 'the immolation of modern civilization in a vast [nuclear] holocaust', which he predicted 'with almost mathematical certainty' if the present system were to continue, for his pre-war prognosis of the inevitable collapse of Western culture, and argued again for the political unification of the world through federation (1946, 36). In the same article, he came very close to drafting a blueprint for a world federation on the basis of the United Nations Organization which had by then come into existence (1946, 44ff.). Faced with the apparent unrealizability of his goal, he wrote: '[If a world government remains unrealized] mankind must be judged to be not seriously concerned about its own salvation, or the meaning of Man to himself' (1954, 493).

Like Schuman, Hans Morgenthau was also in favour of the idea of a world state. A lawyer by training, he had written a monograph on the theme of the limitations of the judicial settlement of disputes in international relations (Morgenthau 1929; see also Morgenthau 1977, 1–17). This work, published in 1929, formed the basis of a chapter on the same theme in his *Politics among nations* (1948, chap. 23). This book did not appear until after the Second World War, and Morgenthau included in his discussion the rising tension between the United States and the Soviet Union. Nevertheless, the book developed from lectures on international politics he had delivered at the University of Chicago since 1943, and the experience of the first half of the twentieth century, especially the period leading to the Second World War, provided a significant portion of his empirical material (Morgenthau 1948, Foreword).

In this book Morgenthau stated that 'two world wars within a generation and the potentialities of mechanized warfare have made the establishment of international order and the preservation of international peace the paramount concern of Western civilization' (1948, 309). These goals, however, could not easily be achieved. Arguing along lines similar to Schuman's, Morgenthau arrived at the conclusion that the only road to peace was the creation of a world state. In his judgement, 'the argument of the advocates of the world state [was] unanswerable', and 'there [could] be no permanent international peace without a state coextensive with the confines of the political world' (1948, 398–9).

Morgenthau, however, stressed that under the prevailing moral, social and political conditions of the world, a world state could not be established (1948, 398–402). A world community must antedate a world state (1948, 406). On the question of community-building, Morgenthau quoted David Mitrany and gave some support to the view that a world community could grow through a gradual erosion of national loyalties encouraged by increased functional co-operation in the UN specialized agencies (Morgenthau 1948, 412ff.; Mitrany 1966, 10–11).

However, Morgenthau warned that functional co-operation would not succeed where nations were in conflict (1948, 414–15). Therefore, in the end, the creation of a world community presupposed 'the mitigation and minimization of international conflicts so that the interests which unite members of different nations [might] outweigh the interests which separate them' (1948, 415). For this goal Morgenthau suggested the pursuit of skilful diplomacy divested of a crusading spirit and based on the realistic calculations of national interest (1948, pt 10). This, in his view, was the first step in the long road to peace and order in the world community organized as a world state.

It is to be noted that among the three adherents of the world-state idea discussed here, Schwarzenberger attached more significance than did the other two to the drafting of federal blueprints; Schuman was more concerned to stress the magnitude of the disaster which he saw as lying ahead than to engage in the drafting of federal schemes; and Morgenthau found it more important to spell out what should be done in the immediate future than to frighten the readers into supporting the cause of federalism. Despite these differences, these writers all accepted the view that, whether or not immediately realizable, world government was in principle the most appropriate mechanism for the maintenance of world order.[1]

Whether these writers should be regarded as resorting to a stronger form of the domestic analogy than did reformed-League advocates, such as Woolf, or whether, on the contrary, their commitment to the world-state idea should be treated as an instance of the rejection of this analogy will depend on how the term 'domestic analogy' is defined. According to the terminology adopted in chapter 2, they must be said to have accepted the domestic analogy in the 'cosmopolitanist', as opposed to 'internationalist', form. What is clear is that these three writers, together with a number of others who argued along similar lines, were objecting to the form of domestic analogy as embodied in the Covenant of the League of Nations.

The advocates of 'welfare internationalism'

The same point can be made with respect to the third group of thinkers, who criticized the League for its reliance on nineteenth-century liberalism. Among these critics were E. H. Carr, J. L. Brierly and David Mitrany.

1 E. H. Carr

To the student of International Relations, Carr is well known for his criticism of idealism. He was indeed severely critical of international constitutionalism, many variations of which we have already seen. He was generally sceptical of an approach to the problems of international politics which tried to seek a 'set of logically impregnable abstract formulae', and, in particular, he dismissed the attempt to strengthen the rule of law in international society by increasing the formal power of its judiciary (1939, 42, 253–4, 261–3).

Despite his attacks on idealism, Carr in turn offered a number of prescriptions in his war-time publications. These included *The twenty years' crisis* (1939), *Conditions of peace* (1942), and *Nationalism and after* (1945). In all these Carr stressed the bankruptcy of nineteenth-century liberalism and lamented its application to the international sphere in the peace settlement of 1919 (1939, chaps. 3–4; 1942, pt 1, 238; 1945, 60–1).

Nineteenth-century liberalism held that the liberty of individuals could be secured by a liberal democratic constitution based on the separation of powers and representative government; it left the economic well-being of individuals to the working of an invisible hand, which, on the basis of the assumed harmony of interests, was supposed to produce well-being for each and all. When transposed to the international level, liberalism meant that an international government or organization be modelled more or less along the lines of a liberal democratic constitution, with nation-states as its constituent units, while leaving economics to its own devices through the institution of free trade. The liberal concern for the rights of individuals and freedom from constraints, when translated into international theory, produced the idea of national self-determination, and the doctrine of the fundamental rights and obligations of states.

Carr rejected this line of approach since he believed that nineteenth-century liberalism had been shown to be inadequate even within the domestic sphere (1942, Introduction, pt 1). According to him, the transition from nineteenth-century bourgeois democracy to twentieth-century mass democracy meant that the function of the state had to transcend the mere protection of the political liberty of propertied individuals, and encompass an attempt to equalize well-being and raise the living standards of the masses. The planned economy and the 'social service' state were in his view the twentieth-century imperatives in the realm of domestic politics (1942, chaps. 2, 4, 6).

Such a perception, combined with his dislike of rationalism, led Carr

101

to produce a vision of future international co-operation different from the proposals of the kind advanced by the old-fashioned liberal, and legalistic, thinkers of his time, as well as by their nineteenth-century predecessors. Carr's suggestions for the future included prudential realism in foreign policy with regard to the problem of peaceful change between 'have' and 'have-not' states, functional internationalism in European co-operation and economic planning at the international level. We shall examine these in turn.

First, Carr rejected a judiciary and legislature as a means for peaceful change in international relations. He nevertheless suggested that an instructive analogue might be found in domestic society (1939, chaps. 12–13). This was the way in which in some countries the turbulent relations between capital and labour had eventually produced on both sides a willingness to submit their disputes to various forms of conciliation and arbitration. This, according to Carr, had resulted in creating 'something like a regular system of "peaceful change"' (1939, 269ff., 272). Such a development had been possible through contest and compromise, and Carr noted, the ultimate right to resort to the weapon of the strike had never been abandoned except under repressive regimes (1939, 270–1). He considered whether a parallel development was possible in the international sphere between the satisfied and dissatisfied nations.

His conclusion was a tentative one. Whether such an analogy was valid or not was not something which could be answered in an *a priori* manner. Such a question, in his view, would have to be settled by the test of experience (1939, 272). But if a parallel development were to take place, it would have to be the result of a long period of experience in which statesmen would learn to bargain without fighting. And such a development would be possible, Carr thought, only if statesmen did not lose sight of the element of power and that of morality. They would therefore have to yield to a threat when the prospect of war was hazardous. Carr's model here was an employer who conceded the strikers' demands by pleading inability to resist, and a trade union leader who called off an unsuccessful strike pleading that the union was too weak to continue (1939, 272). Moreover, in Carr's view, statesmen would have to learn to give in when the demands faced were reasonable. He considered this as analogous to the peaceful solution of industrial disputes through 'a spirit of give-and-take and even of potential self-sacrifice' on the basis of the mutually perceived justice and reasonableness of the claims (1939, 279). Thus, skilful diplomacy, on the model of skilful bargaining in industrial disputes, which took full cognizance of the reality of power, and yet did not lose sight of the reasonableness of the claims, however difficult in practice, was, in Carr's opinion, the only realistic means for peaceful change in international relations (1939, 272, 283-4).

Here it might be suggested that Carr's commendation of prudential realism, while explained in terms of a domestic analogue, was not in fact based on analogical reasoning. Like Manning's remark, noted earlier, that the effective functioning of a social system presupposed a sufficiently prevalent disposition among its units at least to tolerate it, the idea that prudential realism was a key to success in peaceful change might be regarded as an axiomatic statement. There is some truth in this interpretation: if the avoidance of war was a defining condition of 'prudential realism', and if every government acted prudentially and realistically by that criterion, then war would necessarily be ruled out.

This, however, does not seem to be the true import of Carr's message. What he was suggesting was that statesmen should try to combine the considerations of power and morality as best they could, and that this would make the world a little more peaceful place to live in. If this interpretation is accepted, then Carr's commendation of prudential realism will not be treated as a logically impregnable abstract formula. If so, the strength of his commendation would depend on the persuasiveness of his empirical evidence.

It may, however, still be insisted that his empirical evidence need not have come from the domestic sphere. Indeed, it can be admitted that prudential realism is not a social technique which is distinctive of domestic society. Morgenthau, for example, suggested certain guidelines for diplomacy designed to mitigate international conflict, and these were substantially similar to Carr's idea of prudential realism. But, unlike Carr, Morgenthau tried to show the effectiveness of his suggested guidelines in the light of various examples from diplomatic history itself, and not by any domestic analogues (Morgenthau, 1948, 439ff.). However, given that Carr himself explained his prescriptions here in terms of what he regarded as a parallel experience in the domestic sphere, he can be said to have resorted to the domestic analogy, although it was perhaps unnecessary for him to do so.

Second, Carr argued that under the twentieth-century conditions of industrial production and military technique, the nation-state was no longer an appropriate unit for the assurance of military security and economic well-being. But he was equally critical of the idea of a universal political organization based on a well-defined constitution. What he favoured was regional co-operation in Europe with regard to urgent and practical matters, such as relief, transport, reconstruction and public works (1945, 38ff.; 1942, chap. 10; 1941). He considered that international co-operation in these areas could be developed on the basis of the 'so-called "technical organs" of the League', which, in his view, displayed a far greater vitality than its political organs, and also on the basis of the existing machinery of Allied war-time co-operation in various fields (1942, 244ff.; 1945, 43ff.). In short, he adhered, at least partly, to the 'functional' approach. This approach is usually associated with the name of David Mitrany whose ideas will be discussed shortly.

In line with functionalism, Carr maintained that the question of the shape and size of the requisite international institution should be determined by the end in view (1945, 47–8; Mitrany 1943, 32–3). What is noteworthy is that he explained the functionalist vision of the multiplicity of overlapping international agencies along the lines of pluralism, as follows:

> In the national community the concentration of all authority in a single central organ means an intolerable and unmitigated totalitarianism: local loyalties, as well as loyalties to institutions, professions and groups must find their place in any healthy society. The international community if it is to flourish must admit something of the same multiplicity of authorities and diversity of loyalties.
>
> (1945, 49)

It is clear that in Carr's view the liberty and well-being of the men and women of Europe could be best protected if they were to be governed by many functionally differentiated international institutions, just as in the domestic sphere the power of government should not be concentrated in one body.

It is of great interest to note here an incidental remark David Mitrany made on the doctrine of pluralism. According to him, there was a significant revulsion in philosophical outlook which marked the post-war (First World War) period. This was the revulsion against the doctrine of sovereignty. He wrote: 'The doctrine of state sovereignty is now staggering under a double attack. It is being assailed from within by the pluralist school of political thinkers, and at the same time the external side is being courageously assailed by a growing number of international jurists' (1975a, 94). No doubt, Carr was not in agreement with those 'courageous' jurists (see Carr 1939, 249 n. 1). None the less, his accommodation of the pluralist doctrine in his second approach to the problem of world order indicates that his proposal contained an application to the international sphere of what was at that time regarded as an important doctrine within the sphere of domestic politics.

His third approach to future world order was closely linked with the second, but it is here that his rejection of nineteenth-century liberalism in the domestic sphere clearly affected his international thinking. In his opinion, the 'substitution of the "service state" for the "nightwatchman state" [meant] that, internationally also, the truncheon [would have to] be reinforced by the social agency and subordinated to it' (1945, 61). Carr noted, however, that in the period after the First World War, it was as a means of enhancing their national strength that the policy of planned economy was substituted for *laissez faire* in major countries. In his view, planned economy was therefore 'a Janus with a nationalist as well as a socialist face', and the 'socialization of the nation' was accompanied by the 'nationalization of socialism' (1945, 23, 19). It was clear to him that internationally disruptive tendencies were inherent in the juxtaposition of a multitude of planned national economies (1945, 45–7).

This did not lead Carr to say that economic planning would have to be abandoned. He argued that the internationally disruptive tendencies resulting from the coexistence of planned national economies should be mitigated by 'a reinforcement of national by multinational and international planning' (1945, 47).

2 *J. L. Brierly and David Mitrany*

A line of argument in many ways similar to Carr's was put forward at about the same time by an eminent international lawyer, J. L. Brierly. Like Carr, he was against an *a priori* reliance on the domestic analogy and criticized the view that all disputes could be settled by compulsory arbitration. In his judgement, the judicial machinery was already far ahead of international organization on any other side, and it was not likely that it would need any major amendment (1944, 34–5, 38–9, 46, 118).

While being critical of the domestic analogy, Brierly, like Carr, conceded that municipal law sometimes confronted situations which were fundamentally similar to those which were normal in international law. This was so, according to Brierly, whenever municipal law had to deal with demands by large groups and factions rather than by individuals. Thus, industrial disputes and civil strife were to domestic law what international disputes and wars were to international law (1944, 47ff.).

Being more legalistic than Carr, however, Brierly stressed that even in those states where revolutions and civil wars were quite as endemic as war was in international society, 'none of them ever [accepted] the view that for law to go on forbidding them [was] so unrealistic that it might as well admit the legality of actions which experience [had] shown it [was] unlikely to be able to prevent' (1944, 50–1). Brierly condemned the defeatist attitude which international law alone took towards the reign of force. It was certain, he wrote, that any plan for strengthening the influence of international law would have to start by forbidding states to use physical force against one another except in circumstances which were to be defined by the law. Moreover, a general ban on the use of force, unlike the Kellogg–Briand Pact, he thought, would have to be supported by a system of sanctions. However, he saw no possibility in the near future of establishing anything more centralized than a system of collective security based on the co-operation of the Great Powers (1944, 51ff., 75ff.).

Brierly's advice did not end here. He maintained that Machiavelli's maxim that the foundation of all states was good laws and good arms should be applied to international society. He contended that in addition to the general ban on the use of force backed by a system of collective security, international society would have to concern itself more positively with the general welfare of states. Brierly's main proposal here was the transformation of international law from the traditional *laissez-faire* system towards a more creative system which would enable states to co-operate more closely for the welfare of their citizens (1944, 58–9, 95ff.).

Brierly's prescriptions were therefore more radical than his initial rejection of the domestic analogy seems to indicate. None the less, he was in line with Carr in stressing that the resolution of international disputes could not be left to judicial methods alone, and that a system of collective security would have to be underpinned by a greater degree of co-operation between states in the economic and social fields. This undoubtedly was a reflection of the transition which had taken place within the domestic sphere from old liberalism to the doctrine of the welfare state.

The same transition provided a foundation also for Mitrany's functionalist approach to international co-operation. In his view, the difference between national government and international government was a matter of scale. The latter dealt with those things which could not be handled well, or without friction, except on an international scale. But the purpose of the two were the same: equality before the law, economic well-being and social justice (1975a, 98–9, 125).

Mitrany criticized the League of Nations for being essentially an application of the philosophy of *laissez faire* in international society. He remarked strikingly: 'It is no use putting a policeman at the street corner to keep the traffic in order and to watch for burglars if at the same time the water and food supply for that street is being cut off' (1975a, 182). The Covenant was concerned primarily with defining the formal relationships of states, in a negative sense, and only vaguely with initiating common activities, he noted. The economic, financial and other sections of the League were mere secretariats, and so in fact was the International Labour Organization (ILO). What he wished to see instead was executive agencies with autonomous tasks and power. They would not merely discuss but would do things jointly, he speculated (1975a, 125).

Here it is important to note Mitrany's own account of the two sets of experience which were vital in the making of his approach. Both these experiences were from within the domestic sphere, and Mitrany had studied them with great interest.

The first of these he encountered when, as an Assistant European Editor of the Carnegie Endowment's project, he edited European contributions to the economic and social history of the First World War. His study of the various manuscripts revealed to him that, under the impact of the new kind of warfare, which had made economic resources and industrial potential a decisive factor, the main belligerents, no matter how great the historical, constitutional and social variations, responded to the practical war-time needs in similar ways everywhere, by improvising similar and novel executive and administrative arrangements. This was a remarkable confirmation of the functionalist thesis that under given conditions there was a close relation between the function of government and the structure of government, and that needs breed institutions without rigid advance planning (1975a, 17–18, 136).

The second experience came from the United States, in the form of President Roosevelt's New Deal and the Tennessee Valley Authority (TVA), whose birth and progress Mitrany observed closely as a visiting professor at Harvard University. According to Mitrany, the 'New Deal was a functional evolution all along the line' (1975a, 129). The TVA's central purpose was 'water control, with electric power as a corollary, affecting a river system that spread over seven of America's "sovereign" states', and which presented 'problems and opportunities too big for individuals or local governments to handle' (1975a, 26, 162). This, he witnessed, transformed the 'Federal Government' into a 'national government' without any change in the text or forms of the constitution. This was possible, he thought, because the TVA 'was a new administrative but not a new political dimension' (1975a, 27, 26). He described the experience of the TVA further:

> Each and every action was tackled as a practical issue in itself; no attempt was made to relate it to a general theory or system of government. Every function was left to generate others gradually; and in every case the appropriate authority was left to develop its functions and powers out of actual performance . . . It has been a purely functional development at every point.   (1975a, 27)

Mitrany considered such a pragmatic approach, as opposed to the method of constitution-making, which he considered as a nineteenth-century preoccupation, as an appropriate mode of international co-operation in future. Moreover, his concern for the international management of welfare issues, as in the case of Carr and Brierly, was a clear reflection of the change in perception which had taken place within the sphere of domestic politics as regards the proper function of the government (1975a, 106ff.).[2]

3 The element of domestic analogy in 'welfare internationalism'

An important question arises here as to whether these three writers can be said to have resorted to the domestic analogy when, influenced by the change in domestic political concern, they advanced proposals in favour of the international management of economic and social welfare.

As a brief discussion in chapter 2 has indicated, the answer to this question seems to be in the affirmative, but with an important qualification. The qualification is that, unlike the more usual kind of domestic analogy (such as contained in a proposal for an international police force) the type of proposal advanced by Carr, Brierly and Mitrany with respect to welfare issues does not involve the personification of states. None the less, an analysis of the structure of their thought reveals an element of the domestic analogy. Their views can be summarized as follows.

Recent experience from within the domestic sphere of major countries shows that an appropriate institutional response is required not only by the problems of 'law and order' but also by those of 'economic and social welfare'. However, the international system has lagged behind this development, and there is a lamentable tendency to concentrate attention on the 'law and order' issues in isolation. Some problems of welfare may appropriately be dealt with within the domestic sphere, by each state individually, but there are some welfare issues which cannot satisfactorily be handled in that way. These problems are international problems. Just as 'domestic' welfare issues require an appropriate domestic institutional response, so 'international' welfare issues, in this sense, require an international institutional response.

In other words, these writers' suggested solution for what in their judgement was properly an international problem (i.e., the cross-national enhancement of the welfare of individuals) was inspired by, and was advanced in parallel with their endorsement of those domestic institutional remedies which had been applied by major countries to their (domestic) welfare problems. It is in this sense that these writers' line of argument can be said to incorporate an element of the domestic analogy. It must be stressed, however, that these writers' line of argument concerning welfare issues does not involve the personification of states, and that accordingly what they envisage as 'international welfare' is not the welfare of personified nation-states in international society. Brierly did argue partly along the states-as-persons lines that as domestic government was concerned with the general welfare of citizens so international society, through its laws and institutions, would have to be concerned more positively with the general welfare of states (1944, 95). However, the units of these writers' main concern were individuals, not states.

This distinctive feature of their mode of thinking can be illuminated when we compare strikingly similar passages from Immanuel Kant and E. H. Carr. As we noted in chapter 1, Kant stated:

> What avails it to labour at the arrangement of a Commonwealth as a Civil Constitution regulated by law among individual men? The same unsociableness which forced men to it, becomes again the cause of each Commonwealth assuming the attitude of uncontrolled freedom in its external relations, that is, as one State in relation to other States; and consequently, any one State must expect from any other the same sort of evils as oppressed individual men and compelled them to enter into a Civil Union regulated by law.
>
> (Forsyth, Keens-Soper and Savigear 1970, 183)

And now wrote Carr in *Nationalism and after*, arguing for the need to reinforce national by international economic planning:

> The pursuit of 'free competition', of an economic principle of all against all, inevitably tends to create those extreme inequalities and forms of exploitation which offend the social conscience and drive the less privileged to measures of self-defence, which in turn provoke corresponding counter-measures. By the end of the 19th century this process had led, as it was bound to lead, to the progressive development of combination at every level and in every part of the system, culminating after 1914 in the most powerful combination yet achieved – the modern socialized nation.   (1945, 46)

109

'Yet, what avails it to labour at the arrangement of a Commonwealth', one almost imagines Carr muttering to himself as he continued:

> But a further stage has now been reached. What was created by a cumulative process of combination between individuals to protect themselves against the devastating consequences of unfettered economic individualism has [through the process of 'nationalization of socialism'] become in its turn a threat to the security and well-being of the individual, and is itself subject to a new challenge and new process of change. (1945, 46)

What is striking is not only the remarkable resemblance of the two passages, but also the fact that, whereas Kant had, in the passage cited above, talked in terms of the state in its external relations with other states, Carr was seeing the hazardous impact of international economic anarchy with reference to the individual men and women living in separate national communities. Kant, while starting from the individual in his theorizing, nevertheless personified states; Carr, by contrast, took individuals as the units of his concern even in matters of international organization.[3]

Another interesting illustration of the distinctive feature of welfare internationalist thought is found in Brierly's proposal for an international protection of human rights. He favoured a relatively modest approach in this field, and suggested an international convention obliging states to incorporate in their own municipal laws a procedure for protecting certain basic rights of their own subjects (1944, 116). He considered that such an agreement would contribute towards the protection of basic rights, such as the freedom of speech, of the press and of thought, within separate national communities. This, according to Brierly, was in turn an indispensable condition of peace, for it was through the infringements of such basic rights that totalitarian governments manipulated their peoples into fighting an aggressive war (1944, 116).

Brierly's argument here clearly did not involve the personification of states. Had it done so, he would have suggested that as domestic constitutions often contained the declaration of the basic rights of citizens, so would international law have to clarify the basic *rights* of states. This was not Brierly's idea here. His point was that the protection of basic rights of citizens would have to be reinforced by an international instrument clarifying the *duties* of states in this respect.

It should be added here that besides their recourse to the domestic analogy in their welfare internationalist stance as such, the three writers considered here resorted to the analogy in other areas also. Thus, as we noted, Carr resorted to it in discussing the methods of peaceful change. Brierly insisted that international law would have to ban the use of force just as any domestic legal system. Even Mitrany, somewhat unexpectedly, maintained that a 'certain degree of fixity would not be out of place' in those areas related to 'law and order' and 'others of a more formal nature' (1975a, 116–17). Under this category, Mitrany had in mind a hierarchy of international courts and security arrangements organized on an interlocking regional basis. For the latter, he hinted at the possibility of using the British Committee of Imperial Defence as a model (1975a, 117).

One further observation to be added here is that the domestic analogy is involved also in Mitrany's functionalist line of thought regarding community-building across the borders of states. What underlies his vision is an empirical hypothesis about human nature, according to which human beings tend to show loyalty towards those institutions which satisfy their welfare needs. It is because of this that, according to Mitrany, national loyalties disruptive of world order could be superseded by loyalties towards international institutions satisfying the welfare needs of men and women located in separate national communities. If empirical substantiation of this hypothesis about human nature is drawn from the international sphere, the functionalist argument becomes less dependent on the domestic analogy. However, to the extent that substantiation is based crucially on experience from within the state, the domestic analogy must be said to be involved in the functionalist argument about community-building across the borders of states (see Mayall 1975, 254).

The defenders of the nineteenth-century system

Our fourth and final group of commentators on the League comprised those who saw in its inability to maintain world order the superiority of the pre-League system of international law in the area of the control of force. According to Wolfgang Friedmann, there were some international lawyers who, with the League collapsing and the Kellogg–Briand Pact still-born, took this attitude (1941, 15–16). Unfortunately, Friedmann did not say who these were, but Edwin Borchard and his mentor, John Basset Moore, appear to fit this category well. The example of Borchard is particularly striking because of his uncompromising insistence on the superiority of pre-1914 international law to its post-1919 counterpart which he expressed in numerous writings for over a quarter of a century well into the period after the Second World War (Moore 1933; Borchard 1934; Briggs 1951, 708–9). An anonymous reviewer of *Neutrality for the United States*, which

111

Borchard published in 1937 with W. P. Lage, remarked that Borchard was well-known as one of the foremost opponents of the American supporters of the League of Nations and perhaps of all plans of international reorganization.[4] Similarly, an obituary note on Borchard described him as having been 'profoundly skeptical of general international organizations' (Briggs 1951, 709).

Borchard was not in fact critical of all aspects of international law developed since the Great War. He was not opposed to adjudication as a means of settling international disputes, although he saw no point in according the power of obligatory jurisdiction to international tribunals, and considered diplomacy as a more important mechanism for adjustment (Borchard 1943, 47, 52). Nor was he against a possible development, after the Second World War, of international co-operation in the economic and social fields facilitated by some international institutions, which, if appropriate, he thought, might gradually increase their measure of control (1943, 54).

However, he did not see the absence of an international legislature as a major weakness of international law, for states had learned to co-operate by treaty in hundreds of fields when the need arose (1943, 52). Moreover, he was firmly convinced that the contemporary trend in international law and legal thinking, according to which belligerents were to be divided into aggressors and victims and the third party was expected to favour, or come to the rescue of, the victim states, was entirely mistaken. He stated: 'Many of the political errors of recent years have been due to the easy assumption that there is a close analogy between the law within a state, whereby the unruly are hailed before the civil authorities, and the international system, in which no one can hail an unruly nation before the bar of justice without producing conflicts' (Borchard and Lage 1937, 2). Borchard added that the system of collective security was not only unlikely to work, but also likely to extend and intensify conflicts without in any way resolving their underlying issues (Borchard and Lage 1937, pt 3, 1).

What Borchard proposed instead was to return to the system which had prevailed before the First World War. According to him, the nineteenth century was not a period of 'international anarchy', and the Hague Conferences symbolized 'the high-water mark of the trend toward harmony' (1943, 50). The reformer of international law, according to him, made a grave error in 1919 by acting in hysteria, mistakenly assuming international society to be amenable to the kind of control operative in the domestic sphere, and ignoring those institutions which 400 years of history had cultivated in the international system. He concluded therefore that there was no way but to return to the

112

pre-1914 system of international law supported by conciliation through diplomacy designed to eliminate the real sources of conflict (Borchard 1938; Borchard and Lage 1937, 348).

In presenting the views advanced by Borchard, however, it is important to point out that he was writing primarily from the angle of the United States. *Neutrality for the United States* shows his adherence to the position that American national interests, as well as the distinctively American contribution to the theory and practice of international relations, lay in its maintenance of strict neutrality *vis-à-vis* European wars (Borchard and Lage 1937, 23–4, 32). He desired the United States to be a leading neutral power, capable of protecting the rights of other neutral states and acting as 'the trustee for civilization in a shell-shocked world' (Borchard and Lage 1937, 346). Despite this American bias, however, it is also clear that Borchard considered the older system of international law to be more conducive than the twentieth-century system to the maintenance of order in the international system as a whole (Borchard and Lage 1937, 348). Thus his line of argument was diametrically opposed to that of Leonard Woolf, with whose ideas we began this chapter.

In the next chapter we shall examine which of the four lines of thought identified in this chapter contributed to the birth of the United Nations, paying special attention to the role played by the domestic analogy in the establishment of this new world organization.

7 THE DOMESTIC ANALOGY IN THE ESTABLISHMENT OF THE UNITED NATIONS

In chapter 6 we saw four major patterns of thought emerge against the background of the perceived inadequacies and the eventual collapse of the League of Nations. To recapitulate, these were: (1) a reformed-League idea (e.g., of Woolf), which held that a new organization incorporating the basic features of the League, with certain necessary improvements made, should be established after the war; (2) federalism (e.g., of Schwarzenberger), a radical view, which stressed the necessity to replace the sovereign states system by a federal union, though not necessarily encompassing the whole world at the initial stage; (3) the approach (e.g., of Mitrany) which stressed the importance of international co-operation in the economic and social fields; and (4) the view (e.g., of Borchard) that in the area of the control of force international law should revert to the pre-1914 system.

These were not in fact exhaustive of all the ideas which developed in the period regarding how best to rearrange the framework of the states system. For example, Carl Schmitt, a German legal theorist, notorious for his support of Hitler, formulated in 1939 the idea of non-intervention between a number of blocs, each led by a Great Power, as a basis of world order. What he envisaged was a reciprocal adoption, by each of the Great Powers, of the principle of inter-bloc non-intervention on the model of the Monroe Doctrine. This was a barely disguised attempt to justify and protect German preponderance in Europe and was based on the Nazi doctrine of *Lebensraum* and *Herrenvolk* (Schmitt 1939; see also Schwarzenberger 1943, 28–9; Brierly 1944, 76–7; Morgenthau 1977, 15).

None the less, the four approaches outlined in the previous chapter were dominant. In this chapter, we shall examine which particular lines of thought, among the four identified, had influenced the making of the Charter, and pay special attention to the part played by the domestic analogy in the birth process of the United Nations. It is, however, not our purpose here to give a detailed account of the conferences which led to the creation of the new world organization.

114

The idea of a world federation

Of the four approaches listed above, (2) and (4), the radical and conservative extremes, had little direct influence on those government officials who played a major part in the establishment of the United Nations. The fact should not be ignored, however, that arguments for federalism were widely canvassed in the initial phase of the Second World War. The frontal attack on state sovereignty was seen as a new panacea for world ills. This violent flirtation with the idea of federal union, however, was a symptom of despair, a psychological escape from the war. After 1940 this tendency declined both in numerical support and propagandist activity. During 1943 and 1944, opinion veered away from federalism and swung towards a more favourable view of the revival of the League of Nations (Thomson, Meyer and Briggs 1945, 158, 183, 308).[1]

The idea of reviving the League of Nations itself, however, was rejected at an early stage as being out of the question by those who directly participated in official postwar planning. Cordell Hull, who as secretary of state took the initiative in planning for postwar organization in the United States, remarks in his memoirs without any further explanation: 'As to whether to revive the League of Nations or set up a new international organization, we decided in favor of the latter' (1948, 2:1639). This decision was taken between the spring and summer of 1943, and by 'we' Hull meant the political subcommittee of the non-partisan Advisory Committee on Postwar Foreign Policy (1948, 2:1634ff.)

It is generally understood that the reasons for not reviving the League itself were threefold. By 1942, as H. G. Nicholas puts it, 'the League reeked with the odour of failure' (1975, 2). The Soviet Union would have been too proud to consider rejoining the League after having been expelled from it over the Russo-Finnish War in the dying days of that institution. And in the United States it was commonly felt that it would be more prudent to seek public support for a new organization than to revive the old controversy over the country's entry into the League (Nicholas 1975, 2).

A reformed-League idea, therefore, became the single most significant force in the process of planning and negotiations which led eventually to the adoption of the Charter in 1945. This is not to say, however, that those who worked for the foundation of the United Nations never considered their effort as being aimed at the ultimate ideal of a world federal union. Some appear to have done so.

A clear indication of an attachment to the ultimate goal of a world federation is found in none other than President Roosevelt. According to Thomas Greer, who studied Franklin Roosevelt's ideas closely, the president believed that 'at some distant time a world federation would evolve', and stressed that 'the conception of the United Nations was not that of an *ultimate* organization' (1965, 198). It was, in Roosevelt's view, only a stepping stone to greater security, and towards the greater unification of mankind. This is reminiscent of Woodrow Wilson's idea noted in chapter 5.

The unconventional first words of the Charter, 'we the peoples of the United Nations', were derived from the federal Constitution of the United States, and they might also be taken to indicate the drafters' attachment to the ultimate goal of a world federation. Some might, of course, have read such an idea into these words. Senator Sol Bloom, a member of the American delegation at the San Francisco Conference, at whose insistence the wording was adopted, certainly wished to impregnate what was essentially a loose association of sovereign states with a democratic sentiment, and a democratic ideal may be said to be more closely linked with a federal structure than a confederal or looser bond (Bloom 1948, 2–4, 278; Forsyth 1981, 186). Whether Bloom himself saw this new association as a first step towards a closer union, however, is uncertain from his autobiography.

The nineteenth-century system

If the radical approach of federalism has only a negligible and indirect influence on the creation of the United Nations, the conservative outlook of the kind expressed by Edwin Borchard also had little direct impact on the formation of the new organization. He was clearly against the tide of the mid-1940s in the United States inasmuch as it was one of the central concerns of the governmental planners of postwar arrangements to create an effective system of sanctions against aggressor nations and to secure American co-operation in such a system. Borchard, by contrast, was an isolationist, and favoured the traditional conception of war as embodied in the positive international law of the previous century, which saw no legal distinction between aggressors and victims, or to use the terminology of Hans Kelsen, 'delict' and 'sanctions' (Leuchtenburg 1963, 222; Kelsen 1967, 3–173).

In this connection, it is pertinent to note the following observation by Evan Luard on Article 51 of the Charter, which provides for the right of self-defence, individual and collective:

> It is arguable that [the insertion of this article at the San Francisco Conference] brought a significant alteration in the emphasis of the

Charter taken as a whole. . . . [The United Nations] might now become a system in which breaches of the peace were met in the first place by action taken by individual states or groups of states, while only at some subsequent stage would the Security Council be called on to take action if necessary. In other words, it made it substantially . . . more likely that conflict situations would be dealt with in the traditional way, as for hundreds of years before.   (1982, 54)

In a similar vein, Alfred Verdross argued as follows:

Since enforcement action under the Charter is impossible against a great Power, reactions against such a State, if guilty of an act of aggression, are not governed by the Charter, but by general international law. According to the spirit of Article 51 of the Charter, it is true that measures of individual and collective self-defence are intended to be only provisional, until the Security Council takes the necessary steps to restore the peace. But if the Security Council is paralysed, these measures change their character. Nothing remains but collective self-defence, or the old measures of self-help. In such a tragic situation they replace the new system of collective security under the authority of a central organ of the international community.
(1954, 348)

Thus, according to Verdross' interpretation, the institution of the veto enables the reintroduction of the old conception of self-help and war through Article 51, while according to Luard this article tends by itself to resurrect the old system of dispute settlement. Josef Kunz has also advanced an argument similar to that of Verdross (Kunz 1968, 605).[2]

It is important, however, not to confuse consequences with intentions. Whatever the legal and political implications of Article 51, the reason for its adoption was primarily to placate the anxiety of the Latin American states to protect their right to use force in collective self-defence without prior authorization by the Security Council (Russell 1958, 688ff.). This, it may be argued, would amount to the retention of the old conception of war. But Article 51, as is well known, delimits the legitimate use of force in self-defence to those cases where an armed attack occurs against the member-states (Akehurst 1984, 221–2). This article, despite its reference to the right of self-defence as 'inherent', cannot therefore be taken by itself to preserve for the member-states the right of self-defence under general international law, let alone resurrect the nineteenth-century institution of war as a whole. At any rate, there is no indication in historical sources, such as Russell 1958, that this article was inserted at the San Francisco Conference because the member-states preferred the nineteenth-century conception of war, and its concomitant institution of the laws of war and neutrality, to the contemporary trend towards collective security set by the

117

Covenant and the Kellogg–Briand Pact. Moreover, crucially for our argument, a French proposal at San Francisco to specify in the Charter that 'the status of neutrality is incompatible with membership in the Organization' was accepted in principle as inherent in the Charter system (Russell 1958, 676 n. 61). Thus, while Article 51 may have opened the door for a revival of the traditional method of dealing with international conflicts, it was not the intention of the drafters of the Charter to follow the lines persistently advocated by such conservative writers as Borchard, and to reintroduce the nineteenth-century system of the laws of war and neutrality.

Even with respect to the veto, it is uncertain how far the power accorded to the permanent members of the Security Council reflected a general belief in the superiority of the old-type international law and of the method of conflict resolution reflected in it. True, the idea of the Concert is implicit in the principle of Great Power unity. But the veto appears primarily to have been a concession made to the reality of the might of the Great Powers who *each* wished to preserve their freedom of action in joining a new world organization.

Stalin wished to avoid repeating in the United Nations the Soviet experience of expulsion from the League (Churchill 1948–54, 6:311; Hull 1948, 2:1700–1). The United States Senate, Roosevelt feared, would not ratify the Charter if the veto power could not be secured (Sherwood 1949, 2:846–7). Churchill was also in favour of the veto as a means of preventing any encroachment on British Imperial interests (Sherwood 1949, 2:846). It appears primarily to have been the co-incidence of these wishes and fears, rather than coherent adherence to the theory advocated by writers like Borchard, which led to the adoption of the veto in the Charter of the United Nations.

Welfare internationalism

In addition to the reformed-League idea, which was a predominant factor in the formation of the United Nations, the third approach noted above, which stressed international co-operation in the economic and social spheres, was also influential in postwar planning.

In comparison with Woodrow Wilson's 'Fourteen Points', whose main concern was to establish international order on the basis of national self-determination, the Atlantic Charter, drawn up by Roosevelt and Churchill in 1940, is noteworthy for the stress it placed upon international co-operation for 'economic advancement and social security' (Latané 1932, 2:846–7; Russell 1958, Appendix B). According to Thomas Greer, Roosevelt had accepted the view in 1937 that the best chance of peace lay in a co-operative effort to solve the social and economic problems of the day (Greer 1965, 170). In line with such a belief, and apparently also in accordance with the view that habits of co-operation should expand gradually through institutionalized collaboration on practical issues, Roosevelt decided that the first steps should be taken by a series of conferences on food and agriculture, monetary relations and other economic and social subjects (Russell 1958, 66).[3]

Thus, at Roosevelt's insistence, a plan was developed early in 1943 for the convocation of a conference on food and agriculture at Hot Springs, Virginia, which led to the establishment of the Food and Agriculture Organization (FAO) (Hull 1948, 2:1643). This was followed in July 1944 by the United Nations Monetary and Financial Conference at Bretton Woods in New Hampshire, which led in December 1945 to the creation of the International Monetary Fund and the International Bank for Reconstruction and Development. Similarly, an international conference on civil aviation held in Chicago in 1944 led to the establishment of the International Civil Aviation Organization (ICAO) provisionally in 1945 and permanently in 1947 (Russell 1958, 172–3). The United Nations Educational, Scientific and Cultural Organization (UNESCO) was formally agreed upon in November 1945, and was established in the following year, while the World Health Organization (WHO) was created by the United Nations Organization itself in 1948 (Russell 1958, 173; Nicholas 1975, 161).

In the meantime, there was also a move in the International Labour Organization (ILO), which had survived the collapse of the League, to expand its role in economic and social affairs, and, in particular, to concern itself with the problem of unemployment. The United States, however, strongly opposed such a move in view of its other proposals for dealing with the general question of international economic co-operation. In the event, at its 1944 Philadelphia Conference, the ILO adopted a declaration which among other things pledged the full co-operation of the organization with other international bodies which would also be working for effective international and national action to achieve general objectives of full employment, higher standards of living and other social and economic goals (Russell 1958, 170–1).

In view of the fact that a number of 'specialized agencies' were being negotiated and established in the economic and social spheres, the planners of the postwar general organization acted on the assumption that provisions would have to be made to co-ordinate these agencies as well as the technical organizations active before the war, such as the ILO (Russell 1958, 306). This was in line with the Bruce Report of

August 1939, whose main proposal was to establish for the League of Nations a Central Committee for Economic and Social Questions. Though the war in Europe prevented the implementation of this report, the Central Committee was to exercise control over the economic and social agencies of the League (Walters 1952, 2:762; Russell 1958, 305). The planners of the new organization in effect put the Bruce Report into practice in suggesting the establishment of the Economic and Social Council as one of the principal organs of the United Nations (Reynolds and Hughes 1976, 70).

The way these 'specialized agencies' of the United Nations emerged has been compared by Evan Luard to the manner in which 'the British Empire is supposed to have done, in a fit of absence of mind' (1982, 38). The creation of these agencies, however, may more appropriately be compared to the setting up of numerous agencies in the United States under Roosevelt's New Deal policy (Leuchtenburg 1963). It will be recalled that David Mitrany, whose idea may be said in effect to have been followed in the creation of the UN specialized agencies, had himself been much inspired by the New Deal policy in developing his approach. How far American proposals for new international agencies were consciously derived from domestic sources is uncertain. It does appear, however, that the idea of responding pragmatically to the urgent economic and social problems of the day by setting up new agencies was very much in the air, or in fashion at that time. The idea which underlay the establishment of these agencies was that just as certain domestic social and economic problems necessitated an appropriate institutional response within the domestic sphere, so those social and economic problems, which were international in character inasmuch as their full solution could not be had without international co-operation, required similarly appropriate institutional remedies at the international level. This line of thought, we have argued, embodies the domestic analogy, which, however, does not involve the personification of states.[4]

The police analogy

The stress placed on international co-operation in economic and social affairs was an important feature of postwar planning. Another innovation which the planners of the new organization considered as vital was in the area of enforcement. They in effect followed the advice given by Brierly, according to whom, as we saw, Machiavelli's maxim that the foundation of all states was good laws and good arms should be applied to international society. And it is here, in the ideas about enforcement, that reliance on the domestic analogy was most conspicuous. The analogy used was that of a police force as shown by Roosevelt's well-known term 'Four Policemen'.

Roosevelt wished to establish an enforcement agency consisting of the United States, the Soviet Union, Great Britain and China as one of the central organs of the new institution with 'power to deal immediately with any threat to the peace or any sudden emergency' (Sherwood 1949, 2:780). In explaining his ideas to Stalin at the Teheran Conference of November 1943, the president cited the Italian attack on Ethiopia in 1935 as an example of the League's failure to deal promptly and forcibly with an act of aggression. The president remarked that had the Four Policemen existed at that time it would have been possible to close the Suez Canal and thereby prevent Mussolini from attacking Ethiopia (Sherwood 1949, 2:780).

Later, Roosevelt stated in his speech to the Foreign Policy Association: 'The Council of the United Nations must have the power to act quickly and decisively to keep the peace by force, if necessary. A policeman would not be a very effective policeman if, when he saw a felon break into a house, he had to go to the Town Hall and call a town meeting to issue a warrant before the felon could be arrested.' The 'Town Hall' here, however, was a metaphor for the United States Congress, not a central organ of the proposed United Nations (Sherwood 1949, 2:817–18).

From the viewpoint of the domestic analogy, it is interesting to note Cordell Hull's remark that Roosevelt often expressed his views on international relations in terms of the situation in the United States. For example, the president said that he wished to have the United Nations located somewhere 'in the nature of an international District of Columbia' (Hull 1948, 2:1682). When confronted with the Soviet demand at the Dumbarton Oaks Conference that a member of the Security Council, even when itself involved in the dispute brought forward, should be entitled to vote, Roosevelt is reported by Hull to have said to Ambassador Gromyko that 'when husband and wife fell out with each other they stated their case to a judge and abided by his ruling: they did not vote in the case' (1948, 2:1700). Hull continues: 'This principle, that any party to a dispute could be heard but could not vote, [the president] said, had been imbedded by our forefathers in American law' (1948, 2:1700).

In spite of these few examples, an explicit reliance on the domestic analogy is in fact extremely rare in the birth process of the United Nations. This is in clear contrast to the case of the League of Nations where, as we saw, there were abundant instances of this analogy in explicit forms. This difference is hardly surprising, since the major powers, the United States and Great Britain in particular, had commonly accepted that a new organization to be established after the war would have to be something resembling the League of Nations. Therefore, inevitably, in formulating their ideas about the new organization they consciously built on the League. Since they were not creating a new organization from nought there was little need to conceptualize it in terms of any domestic model, unlike in the case of the establishment of the League of Nations itself.

Thus, for example, Ruth Russell's detailed account of the creation of the United Nations reveals that the United States Department of State planners, who had decisive influence on the eventual outcome, consistently referred to the League of Nations Covenant as a basis, and tried to reform it in whatever direction they considered appropriate (Russell 1958, pt 2). In Great Britain, too, the importance of the Covenant as a basis for any future security organization was fully acknowledged. Thus Churchill, while himself emphasizing the importance of regional security arrangements, warned against casting aside 'all the immense work' accomplished by the League (Russell 1958, 105). And a cabinet memorandum of July 1943 entitled 'United Nations plan for organising peace' stated: 'It is improbable that the League of Nations can be revived in its old form, but it is highly desirable that some international machinery, embodying many of the good features of the League, should be established on the conclusion of hostilities' (Reynolds and Hughes 1976, 126).

The birth of the United Nations Charter thus gives a very clear illustration of the tendency for the domestic analogy not to be used explicitly when a proposal for a new organization can be conceived of as a modified version of an institution already existent in the international sphere.

Regionalism or world organization

Despite the fundamental agreement on the need to endow the new League-like organization with the effective power of enforcement against aggressor nations, there were some initial disagreements among the leading figures over the extent to which the new institution should be based on the regional principle. Prime Minister Churchill held that Great Britain, the United States, Russia, and possibly China, should form a Supreme World Council together with certain other powers. Subordinate to this, he argued, there should be three Regional Councils, for Europe, the American hemisphere and the Pacific, respectively (1948–54, 4:717). The European Council, he urged, should be organized as a 'really effective league, with all the strongest forces concerned woven into its texture, with a High Court to adjust disputes, and with forces, armed forces, national or international or both, held ready to enforce these decisions and prevent renewed aggression and the preparation of future wars' (Russell 1958, 105). The European Council, he suggested elsewhere, should be 'a form of United States of Europe' along the lines suggested by Count Coudenhove Kalergi (Churchill 1948–54, 4:718; Coudenhove Kalergi 1926). The Council was to consist of twelve or so states and confederations, the latter comprising the Danubian, Balkan and Scandinavian blocs. France was to be strengthened, while Prussia was to be divided from the rest of Germany. Bavaria, Churchill thought, might join the Danubian Confederation. The members of the World Council, he proposed, should sit on the Regional Councils in which they were directly interested, and he hoped that the United States would be represented in all three Regional Councils (1948–54, 4:717–18). However, he also stated that he attached great importance to the regional principle. According to him, 'it was only the countries whose interests were directly affected by a dispute who could be expected to apply themselves with sufficient vigour to secure a settlement' (1948–54, 4:718–19). Such a consideration, it will be recalled, was contained in Leonard Woolf's suggestions discussed in the previous chapter. Brierly had also made an identical point (1944, 87).

President Roosevelt's initial ideas about the place of regionalism in postwar organization is a little unclear. His early essay, 'A plan to preserve world peace', submitted in 1923 for the American Peace Award, shows that he broadly endorsed the principles of the League of Nations (Roosevelt 1950, Appendix I). However, by the beginning of the Second World War, he was in favour of the Anglo-American policing of the world, and after the Pearl Harbor attack, he talked of the four powers policing the world against the renewal of aggression (Russell 1958, 96). According to Hull, in the spring of 1943 Roosevelt still favoured a four-power establishment to enforce peace. All other nations, including France, were to be disarmed. Hull wrote: 'At that time he did not want an over-all world organization. He did favor the creation of regional organizations, but it was the four big powers that would handle all security questions' (1948, 2:1642–3).

Hull contends that while he himself did not object to regional and other special arrangements supplementary to the general international organization, he considered the formation of a powerful world-wide association of nations as of supreme importance. He suggests that he and his associates presented their arguments against regionalism in various meetings at the White House, and as a result, the president, by the summer of 1943, began to turn towards their point of view (Hull 1948, 2:1645–6; Russell 1958, 206).

According to Harry Hopkins, however, the president, and the under-secretary of state, Welles, in their meeting with the British in March 1943, were already emphatic that the United States could not be a member of any independent regional body such as a European Council, that they felt that all the United Nations should be members of one body for the purposes of recommending policy, and that this body should be world-wide in scope. They also held that Regional Councils should have advisory powers and that the real decisions should be made by the United States, Great Britain, Russia and China (Sherwood 1949, 2:715).

At any rate, by the time Roosevelt explained his conception of the postwar international organization to Stalin at the Teheran Conference of November 1943, the president seems to have moved towards the idea of a global international organization. It was to consist of three main bodies. First, a world-wide Assembly of all the members of the United Nations, which would meet at various places at stated times for the discussion of world problems and for the recommendation of solutions. Second, an Executive Committee, to consist of the Big Four, together with the representatives of a number of regions. The Committee was to deal with all non-military questions such as economy, food and health. The third body was the Four Policemen, an enforcement agency (Sherwood 1949, 2:7870).[5] Stalin indicated that he preferred the idea of regional organizations, but Roosevelt replied that the United States would be unlikely to wish to participate in a purely European Council (Sherwood 1949, 2:780–1).

We noted above Hull's version of how he and his associates persuaded Roosevelt to accept the need for an over-all global institution by the summer of 1943. In Britain, C. K. Webster played an important role in postwar planning as a member of the newly established Research Department of the Foreign Office, seconded later to Gladwyn Jebb of the Economic and Reconstruction Department (Gladwyn 1972, 108–9, 128; Reynolds and Hughes 1976, chap. 2, 26). Webster reveals in his diary his strong disapproval of the regional principle. His opposition to the Churchillian regional approach is clearly stated in one of the papers which Webster prepared. He wrote: 'A World Council with final responsibility for the preservation of peace in every part of the world is of greater importance than any regional organisation such as the "Councils of Europe and Asia"' (Reynolds and Hughes 1976, 29). Webster was indeed extremely scathing about Churchill's conception as the following remark in his diary reveals:

> The PM talked the vainest nonsense advocating among other things a World Court to settle all disputes i.e. a sort of equity tribunal like the New Commonwealth of which he is President. The regional councils with nothing to do and the 3 Powers running round first to the Council of Europe, then Asia, then Pan America. It would be exceedingly funny if it were not so tragic.
>
> (Reynolds and Hughes 1976, 32).

In the event, as Webster shows, at the May 1944 Dominion Prime Ministers' Conference, Churchill was confronted by concerted opposition to his ideas, and was forced to accept the plan prepared by the Foreign Office for the Conference. Webster had played a substantial part in drafting this plan (Reynolds and Hughes 1976, chap. 3). It is noteworthy that in his diary he refers to this plan as 'my plan', and also comes very close to claiming the authorship of the Charter itself (Reynolds and Hughes 1976, 28, 70, 88–9). Across the Atlantic, Cordell Hull was praised by Roosevelt as the 'Father of the United Nations' (Hull 1948, 2:1727–8). Indeed, by the summer of 1944 there was no fundamental difference between the official American and British lines. Webster described the American proposals for the Dumbarton Oaks Conference as 'simply a reformed Covenant', and in essential respects so also was the British plan (Reynolds and Hughes 1976, 38).

The Covenant and the Charter

The history of the Dumbarton Oaks Conference and the San Francisco Conference need not be dealt with here, since the outline of this history is readily available in many works on the United Nations (Nicholas 1975; Luard 1982), and the detailed analysis of the kind contained in Russell's work is beyond the scope of the present discussion. At this stage in the emergence of the Charter, the general framework had been agreed on, and the discussion tended to be on matters of detail. Even with respect to the veto, the controversy over which was finally settled while the powers met in San Francisco, there was agreement from the start that none of the Great Powers should be subjected to enforcement measures by the Security Council (Reynolds and Hughes 1976, 40ff.; Luard 1982, 29ff.). At any rate, in its essential respects, the final outcome remained the body which the four powers had conceived at Dumbarton Oaks, and this in turn,

125

following the American line, was closely based on the reformed-League idea.

Thus, in the place of the Council of the League was established the Security Council, and the Assembly was replaced by the General Assembly, while the new Secretariat remained, as in the League, permanent and international, under an elected Secretary-General. In addition, in the place of the Permanent Court of International Justice was created the International Court of Justice. These were virtually identical in structures and functions, but while the Permanent Court was not actually a League organ in that the members of the League were not automatically parties to the Statute of the Court, the International Court of Justice was made an integral part of the United Nations. As we noted, the Economic and Social Council was added in line with the Bruce Report of 1939 which, had it not been for the war, would have led to the establishment of a comparable body under the League. And the League's Mandates Commission found its UN counterpart in the Trusteeship Council.[6]

There were some significant differences between the Covenant and the Charter, however. Here we may focus on the issue of the control of force, since this was the aspect with respect to which the makers of the Charter were most anxious to advance beyond the Covenant on the basis of closer approximation to domestic society.[7]

Whereas the Covenant did not prohibit resort to war completely, the Charter bans the threat and use of force by member-states against the territorial integrity and political independence of any state, or in any other manner inconsistent with the purposes of the United Nations. Moreover, whereas under the League each member retained the competence to decide whether the conditions for an enforcement action existed, under the Charter this competence is vested in the Security Council. In the League each member was obliged to take non-military sanctions, and authorized to resort to military measures when it decided that a member-state had resorted to war in breach of the Covenant. By contrast, in the United Nations the Security Council makes binding decisions on what enforcement measures, military or non-military, should be taken when it determines that there exists a 'threat to the peace, breach of the peace, or act of aggression'. But the Security Council is not required to determine the existence of these conditions in the light of whether any state is in breach of the law, unlike under the Covenant, where sanctions were to be directed only against those states resorting to war unlawfully. Therefore, enforcement measures under the Charter, unlike those under the Covenant, cannot necessarily be interpreted as having the character of 'sanctions' against 'delicts' or unlawful acts (Kelsen 1967, 34–6, 47–9).

The Security Council was to be equipped with a Military Staff Committee composed of the chiefs of staff of all the permanent members. This body was to make advance plans for the organization and deployment of military forces which member-states would place at the disposal of the organization, and when the Council acted, the Committee would serve as its strategic adviser (Nicholas 1975, 16; The Charter of the United Nations, Arts. 43, 45–7). But already in April 1947 the Military Staff Committee reported to the Security Council its inability to agree on the armed contributions that permanent members should make. By August 1948 the Committee announced the virtual cessation of activity (Nicholas 1975, 50). Roosevelt's 'Four (and now Five) Policemen' never came into existence.

Another important difference is that the League principle of unanimity, both for the Assembly and the Council, was abandoned in the Charter. But precisely because the League of Nations was a decentralized system the effectiveness of the League did not depend on its organs being able to reach decisions, but upon the observance by the individual members of their obligations under the Covenant. By contrast, since under the Charter enforcement action can only be taken if the Security Council so decides, it was necessary to provide against the possibility of deadlocks by introducing some form of majority voting. But the Charter could do this only at a very high price: the Great Power veto on non-procedural issues (Brierly 1958a, 319–21).

Indeed, the institution of the veto has been criticized as having made the United Nations more backward than the League. Brierly, one of the critics, has remarked: 'we must realize that what we have done is to exchange a scheme [i.e., the Covenant] which might or might not have worked for one which cannot work [in those circumstances in which there is a real threat to world peace]' (1958a, 324). In his view, 'we have returned . . . to the idea which underlay the Concert of Europe in the nineteenth century' (1958a, 326). The United Nations, which is apparently more centralized than the League, and can be regarded as an attempt to transform the structure of international society one step closer to that of domestic society, was made from the start to depend on the age-old principle of the unity of the Great Powers (Kelsen 1967, 33–51). In the more sympathetic words of C. K. Webster, the Charter embodies an attempt at 'harmonising the Great Power Alliance theory and the League theory' (Reynolds and Hughes 1976, 71). In the last years of the Second World War there was still enough hope for continued solidarity among the Great Powers allied against the Axis

Powers to enable a distinguished historian–diplomat to make such a remark with confidence and pride. It is ironic that Carl Schmitt's idea noted at the beginning of this chapter, to which the liberalism and universalism of the Charter are opposed, has come to resemble what might be seen as an unwritten code of conduct of the Superpowers in the postwar era (McWhinney 1964; Cohen 1981; Keal 1983).

8 THE DOMESTIC ANALOGY IN CONTEMPORARY INTERNATIONAL THOUGHT

In chapter 6 we identified four dominant approaches to world order which emerged against the background of the perceived inadequacies and the eventual collapse of the League of Nations. In the light of these four approaches, we discussed in chapter 7 the place of the domestic analogy in the birth process of the United Nations. If, as we saw, a reformed-League idea and welfare internationalism were the two major influences in the shaping of the new world organization, these and the other two approaches all continue to find support among the writers and practitioners of the postwar era, although some modified or new approaches have also emerged.

A reformed-UN approach within the bounds of legalism

Clark and Sohn's oft-cited work, *World peace through world law* shows that the idea of improving on the League, and now on the United Nations, but remaining within the old legalistic mould, still continues to find many adherents. A distinguished Harvard-educated legal practitioner, Grenville Clark has engaged in the study of world order since before the war. A proposal contained in a short pamphlet he published in 1940 under the title *A memorandum with regard to a new effort to organize peace* was in many ways an adaptation of the American Constitution, and advocated the unification of democratic countries. A generation younger than Clark, Louis Sohn has taught courses such as 'United Nations law' and 'Problems in the development of world order' since 1951 at the Harvard Law School (Clark and Sohn 1966, lii). The two authors began their collaboration in 1945, which resulted in the publication of a small book, *A plan for peace* (Clark 1950). This, however, was only an outline, and they soon began to work together to fill in the details (Cousins and Clifford 1975, 46). In the first edition of *World peace through world law* the authors claim that at least 2 thousand persons from various parts of the world have commented on the preliminary drafts (1958, xxxv). In 1959, the American Bar Association awarded Clark its Gold Medal, referring to the book as a 'major contribution to world literature' on the subject of law and peace (Cousins and Clifford 1975, 5). In the second edition at least twenty-five hundred persons are said to have corresponded with the authors about their project (1960, xii-xiii). Translations of the entire book, or of its Introduction summarizing its main features, are available in thirteen languages (Clark and Sohn 1966, 380 n.). Clearly, the book can claim to be among the best-known in the genre.

The first edition contains an extremely detailed project for a thorough-going revision of the United Nations Charter, and the second edition retains the proposal without significant alterations. The authors' concern for details is based on their belief that a need for a 'world law' has already been demonstrated, and that what is now required is concrete and specific proposals to encourage discussion (Clark and Sohn 1958, xi, xxxiii). They express their optimistic belief that the proposed system can be in full operation within less than two decades of its publication (1960, xliiiff., liv). Disappointed by the apparent lack of progress, the authors, in the third edition of the book, add an alternative to the whole scheme: a proposed Treaty establishing a World Disarmament and World Development Organization, designed to operate alongside the existing machinery of the United Nations. It emerges, however, that the reformed United Nations which they have proposed from the beginning, and the World Disarmament and World Development Organization which they now offer as an alternative to revising the Charter itself are very similar in their structures and functions. Indeed, as the authors claim, the fundamental philosophy or basic plan set forth in the first edition of their book has remained unaffected despite certain stage-by-stage modifications (1966, xiv). The central pillar of their 'fundamental philosophy' is undoubtedly a belief in the validity of the domestic analogy.

It is unlikely, however, that Clark and Sohn used any specific constitution as a model in arriving at their revised Charter or proposed treaty, although there are a few references, mainly for the purpose of illustration, to the British parliamentary system and the United States Constitution (1966, xxiii, 15, 309, 365–8). Indeed, Sohn recalls criticizing Clark's aforementioned 1940 memorandum for its dependence on the American model: in Sohn's view this model might be familiar to the American people but 'other nations might prefer to build around international rather than national precedents' (Cousins and Clifford, 46). It is pertinent to note here that Sohn as a young lawyer had emigrated from Poland to the United States (Clark and Sohn 1966, lii).

130

It is clear, however, that what guided the two authors' thinking in arriving at their project was the notion that the members of the United Nations would have to accept a legal system more closely analogous in certain fundamental respects to a domestic legal system than is the Charter of 1945 itself. In their judgement, peace cannot be secured without universal and complete national disarmament together with the establishment of institutions 'corresponding in the world field to those which maintain law and order within local communities and nations', namely, 'clearly stated law against violence, courts to interpret and apply that law and police to enforce it' (1966, xv-xvi).

For the achievement of these purposes, the General Assembly is to be radically reformed.[1] It is to have a legislative competence with regard to disarmament and the maintenance of peace. A minimum of one, and a maximum of thirty representatives would be sent to the Assembly by each member-state in proportion to its population. These representatives would, after a time, be elected by a popular vote in each state, and would vote as individuals, not as government delegates. Voting in the Assembly is to be by a majority. A seventeen-member Executive Council, to be elected by the General Assembly from its own members, would substitute the Security Council, but remain subordinate to the Assembly. Through its Standing Committee on the Peace Enforcement Agencies, the Assembly would watch over the new United Nations' vital activities, such as inspection on disarmament, control over nuclear energy and outer space, and the management of the proposed UN Peace Force. The International Court of Justice (ICJ) is to be accorded compulsory jurisdiction over certain kinds of international dispute, and to be augmented by two other new organs, the World Equity Tribunal and World Conciliation Board.

The proposal envisages economic sanctions and the use of the UN Peace Force, a full-time force of between 200,000 and 600,000, to be stationed in various parts of the globe. These measures are to be used against any member-state in breach of the new Charter, any laws enacted thereunder or the judgement of the ICJ. The use of nuclear weapons is not excluded as a last resort. The recommendations of the World Equity Tribunal, when backed by the General Assembly, may also become enforceable.

In addition, a World Development Authority would be created in order to diminish the immense economic disparity between the underdeveloped and industrialized regions of the world because in Clark and Sohn's view this is a source of international conflict. This and all the other vastly expanded activities of the UN are to be financed by a new Revenue System based on tax to be collected by each

131

member-state specifically for the running of the new world organization. In order to protect member-states and individuals from the potential abuse of power by the immensely strengthened United Nations, there is to be a Bill of Rights, but this is not designed to protect the individual against the action of his or her own government.

Given the very far-reaching powers to be accorded to the new United Nations, it is not surprising that Clark and Sohn's project is often classified as a federal, world government plan. It may in this connection be recalled that James Lorimer's proposal formulated in the latter part of the nineteenth century came close to being itself a federation, but did not qualify as one. Clark and Sohn's reformed United Nations would be even more centralized than Lorimer's proposed international government. For example, individuals in violation of the Charter or any laws enacted by the General Assembly are, where appropriate, to be directly punishable by the UN, and those individuals in dispute with the UN are permitted, as a final resort, to appeal to the International Court of Justice (Clark and Sohn 1966, 306, 326). More decisively, the law to be enacted by the Assembly are not 'international law' but 'world law' binding on government officials and individuals directly (Clark and Sohn 1966, xvi, 15). Clark and Sohn even provide for a United Nations citizenship to be accorded to the nationals of all member-states in addition to their local citizenship, although this provision is intended entirely for its possible psychological effect of enhancing individual loyalty to the new world institution (1966, 15–16).[2]

However, the authors themselves state that the proposed United Nations would be an organization of strictly limited powers in no way comparable, for example, to a federation of very wide powers such as the United States of America (1966, 365). Thus the new United Nations would have no authority (as distinguished from the right to recommend) in such matters as international commerce and travel, a world currency, or in respect of various other subjects analogous on the world scene to powers expressly granted to the government of the United States by the Constitution of 1787. On the contrary, the authors claim, the powers of the new United Nations would be carefully restricted to certain matters directly related to the prevention of war (1966, 366). On balance, it would seem correct to conclude that, despite the extensive character of the alterations to be made to the existing United Nations, the Clark and Sohn proposal falls short of envisaging a full federal merger of its member-nations.

There are, in the postwar period, many other proposals within the legalistic framework which are less far-reaching than the Clark and

Sohn project. Among them, for example, are many proposals for expanding the power and functions of the International Court of Justice (Dalfen 1968). But these proposals can in effect be regarded as subspecies of the more comprehensive project formulated by the two authors.

Against the sovereign states system

It will be recalled that three prominent members of the 'realist' school, Schwarzenberger, Schuman and Morgenthau, all accepted the view that the division of the world into sovereign states was the source of world anarchy, and that world peace required the establishment of a world state. The three writers continued to express this view through the successive editions of their major publications. The third edition of Schwarzenberger's *Power politics* appeared in 1964 with a new subtitle, *A study of world society*. Although the consideration of how best to organize the world after the Second World War, which constituted Part III of the first edition, had to be greatly revised, Schwarzenberger still remarked, in the corresponding part of the third edition: 'the federal pattern is the most clear-cut alternative to power politics', 'it is a possible answer . . . to the scourge of war' and '[he] stands by all the points and proposals made in the previous editions' (1964, 526–7, 532). The seventh edition of Schuman's *International politics* was published in 1969, and the fifth edition of *Politics among nations* by Morgenthau appeared in 1973, without any fundamental modification to those parts of their argument by which a world state was defended as an ideal solution to the problem of world order (Schuman 1933, bk 4; 1969, chap. 7; Morgenthau 1948, pts 9, 10; 1973, pts 9, 10).

The idea that it is futile to attempt to maintain global peace through an international organization, such as the League of Nations or the United Nations, which necessarily operates within the framework of the sovereign states system also found an impassioned advocacy in Emery Reves' *The anatomy of peace*, first published in the United States in 1945, and a similar line of argument was put forward by Walter Schiffer in his scholarly work, *The legal community of mankind* (1954). Also published in 1954 was Frederick Schuman's *The commonwealth of man*. While acknowledging the possibility that the new balance of power and skilful diplomacy between the United States and the Soviet Union might enable a peaceful interval, Schuman adhered to the view that a lasting peace was not likely to be achieved without a world state (1954, 490–2).

All these writers in principle accept the idea (though not necessarily with the same degree of conviction) that the goal of world peace could not be achieved unless the totality of mankind is organized as a single state. They can thus be considered as recognizing the validity of the 'cosmopolitanist' form of the domestic analogy. However, not all those who in principle accept this type of domestic analogy will actually go on to propose the establishment of a world state. This is because a world state, however necessary it might be thought to be, is not usually considered as an easily attainable goal (Reves 1946, 245; Schuman 1954, 492). Given the improbability of their high ideal being achieved, those who object strongly to the sovereign states system may provisionally abandon the ultimate federal goal, and focus on what practical measures might be adopted to make small improvements to the inevitably precarious, but not easily alterable world conditions. They may also abandon advancing explicit prescriptions altogether, and instead concentrate on publicizing the view that in the absence of world government world instability is inevitable. If these alternative concerns are labelled 'realist' then there is in a sense only a thin divide between the realists and the utopians.[3]

A rather extraordinary illustration of this point is found in the life of Cord Meyer. Partly under the influence of Grenville Clark, Meyer became, in the early postwar period, the first president of the United World Federalists, an American association which unified various world federalist groups which had come into existence (Meyer 1980, 43–4). There are a few references to Meyer as a prominent world-state advocate in the writings of Frederick Schuman and Inis Claude, for example (Schuman 1954, 44 n., 438, 455; Claude 1962, 218, 249–50). Although his own proposal was closer to Clark and Sohn's re-formed-UN idea than to a full-fledged world federal state, Meyer was also impressed by *The anatomy of peace* by Reves, a world-state advocate, whom he had met when attending the San Francisco Conference as an assistant to an American delegate (Meyer 1948; 1980, 37). Frustrated by the apparent unattainability of his ideal, however, Meyer was soon to abandon his association with the world federalist movement. In the belief that a reformed UN, approximating a world federation in a limited sphere, would not be established in the face of Soviet communism, which he saw as aggressive, and, because of its secretiveness, inevitably opposed to inspection on disarmament, he came to devote himself to the American policy of anti-communism (Meyer 1980, 55ff.). His chosen career now was active service in the CIA. But, in his own mind, this was only a necessary means to an end. As he insists in the concluding part of his autobiography, his ideal remains a peaceful world organized as a federation in which the Soviet

Union would have been liberalized through the concerted effort of the internal and external oppositions to the existing regime (1980, chap. 18).

Of course, neither a belief in the validity of the domestic analogy nor the 'realist' prescription would alone be sufficient to lead one to become a member of a secret service. In fact there is a degree of tension between Meyer's very explicit anti-communist stance, and, for example, Morgenthau's commendation of foreign policy devoid of the spirit of ideological crusade. Nevertheless, in the case of Meyer, it was as a means to the almost unattainable goal of establishing a world state that he chose to work for the secret service of his country.

The domestic analogy in diagnosis

The diagnosis of the international system as inherently unstable and war-prone because of its division into sovereign states is commonly held among the contemporary writers on international relations. Prominent among them is Kenneth Waltz whose *Man, the state and war* appeared in 1959.

Among students of International Relations, Waltz is well known for having formulated a tripartite classification of the causal theories of war. According to what he calls the first image, the primary cause of war is to be found in the nature of man, and according to the second image, war occurs because some states have war-prone internal structures. The third image points to the nature of the international system as such as the fundamental cause of war. What is perhaps less well known is the fact that Waltz categorizes causes of war into two types: 'efficient' or 'immediate' causes, which make a particular war occur; and 'permissive' or 'underlying' causes, without which war could not occur at all. What is probably not remembered by many readers of his book, however, is his reference to two possible scenarios of war: one is where state A wants X from state B, and resorts to war to obtain it; and the other is where A and B, because of their mutual suspicion, intensify their competition for security until one or the other is forced to resort to a preventive war. With reference to the first scenario, Waltz suggests that the 'efficient cause' of the war is A's desire for X, and its 'permissive cause' is the absence of the mechanism of war-prevention from the international system. It is a little unclear why Waltz should think of A's *desire* for X as a phenomenon of the first two images, but he stresses that the 'permissive cause' of this and all other types of war is located in the third image. According to Waltz, however, the second scenario shows that the 'permissive cause' found in the structure of the international system might itself turn into an 'efficient cause' of war.[4]

The above summary shows that Waltz is not offering his three images as alternative hypotheses of equal weight, but that he is committed to the view that the structure of the international system is the most profound cause of war. However, attention must also be drawn to an important fact that what Waltz calls the 'permissive' cause of war is not a cause properly so-called, but a logically necessary condition of all wars. After all, if there were something in the international system that was capable of preventing war, then, logically, war could not occur. No empirical knowledge is required to establish this simple truism. Another important point to note is the fact that the logically necessary conditions of all wars can be found in the first two images also. The latent capacity of man to kill other men, and man's limited sociability are among the logically necessary conditions of war in the first image. A necessary condition of war at the second-image level may be the conception (and the organization which reflects this particular conception) of the state as a body entitled to defend itself against an external enemy even by recourse to force, and to demand the co-operation of its citizens in pursuit of that purpose.

Despite the obvious fact that what Waltz calls a 'permissive' cause of war can thus be found in all the three images, Waltz insists on the view that somehow the third image is of particular significance. This curious bias on his part could be explained as a consequence of his implicit commitment to the fundamental tenet of the domestic analogy: that the disorderly features of the international system, exemplified by the recurrence of war, are due to the absence from the international system of those mechanisms which sustain social order within the borders of states. Waltz admittedly is not an advocate of a world state or of its negative surrogates (Waltz 1959, 228). Yet, at the level of diagnosis, as opposed to prescription, he seems unselfconsciously to have been guided by the domestic analogy.[5]

Opposition to state sovereignty at the regional level

An intense mistrust of the sovereign states system exhibited by world federalists, such as Emery Reves, is also shared by those who work towards the unification of states in a particular geographical region. In this connection, the name that could not go unnoticed is that of Jean Monnet, the first president of the High Authority of the European Coal and Steel Community (ECSC). The winner in 1975 of the Grenville Clark Prize, he is much respected as the father of European unification (Monnet 1978, 498).[6]

Monnet is by no means a world federalist. His desire to see a United States of Europe is not based on the gradualist notion that this could serve as a first step towards a United States of the World. His concern is to create a European entity which could eliminate internecine wars from among the Europeans, and which could also be economically and politically strong in an era in which, according to him, only larger states would have the real capacity for economic prosperity and social progress within (1978, 222).

Nevertheless, Monnet's firm belief that true co-operation cannot be achieved within a framework of Europe divided into sovereign states is identical, albeit applied to a smaller geographical area, to the position of those who argue for a world state. It is unsurprising, therefore, to find Monnet express his dissatisfaction with some of the early postwar attempts to facilitate co-operation in Europe through an international organization of sovereign states, such as the Organization for European Economic Co-operation and the Council of Europe, established in 1948 and 1949 respectively. Of the former he writes: 'I could not help seeing the intrinsic weakness of a system that went no further than mere co-operation between Governments'; and of the latter he remarks: '[It] confirmed my belief that this approach would lead nowhere' (1978, 271–2, 273). These strongly critical remarks are reminiscent of those found in the writings of Saint-Simon, whose radical proposal to unite Europe under one sovereignty had appeared in the immediate aftermath of the Napoleonic Wars.

As if to echo Monnet's conviction of the need for a European entity that would transcend the sovereignty of its member-states, a proposal came in March 1950 from the West German Chancellor Adenauer for a complete union between France and West Germany, with a merger of their economies, their parliaments, and their citizenships (Monnet 1978, 285). Adenauer drew on a similar British offer of 1940 made to France. But his practical preoccupation in making such a radical proposal was the fate of the Ruhr and the Saar. He wanted, in Monnet's words, 'to sublimate national rivalry over these coal and steel resources by uniting Germany and France [under one sovereignty]' (1978, 286). But in Monnet's judgement, an attempt to unite the two countries at a stroke was not realistic at that time. What was needed was not a prior constitutional union intended to remove a particular practical difficulty, but, on the contrary, a method specifically designed to solve the problem itself. 'Unity would gradually be created by the momentum of a first achievement', he speculated (1978, 286). It is understandable why Monnet is sometimes described as a 'functionalist', although it should also be noted that Mitrany, closely associated with this approach, is well known for having criticized the movement toward unity in Europe as an attempt to create a larger entity in one part of the world, with divisive consequences at the global level (Spinelli 1966, 15–16; Mitrany 1975a, 228–9; 1975b, 56–9).

Now firmly convinced of the need to establish, as a first step, a joint Franco-German control of the resources of the Saar and the Ruhr, Monnet was ready to convince others; but, first of all, the idea of joint control had to find an appropriate institutional expression. In this respect he says he had no experience to fall back on 'except the negative experience of international co-operation, whose institutions were incapable of decision-making ... History offered no precedent' (1978, 294). By April 1950, however, Monnet, in collaboration with Etienne Hirsch, his close associate at the French Planning Commissariat, and Paul Reuter, a young professor of law and adviser to the French Foreign Office, was able to produce a draft, proposing 'to place the whole of Franco-German coal and steel production under an international [sic] Authority open to the participation of the other countries of Europe' (Monnet 1978, 295). In subsequent drafts, 'an international Authority' became 'the High Authority' and its competence came to be characterized as 'supranational' (Monnet 1978, 297). The final draft, accepted by the French Foreign Minister, Robert Schuman, became in substance the famous Schuman Plan of 9 May 1950. Negotiations to convert the Schuman Plan into a treaty began in June that year among the delegates of France, West Germany, Italy and the Benelux countries. The French delegation was headed by Monnet himself (Monnet 1978, 298ff.).

The treaty establishing the European Coal and Steel Community, signed in Paris in April 1951, served as a model not only for the failed 1952 European Defence Community Treaty, but, more importantly, also for the 1957 Rome Treaties creating the European Economic Community (EEC) and the European Atomic Energy Community (Euratom) (Spinelli 1966, 33, 49). The idea of setting up an Atomic Energy Community along the lines of the ECSC was itself due to Monnet's initiative (Monnet 1978, 400ff.).

With the advent of the EEC and Euratom, the Common Assembly, the Council of Ministers and the Court of Justice of the ECSC, with new duties and powers accorded to them, became common institutions of the three Communities, and in 1967 the High Authority of the ECSC was merged with the Commissions of the EEC and Euratom to form the European Commission. It was because of their common origins and their consequent structural similarities that the three European Communities could merge to this extent to form what is now usually called the 'European Community'.

In view of these developments, Monnet's reference to his April 1950 draft proposal for a Coal and Steel Community as 'the European Community's true founding document' is not an exaggeration (1978, 295). However, how Monnet and his associates arrived at this important draft proposal is not known in detail, nor is there well-documented history of the negotiations leading to the conclusion of the three Community treaties (Jacobs and Brown 1983, 245). Therefore, whether any particular domestic model may have guided the birth process of any of the three Communities is not known. None the less, reliance upon the domestic analogy is implicit not only in the ultimate ideal of the United States of Europe, upheld by Monnet among others, but also in the idea of creating an institutional framework by which various sectors of the member-states' domestic economies are to be united to form a 'common market'. Merry and Serge Bromberger's account, moreover, shows that Monnet's original draft for a coal and steel community embodied the idea of transferring the principle of planned economy to the supranational level, but that this element was diminished in the final product, the ECSC Treaty (Bromberger and Bromberger 1969, chap. 8, esp. 97). If so, the kind of domestic analogy involved in the original proposal of Monnet and his associates was of the same type as that which was embodied in the welfare internationalism of the 1930s and 1940s upheld by Carr, Brierly and Mitrany.

The domestic analogy in the neo-functionalist strategy for integration

If Jean Monnet was among the leading practitioners of unification in Western Europe, Ernst Haas, an American political scientist, is one of the best-known analysts of the process of integration in the postwar period. A brief observation on Haas' reliance on the domestic analogy is appropriate here.

Haas' scenario of how integration might proceed is known as 'neo-functionalism' because of his self-conscious attempt to refine Mitrany's doctrine (Haas 1964, esp. 26–50; Nye 1971, chap. 2; Pentland 1973, chap. 4). It may be recalled that Mitrany's 'functionalist' strategy for integration could be said to involve the domestic analogy to the extent that citizens' tendency to exhibit loyalty to those domestic institutions which satisfied their welfare needs was implicitly assumed by him as evidence for the tendency of men in general, whatever their location, to show loyalty to international institutions, similarly fulfilling their welfare needs. Haas' scenario of community-building takes a different form, and yet its dependence on the domestic analogy is indubitable. In Haas' own, somewhat abstract, formulation:

> The *neo-functional* approach rests its claim to fame on an extended analogy . . . It borrows the postulates of actor perception and behavior which are said to explain the character of a pluralistically organized national state; it notes that certain of these seem to coincide with behavior at the regional level and therefore holds that the rest of the behavior is also explicable in terms of the pluralistic national model.
>
> (1970, 623)

In line with the pluralist doctrine of politics, popular in the United States in the 1960s, Haas holds that some societies, such as the contemporary American society, exhibit a high degree of internal order because conflicting groups, each in pursuit of its own interests, co-operate rather than fight to resolve their conflicts. Three factors contribute to this peaceful process of conflict resolution. First is the basic homogeneity of political culture and ideology. Second, closely linked to the first, is the fact that cleavages which separate groups within a society tend to cut across one another, thereby preventing the division of society into clearly defined groups in confrontation with one another. Third is the contribution of the central authority in enabling co-operation between conflicting groups. Haas considers that through successful conflict resolution, the central authority enhances its prestige, thereby increasing its conflict-resolving potentials (Haas 1958, 6; 1961, 367–72; 1968, 152–3; Pentland 1973, 110–11). In Haas' view, these conditions, which are thought to obtain in certain domestic societies, such as the contemporary American society, are already present transnationally in postwar Western Europe as a whole. The opening paragraph of one of Haas' articles states this clearly:

> The practices associated with regional integration in contemporary western Europe correspond to a type of society and economy variously labeled 'post-industrial', post-bourgeois' or merely 'the New Europe'. This New Europe evolved historically from the interconnected strands of capitalism, industrialism and pluralistic democracy. It resembles in any [sic] respects the type of economy and society familiar to us in North America. Regional government in such a society is thus merely an adaptation on the scale of half a continent of forms of social and economic organization which evolved historically at the national level.
>
> (1968, 149)

Thus, Haas believes that regional integration in Western Europe would come about through a process similar to the evolution of the

American nation, through an interplay of social solidarity and central guidance. In this regard it is interesting to note Haas' remark that the 'court of the Communities has recently pronounced its equivalent of Marbury v. Madison in the *Van Gend* Case, laying down clearly the supremacy of Community law and holding that it applies directly to the individual citizen' (Haas 1968, 162–3; for Marbury v. Madison, see Lees, Maidment and Tappin 1982, 27–8; for the Van Gend Case, see Stein 1981).

The neo-functionalist approach attracted much attention among the scholars and practitioners in the 1960s (Pentland 1973, 132). Clearly, however, there is no guarantee that a movement towards regional integration, once inaugurated, will continue to progress incrementally. The neo-functionalist doctrine came to be largely discredited when, among other things, its postulated goal of a closely knit political community, predominantly governed by supranational institutions, came to be considered as unlikely to be realized through the process of community-building it had envisaged (Haas 1976; Pentland 1973, 146).

In attempting to formulate a scenario whereby regional integration might be achieved, Haas had criticized the traditional functionalist distinction between 'welfare issues' and 'power political issues' (Haas 1964, 21, 23, 47; Pentland 1973, 107–10). But this distinction continued to be made by those international legal writers who, along the lines adopted earlier by Brierly, stressed the need for international law to concern itself with the welfare of individual men and women living in separate national communities. We shall now turn to the view held by these writers.

Welfare internationalism at the global level

The essence of 'welfare internationalism', in the words of one of its most distinguished practitioners, C. Wilfred Jenks, is 'to substitute the well-being of individual human lives for the mutual relations of states as the primary concern of international organisation and international policy' (1963, 7).[7] According to him:

> The largest issue confronting international law and international lawyers in our time is (1) how far the law of nations will remain a traditional framework ... [of] ... law valued and respected as a necessary discipline for the mutual relations of states but with little obvious direct impact on everyday life perceptible to the ordinary citizens, or, (2) how effectively it will become a common law of mankind in a welfare world beyond the welfare state, fulfilling in a world community of peace and freedom a part comparable to that of a mature legal system in an advanced civilization. (1970, 1)

To create a 'welfare world', our immediate priorities must be 'to secure peace with justice, to protect human rights, to promote economic stability and growth, and to ensure that the progress of advanced science and technology serves the common interest of mankind' (Jenks 1969, 22–3); and for these purposes we must succeed 'in developing during the next generation a whole series of new major branches of the law of which, despite immense and most encouraging progress during the last half-century [symbolized by the achievements of the ILO], only the beginnings as yet exist' (1970, 6). A substantially similar view has been expressed by a number of other contemporary international lawyers, for example, Wolfgang Friedmann in his *The changing structure of international law* (1964), and B. V. A. Röling in his *International law in an expanded world* (1960).

To the extent that these writers' views can be said to replicate the welfare internationalism of Carr, Mitrany and Brierly, who wrote in the closing phase of the previous period, their line of argument can be considered as involving the domestic analogy. The contemporary welfarist international lawyers' vision is still essentially one of applying the 'welfare state' idea to the international level, so that, through the development of the 'international law of welfare', as opposed to dependence solely on the traditional 'international law of liberty', the world community will become 'a welfare community, just as the nation-state became a welfare state' (Röling 1960, 83). However, in comparison to Carr, Mitrany and Brierly, who formulated their ideas against the background of the perceived inadequacies of the inter-war system of international law, contemporary welfarist international lawyers, whose works appeared mainly in the 1960s and 1970s, seem to rely less explicitly on the analogy from domestic experience. This is because contemporary welfarist international lawyers are in a position to base their argument on what they consider as a living reality in the international sphere, namely the emergence and growth of the 'international law of welfare', or what Friedmann has called the 'international law of co-operation' as opposed to that of 'coexistence' (1964, chap. 6). What these writers stress is the need to encourage a further expansion of the new type of international law, rather than, as in the case of earlier writers, to transplant what had hitherto been nearly exclusively of a domestic variety to the new soil of international relations.

Welfarist international lawyers, such as Jenks, Friedmann and Röling, stress the importance of vastly expanding and diversifying the role of international law and international institutions, but they do not produce institutional blueprints of the kind offered by Clark and Sohn.

It should, however, be noted that Jenks, in particular, stresses the role of professional international lawyers in developing international law and institutions in the direction he considers vital, and that in so doing he resorts to a novel form of domestic analogy. The opening statements of the final chapter of his book, *The common law of mankind*, are noteworthy in this respect:

> During critical phases in the development of a legal system the quality of the craftsmanship which practitioners of the law bring to its service can have a decisive influence on the process of development and on the whole texture of the legal system resulting from that process of development. So it was when the great civilians transformed the law of an overgrown city state into the law of an imperial commonwealth; so it was when the glossators laid the foundations of the modern civil law; so it was when the Bench and Bar of England created the common law; so it is today in the case of international law. In every field of professional work, as legal adviser, as legislative draftsman, as advocate and as arbitrator or judge, the contemporary international lawyer has opportunities to build the future law of a world community which no previous generation has been privileged to enjoy on a comparable scale. (1958, 408)

Also worthy of lengthy quotation is the following passage, in which Jenks draws a distinction not dissimilar to that which Thomas Kuhn has made between 'normal science' and 'scientific revolution':

> There is no place for the mentality of the small-town notary in the practice of contemporary international law. We are not dealing with the routine of the established certainties of life but must frequently come to grips with the great unsettled issues on which the future of the world depends. This, it may be objected, is no task for the lawyer, who 'must be orthodox, else he is no lawyer'. It is admittedly not a task in respect of which his voice ever should or can be final, and it is a task which it becomes progressively less necessary and less appropriate for him to undertake in normal circumstances as a legal system develops, but it is, always has been, and must remain, an essential part of his task in the early stages of development of a legal system. The contemporary international lawyer must accept his responsibility as one of architects of a rapidly developing legal system or incur the odium of frustrating the work of his predecessors and contemporaries by perpetuating and reinforcing the weaknesses of a legal system which is failing to keep pace with the needs of an epoch representing an unprecedented challenge to the spirit of man. It is for this reason desirable that the international lawyer should combine with his professional training as a lawyer an instinct for legal and institutional development to which a firm grasp of legal history and a wider background in the political and social sciences can contribute powerfully. (1958, 416–17; see also Kuhn 1962)

143

Thus Jenks' ultimate prescription is that just as legal practitioners have played an innovative role in the revolutionary stages of various domestic legal systems, so the practitioners of international law, with appropriate training, skill and vision, should contribute to the development of international law and institutions in the current critical phase.[8]

A similar view is found in the writings of Myres McDougal of Yale and his associates, whose approach is known as 'policy-oriented' jurisprudence. According to McDougal's conception, lawyers, both within the domestic sphere and in international relations, are strategically placed to make important contributions to the goal of 'human dignity', and for this purpose they should interpret the law and influence decisions with a view to promoting democratic values. To the extent that McDougal's conception of the role of international lawyers derives implicitly by analogy from his assessment of the function of lawyers within democratic states, such as the USA, where lawyers play a considerable part at all levels of decision-making, his approach to the realization of the goal of 'human dignity' can be said to involve the same kind of domestic analogy as found in Jenks. However, McDougal's conception of international lawyers as a progressive force, unlike Jenks', is not tied to the idea of the critical stage in the history of law which, according to Jenks, international law is currently facing in its process of development towards a fully mature system (McDougal and associates 1960, chaps. 1, 2, 12). McDougal's conception by contrast involves the idea that lawyers' 'policy-orientation' towards the values of 'human dignity' should be a constant feature of their profession.

Cosmopolitanism in contemporary international theory

Welfare internationalism upheld by certain contemporary international lawyers is not a monopoly of legal writers. A line of argument sympathetic to it is also found in some contemporary philosophical works on international relations. Charles Beitz's *Political theory and international relations* (1979) and Andrew Linklater's *Men and citizens in the theory of international relations* (1982) are prominent among them.

According to Beitz, the common depiction of world society as a Hobbesian state of nature among sovereign states is empirically inaccurate because 'it fails to capture either the increasingly complex pattern of social interaction characteristic of international relations or the variety of expectations, practices, and institutions that order these interactions' (1979, 179). This point corresponds to the welfarist international lawyers' observation that international law has greatly expanded its scope in the recent period as a result, among other things, of the intensification of international intercourse. Indeed, Jenks had stated that 'contemporary international law can no longer be reasonably presented within the framework of the classical exposition of international law as the law governing the relations between States but must be regarded as the common law of mankind in an early stage of its development' (1958, xi).[9] In a parallel fashion, Beitz remarks that 'international relations is coming more and more to resemble domestic society', so that, increasingly, there is a case for applying domestic principles of justice at the international level (1979, 179).

Beitz, however, is strongly opposed to the conception of international normative principles based on the personification of the states, which he calls the 'Morality of States' view (1979, pt 2). Those who accept such a view 'infer from the analogy of states and persons that states have some sort of right of autonomy in international relations analogous to the right of autonomy possessed by persons in domestic society' (1979, 180). Against this view, Beitz argues that 'the analogy of states and persons is imperfect' and that the ultimate unit of international normative principles must be the individual (1979, 180). Here we find another parallelism between Beitz and welfarist international lawyers who, as we noted, argue for the substitution of the well-being of individual lives for the mutual relations of states as the primary concern of international organization and international policy. Beitz, however, expresses his point somewhat idiosyncratically as follows: 'The appropriate analogue of individual autonomy in the international realm is not national autonomy but conformity of a society's basic institutions with appropriate principles of social justice' (1979, 180). By this he means that whether a state is entitled to exercise its right of autonomy (for example, the right of freedom from intervention) depends on whether the principles of social justice appropriate to that society's stage of socio-economic development are realized within it (1979, 81).

Moreover, Beitz's judgement that there is a substantial degree of economic interdependence in contemporary world society leads him to the view that the principles of distributive justice applicable to domestic society must now be applied at the global level. However, since the ultimate units of global distributive principles are not states but persons located in separate national communities, the principles must be applied with a view to protecting, not the general welfare of the least advantaged states in international society, but the well-being of the least advanced persons and groups of persons in the global community as a whole (Beitz 1979, pt 3, esp. 152–3). Thus, as he himself acknowledges, Beitz's conception of international normative principles is essentially cosmopolitanist as opposed to internationalist (1979, 181–2).

Although Beitz's line of argument is therefore very similar to the welfare internationalism of Jenks and others, whether the former in fact involves the same type of domestic analogy as contained in the latter is a complex question. A close examination of Beitz's structure of thought, however, reveals that his conclusion regarding the cosmopolitanist application of the principles of distributive justice is derived by *logical* deduction from an assumption which he regards as axiomatic, rather than by *analogical* reasoning. His axiom is that a minimum of economic interdependence within a given society is a sufficient condition for the application of the principles of distributive justice within that society. Since this is so, it follows *logically*, and not by the force of any *analogy*, that, given the (in his estimation) sufficient degree of economic interdependence at the global level, the principles of distributive justice must apply globally (1979, pt 3, esp. 161ff.; see, however, Beitz 1983, 595).

Another very important work, *Men and citizens in the theory of international relations* by Linklater, transcends the usual tendency among writers on international relations to accept some version of the Hobbesian view, and presents a theory of international obligation on the basis of the ideas developed by Kant, Hegel and Marx. Linklater's complex argument may be summarized as follows: the purpose of domestic social life is to create conditions under which citizens are treated as of equal worth by virtue of their citizenship; the purpose of international social life must be to progress towards an ultimate condition under which human beings are treated as of equal worth by virtue of their humanity (Linklater 1982).

It may here be recalled that, according to Linklater, 'a progressive development of international relations necessitates the transference of understandings of social relations from their original domestic setting to the international arena' (1982, 193), and that Moorhead Wright, one of the reviewers of his book, criticized him for his heavy reliance on the 'problematic analogy of domestic and international society' (1984, 235). As in the case of Beitz, however, a close analysis of Linklater's structure of argument shows that, despite the appearance of involving the domestic analogy, his argument, too, is in fact a case of logical deduction from an axiomatic presupposition (Suganami 1986).

In Linklater's case the axiom is that the full realization of human potential for self-determining existence (or 'human freedom') necessitates the removal of all those social barriers which impose upon man the institutional distinction between the 'insider' and the 'outsider'. Such a distinction, according to Linklater, necessarily discriminates against those labelled 'outsiders', and thereby hinders the treatment of man *qua* man as a moral being. Linklater's assessment that such barriers have been removed to a considerable extent within the domestic sphere suggests to him that man's major target in the next stage is the dichotomy between 'citizens' and 'non-citizens', which Linklater sees as at present institutionalized in the sovereign states system. But this judgement on Linklater's part is not itself the ground for his belief in the necessity to move towards the ultimate goal of the unity of mankind. The goal is already there in the axiom.

Indeed, Linklater's argument cannot be classed as analogical since the citizen/non-citizen dichotomy, which Linklater wishes to see removed, is an instance of the general category, the insider/outsider distinction. Therefore, what holds true with the latter necessarily holds true with the former, and not on the strength of an analogy. The citizen/non-citizen dichotomy must be removed, according to Linklater, because it is an instance of the more general insider/outsider distinction, which must be removed; and this must be removed because, in his judgement, it interferes with the full realization of human potential for self-determining existence. This is the gist of Linklater's essentially non-analogical, cosmopolitanist thesis.

One qualification must be entered here, however. Beitz and Linklater consider that those values, such as distributive justice, human rights and freedom, which have been pursued with a degree of success within the domestic realm, can profitably be pursued in the world arena through enhanced co-operation of states. They are therefore opposed to the view that there is a sharp functional differentiation to be made between domestic society and international society, and that not all those values appropriate to the former could profitably be pursued in the latter domain. In other words, the two authors can be said to hold domestic society and international society as in principle capable of becoming analogous in their functions.

Beitz, as a political theorist, is concerned with a philosophical defence of the ultimate ideal of the 'welfare world' and only marginally with its institutional structure. In this context it is noteworthy, however, that his cosmopolitanism does not lead him to advocate the cause of world federalism. In his view, 'global normative principles might be implemented otherwise than by global institutions conceived on the analogy of the state' (1979, 183).[10] According to him, 'a variety of

147

configurations of institutions can be imagined (for example, a coordi-
nated set of regional institutions) that would implement the principles'
(1979, 157). Linklater, too, is concerned with a philosophical exposition
of the necessity to transform the currently dominant features of international relations. Thus, he does not offer an institutional blueprint
required for the realization of the values he defends, remarking only
that it is necessary to replace 'the balance of power, with its underlying
state-centric assumption, with a more centralized and principled form
of international government' (1982, 199). The task of working out the
requisite institutional structure for the fulfilment of the kind of goals
set out by these writers is left to legal practitioners and decision-
makers. There are, however, some scholars who do not hesitate to
speculate on the requisite institutional structure for the achievement of
the type of goals defended by cosmopolitanist international theorists,
and among them Richard Falk is probably the best-known contributor.

World Order Models Project: Falk's contribution

Inspired by McDougal's conception of the international law of
human dignity, and in the belief, like that of Jenks, that international
law is now in need of a radical departure, a 'paradigm shift', from its
traditional outmoded structure, Richard Falk, a Princeton Professor of
International Law, has written a book entitled *A study of future worlds*
(1975). This contains a proposal by a team of American scholars,
directed by Falk himself, who, together with a number of other
national and regional groups, participated in the much publicized
World Order Models Project (WOMP). The project was organized by
Saul Mendlovitz in 1967 under the auspices of the Institute for World
Order.[11]

The aim of the American project contained in Falk's book is to
explore the means by which the four essential values of mankind could
efficiently be realized. These are the minimization of large-scale collective violence, the maximization of social and economic well-being, the
realization of fundamental human rights and of conditions of political
justice, and the maintenance and rehabilitation of ecological quality
(Falk 1975a, chap. 1). Falk is concerned to stress that the real problem is
how to enable the transition from the present world system, which he
regards as incapable of satisfying these values, to a system which can
realize these goals (1975a, 2). The knowledge of the institutional structure of the requisite system is less important, in his judgement, than
the identification of the trends of development in the contemporary
world and the knowledge of the strategy which can help strengthen

the desirable trend, leading eventually to the creation of a new system in the next century. Falk is convinced, however, that the new system must have a 'central guidance mechanism', and devotes a chapter to the analysis of its structure (1975a, chap. 4). He insists that central guidance need not take the form of world government, and also warns against 'the fallacy of premature specificity' (1975a, 184, 152–3). In particular, he is critical of Clark and Sohn's project for a revised Charter which, in his view, is based on the erroneous assumption that meticulous demonstration of the rationality of a very detailed project is a major contributory force towards its acceptance (1975a, 347).

Despite all these qualifications, Falk in turn envisages a rather detailed, government-like structure for the world, which can even be characterized as an expanded version of the Clark and Sohn project.[12] The expansion is due to the fact that, unlike Clark and Sohn, who are concerned primarily, and nearly exclusively, with the maintenance of international peace, Falk wants his central guidance mechanism to assist in the realization of many goals which come under the four categories of value noted earlier.[13] It is indicative of the scope of Falk's concern that the survival of the peregrine falcon, endangered by an excessive use of DDT, receives a mention in his book as an ecological problem in need of a global response (1975a, 107). The basic principle which guided Falk in designing his scheme, however, seems very similar to that of Clark and Sohn: Disarm the world, establish an international police force and machinery for the settlement of disputes, and set up any other global bodies necessary for the purposes in mind, ensuring a system of checks and balances and, where appropriate, adding a co-ordinating body to give unity to the whole structure. The outcome is a highly complex, government-like framework for a disarmed world, consisting of 'assemblies', 'secretariats', 'councils', 'boards', 'agencies', 'forums' and 'services', covering a wide range of activity and equipped with 'World Security Forces', a 'World Grievance System' and a 'World Disarmament Service' (Falk 1975a, chap. 4, 235). Although Falk is himself critical of a bland use of the domestic analogy, and of a simple-minded claim that a world government, on the model of a domestic government, is necessary for the creation of world order (1970, viii-ix), it appears that his own vision of an ideal world is heavily dependent on his image of a successfully governed society equipped with multifarious organs within a constitutional framework.

Falk, however, does not commit himself to stating the requisite degree of centralization, and therefore the precise legal character of the proposed government-like structure remains uncertain. This uncertainty is a calculated one. Falk remarks: 'There is a need for institutional agnosticism, for being neither a premature advocate nor opponent of a world government form of power/authority structure' (1975a, 184). He also remarks:

> The degree to which central guidance will entail 'a governmental presence' on a global level depends largely on the character of transition, and on whether the growth of transnational economic, cultural, and social relations can weaken from below the hold which national governments now exert upon the loyalties and resources of their populations: *the weaker the governmental presence becomes on a national level, the smaller the governmental presence that will be needed on a global level.*
>
> (1975a 157, emphasis Falk's; see, however, Watson 1980, 268)

Other notable WOMP proposals

Rajni Kothari of India, the author of another WOMP volume, *Footsteps into the future* (1974), strongly objects to the idea that a world state is a desirable form of political organization. In his view, national autonomy, and its institutional expression, sovereign statehood, is an essential prerequisite for the primary value of personal autonomy (1974, 8ff.). However, Kothari is critical of the way in which the world is at present divided into a large number of sovereign states. In his view, the number must be drastically reduced.

The reduction in the number of sovereign units in the global system is to be achieved by a step-by-step integration of existing states into regional federations. Kothari's idea here is guided by his belief that the power structure of the world must shift radically in favour of currently weaker states. His scheme for a smaller number of larger states is a means for 'abridging the present wide gaps in power and resources and countering the prevailing patterns of dominance and inequality in the world' (1974, 136).

The suggested regional groupings and their total number are tentative (Kothari 1974, 161). It is none the less worth noting that, according to Kothari's scheme, the United States will remain on its own, whereas the Soviet Union is put together with Mongolia, and China with Tibet. India becomes part of the 'South Asia' regional federation together with Pakistan, Afghanistan, Sri Lanka, Bangladesh, Nepal, Bhutan, Sikkim and Maldive Islands (1974, 159–60). In suggesting that the total number of units should not be too small or too large, Kothari refers to the problem of stability in federations. According to him, where the constituent units are too few, as in the case of Nigeria before the Civil War, the federal structure may be precarious, and where they are vast in number, he thinks, the structure may also be ineffective especially when the system is dominated by a few large units (1974, 156–7). The use of the federal analogy in discussing the appropriate number and size of units is understandable, since Kothari envisages the twenty-five or so regional units coming under some form of world organization.

Despite his clearly stated opposition of global centralization, what Kothari visualizes is a more centralized form of the United Nations 'with the express objective of promoting justice and a fair distribution of resources, restraining powerful states and adventurist regimes from violating the freedom and rights of human beings, and ensuring the preservation of nature and its life-sustaining qualities against undue encroachment by human agencies' (1974, 138). For these purposes, the present Economic and Social Council (ECOSOC) is to become the principal executive organ of the United Nations (Kothari 1974, 139). Moreover, 'as a step towards greater federalization of world political processes, a World Parliamentary Assembly' is to be established, consisting of representatives from various national legislatures (Kothari 1974, 139–40). This body is to act as a forum for discussing various issues facing different regions as well as the world as a whole. The various specialized agencies, such as ILO, ICAO, WHO, UNESCO, as well as 'the present institutional structure for dispensation of justice' are to be strengthened (Kothari 1974, 140). Moreover, like Clark and Sohn's proposal, the new UN is to be equipped with a world police force and a 'high-powered Commission on Disarmament' (Kothari 1974, 141). Thus, despite some innovative features of his plan, the overall influence of the domestic analogy upon Kothari's proposal is undeniable.

A project which is comparable in some important respects to Kothari's is contained in Ali Mazrui's *A world federation of cultures* (1976), an African contribution to the WOMP series. If the basic idea of Kothari's work is to accord more power to currently weaker states by creating regional units as constituents of world politics, Mazrui's guiding principle is to give more power to the world's disadvantaged cultures by giving votes in the running of world affairs to regional and world cultural units. What is required at the global level for greater social justice, enhanced economic welfare and diminishing prospects for violence, according to Mazrui, is to encourage cultural interplay and convergence on a more equal footing than at present, which, he hopes, will lead to a higher degree of normative consensus. This in turn, he thinks, is a necessary step towards the realization of those postulated values (1976, 1–15, 473ff.). For the time being, nation-states will remain, and must endeavour to foster cultural unity within (Mazrui

1976, 482). But in addition to the representatives of national units, those of regional units and of the five world cultural blocs, defined in terms of their respective languages (English, French, Russian, Arabic and Chinese) are to participate in the management of global affairs (Mazrui 1976, 473–83).

From such a standpoint, Mazrui proposes the creation of a new world authority (1976, 482ff.). In the place of ECOSOC, which is to be given a central position in Kothari's scheme, Mazrui suggests the elevation of UNESCO to a prominent position in the new structure. Renamed the 'World Council on Science and Culture', UNESCO is to have a number of bureaux under its wing and vastly expand its functions in order to facilitate cultural convergence at the global level. Also to be given an important place are the 'World Council on Mobility and Communication', 'Political and Security Council' and 'Economic and Social Council'. There will be a Military Inspectorate for the limitation of national armaments, and as global police force is to be established under its wing. The 'Economic and Social Council', through its 'Taxation Authority for General Development', is to collect taxes from states and regions. The tax is designed mainly to augment global revenues for general development, but Mazrui also envisages the use of taxation as an instrument of social control and manipulation. Thus, for example, a population poll tax might be collected only from those countries where the infant mortality rate has fallen down to 50 or less per 1000, or whose level of life expectancy has hit the fifty-year mark (Mazrui 1976, 492–3). Mazrui can therefore be said to favour the transfer of a number of important domestic governmental institutions to the international level in order not only to facilitate cultural convergence at the global level but to enhance the general welfare of individuals located in separate national units.

An extensive set of prescriptions for world order which goes far beyond the standard domestic analogy lines is found in *The true worlds* (1980), a contribution to the WOMP series from a transnational perspective by a distinguished Norwegian peace researcher, Johan Galtung. His suggestions are thorough and thoughtful, and the broad range of strategies contained in the book for the achievement of peace, economic well-being, social justice and ecological balance cannot easily be summarized without doing considerable injustice to his careful formulations. Among the suggested strategies are, for example, those for improving the conditions of the exploited individuals in the world through various types of attitudinal, institutional and policy changes towards 'self-reliance' in the 'Center countries', 'Periphery countries', 'Center-Periphery relations' and in the 'Global System' (Galtung 1980,

149ff.). Another set of prescriptions is an intricate programme for the demilitarization of the world, which includes, among many other things, a strategy for gradually reducing scientists' contribution to military machinery (Galtung 1980, 215ff.).

One aspect of Galtung's proposals which is particularly noteworthy from the viewpoint of our investigation is his stress on non-territorial actors. These actors are divided by him into three types: 'intergovernmental' organizations, such as the United Nations, where the members are states represented by their governments; 'internongovernmental' organizations, such as an association of national associations of dentists, where the members are non-governmental, but nationally based; and 'transnational nongovernmental' organizations, where the members are individuals located in separate states. Multinational corporations belong to the second type, and Galtung considers the world hippie movement as of the third type (1980, 305ff.).

Galtung warns that we cannot naively assume that non-territorial actors are on the side of good, since they are often instruments in the hands of territorial actors, or states (1980, 311–12). Moreover, Galtung considers some non-territorial actors, multinational corporations in particular, to be instruments of structural violence or exploitation (1980, 313–15). None the less, he observes that non-territorial actors are far less likely than territorial actors to be engaged in war precisely because of their non-territoriality (1980, 312). The aim, according to Galtung, is therefore to enhance the role of non-territorial actors (in particular the role of 'transnational nongovernmental' organizations, which are least likely to be instruments of states), while countering effectively the potential structural violence which might accompany non-territorial systems (1980, 330).

It is of great interest to observe that Galtung sees a parallel between the role of non-territorial organizations in the world system, which he predicts will rapidly increase, and the role which non-territorial associations, such as trade unions and political parties, have come to play within a domestic sphere, which was initially dominated by territorial units, e.g., provinces and counties (1980, 319, 330). Galtung's idea here is similar to Mitrany's in that they both consider non-territorial organizations as capable of weakening national loyalties, and Galtung is confident that such a vision is not utopian 'for the simple reason that it has happened already inside so many states' (1980, 330).[14]

Unlike the domestic system, however, the world system is largely devoid of a central authority which, in Galtung's view, must be remedied. But he is critical of those who see a panacea in a strong intergovernmental world organization: 'An intergovernmental organization will capture only some of the world's problems and conflicts, namely, those that governments will bring up' (1980, 344). Actors other than governments must be represented in the running of global affairs. In concrete terms, what Galtung has in mind is a world assembly consisting of four houses: a House of States, which is in the nature of the UN General Assembly; a House of Minorities, representing minority groups within states; what Galtung misleadingly calls a House of Supranational Organizations, meaning a house consisting of the representatives of 'internongovernmental' organizations; and a House of Transnational Associations, representing transnational political movements and pressure groups. All the four Houses are to participate in the articulation of world problems, but the power to decide will be given initially to the House of States, and later jointly to that House and the House of Transnational Associations, which Galtung hopes will gradually develop into a House of World Parties (1980, 348–9).

The power of the central authority is to derive from its ability for punishment and reward. Galtung envisages a world police force of the order of magnitude of 100,000 to 1 million men and women, with destructive capacity of the type authorized in the UN peace-keeping operations, and with much wider functions than the control of inter-state direct violence (1980, 351). For example, a world police force might intervene against a suppression of minorities within a state, and also help 'the freedom fighters' to consolidate 'liberated territories' against the 'oppressor' (Galtung 1980, 365–6, 369). But the world authority's power is to depend primarily on its having enormous resources, in terms of capital, goods and know-how, for constructive use for the satisfaction of basic human needs (Galtung 1980, 351). In order to enhance the remunerative power of the world authority, certain multinational corporations are to be 'globalized'. Here Galtung resorts to the same type of domestic analogy as that which underlay the welfare internationalism of the 1930s and 1940s, and argues that 'just as the emergence of the nation-state society led to the national-ization of some key types of economic activity within its border, par-ticularly in the fields of transportation and communication, the emergence of the global society will have to lead to the globalization of some types of production' (1980, 352–3). Accordingly, a world produc-tion authority is to be established, to which the ownership, for example, of the General Motors Corporation, would transfer, and, under the new name of Global Mobility Co-operative, the former multinational corporation is to engage in the production of a very inexpensive and non-polluting means of mass transportation. Also to

154

be 'globalized' are a means of air transport and a means of communication (Galtung 1980, 353–5, 357–8).

These prescriptions are, by Galtung's own admission, broad outlines, however (1980, 372). In more immediate and specific terms, attempts are to be made to build on and modify the existing UN system to turn it into a more adequate central authority. Thus, perhaps as a very first step towards establishing a House of Minorities, Galtung suggests setting up a UN embassy in each member-state to which local citizens could report, among other things, extreme cases of poverty and infractions of human rights norms hidden by the host country (1980, 375). The idea of a world central authority endowed with remunerative power finds a more immediate application in the principle that 'global commons' must be established wherever possible (1980, 375ff.). And, as a first step towards the eventual creation of a world police force, Galtung suggests the establishment of a permanent elite force earmarked for UN service, in the order of magnitude of 100,000 (1980, 380). And, in Galtung's carefully considered opinion, all such moves towards a world less violent in direct and structural terms are to come not from any particular class of individuals, for that would be to privilege that class against the rest of humanity, but from 'all of us' (1980, 423) at all levels through our own activism imbued with the spirit of self-reliance and concern for humanity as a whole (1980, chap. 9).

A WOMP proposal guided by a similar set of ideas to Galtung's, but more restricted in scope, is found in the work by Lagos and Godoy, who write from the Latin American perspective. According to these authors, the sovereign states system would have to remain for the time being, but each national society is to be organized in accordance with egalitarian ideology and democratic socialism to form what they call a 'humanist society' (1977, 88, 100, chap. 6). The international system, too, is to be reorganized in order to realize humanist values, and to suppress direct and structural violence (Lagos and Godoy 1977, chap. 7). Lagos and Godoy's scheme for a reorganized international system, however, is written in a constitutionalist spirit, and is much more reminiscent of Clark and Sohn's work than Galtung's multifaceted strategy. None the less, Lagos and Godoy's commitment to a wider set of values than Clark and Sohn's has made the Latin American WOMP proposal much wider in scope than the American classic (Lagos and Godoy 1977, chap. 8). Moreover, there are some important suggestions in Lagos and Godoy's work which correspond to Galtung's. For example, the two writers propose the appointment of ambassadors of the new world organization to member-states, and, like Galtung's proposal, several sectors of the world economy are to be internationally 'socialized' and to be placed in the hands of relevant world agencies. However, in clear contrast to Galtung's proposal, transnational organizations are only to have consultative status within the new institution (Lagos and Godoy 1977, 139, 147ff., 151–2).

What is particularly noteworthy about Lagos and Godoy's work is their relatively well-considered scenario for the achievement of humanist goals at the domestic and international levels. Transition towards a humanist society is to be achieved by grassroots movements led by progressive intellectuals, pressure groups and political parties. Such movements, Lagos and Godoy speculate, may have a chance of success in some of the well-established democracies in the capitalist area and in some political systems of non-aligned countries, with capitalist or socialistically inclined regimes, which display some of the characteristics of the well-established democracies. But the authors also suggest that a humanist society might come about in countries without a democratic tradition as a result of violent revolution, civil war and other sufferings undergone by the population (1977, 156–7). In their opinion, however, transition towards a humanist society is likely to be realized only in some of the Third World countries and in some developed countries other than what they regard as the Superpowers of the 1990s: the United States, the USSR, Japan, China and the EEC (1977, 154–5). The authors hope that initial moves towards a humanist society in these delimited parts of the world might have a 'demonstration effect' (1977, 163). And, according to their cautious judgement, it is only when the demonstration effect has attained sufficient magnitude, and solid ties have been cemented between these societies and those political and social movements which support similar values within the 'dystopian societies' that the structural changes in the international system can begin to be decisively brought about (1977, 163–4).

The foregoing summary of some of the main WOMP proposals shows that there is a considerable variety among them. Moreover, arguments along the standard domestic analogy lines, with which we are by now familiar, are not given a central place in the WOMP contributors' prescriptions. None the less, there is a strong undercurrent of welfare internationalism in all their writings, and their institutional proposals make a selective but wide-ranging use of the domestic analogy. A World Parliamentary Assembly, a House of World Parties, an enhanced role of ECOSOC and UNESCO, a Taxation Authority and taxation for social control, the 'globalization' of certain sectors of the world economy, a world court and a world police force are among those which have indubitably been inspired by their dom-.

estic analogues. Overall, it can be said that the domestic analogy has worked not as a central pillar, but as an essential ingredient of the WOMP writers' speculation about how best to organize the world.

Opposition to global welfare internationalism

As we noted earlier, common among welfarist international lawyers is the notion that there are two types of international law. One, the traditional type, is concerned with the basic goal of enabling sovereign states to coexist. The other, of a more recent origin, is a body of law designed to protect and enhance the social and economic welfare of individuals living in separate national communities. Wolfgang Friedmann calls the two types of law the 'law of coexistence' and the 'law of co-operation' respectively. It is an enhanced effectiveness of the law of coexistence at the global level and an expansion of the role of the law of co-operation at the regional and global levels that welfarist international lawyers consider as vital for the future of mankind. Myres McDougal and Richard Falk would broadly agree with this position, the former putting more stress on the role international lawyers can play within the existing framework than upon the need for institutional reform, while the latter considering it as vital to transform man's attitude towards global problems so that eventually some form of central guidance mechanism can come to replace the present system of sovereign states (Higgins 1969). Most WOMP writers as well as Beitz and Linklater broadly support the welfarist lines summarized here.

There are, however, some contemporary writers on international law and relations who are critical of the notion that international society should concern itself with those goals, such as human welfare, which go beyond the minimum goal of inter-state coexistence. R. J. Vincent falls into this category insofar as we can judge his position from his defence of the principle of non-intervention. According to him, the observance of this principle is a minimum condition for the coexistence of sovereign states, enabling each to pursue within its boundaries the primary goals of society. Although Vincent does not count the protection and enhancement of the social and economic welfare of its members as among the primary goals of society, he appears in principle to subscribe to the view that there is a functional differentiation to be made between domestic society and international society: in the former, multifarious social goals can be pursued and realized, but the latter should concern itself with the minimum goal of coexistence among its constituent units, sovereign states (1974, 330–1).[15]

THE DOMESTIC ANALOGY AND WORLD ORDER PROPOSALS

A more specific opposition to the global application of welfare internationalism is found in Terry Nardin's *Law, morality and the relations of states* (1983). Central to his argument is the distinction between 'practical association' and 'purposive association' (1983, Introduction). The former consists of those who are engaged in the pursuit of different and possibly incompatible purposes, and who are associated with one another only in respecting certain restrictions (or 'authoritative practices') on how each may pursue his own purposes. By contrast, the members of the other type of association are brought together in a co-operative enterprise to promote shared values, beliefs or interests, and are united by their convergent desires for the realization of a common goal. For example, those who come together for the sake of promoting a candidate for office form a 'purposive association'. According to Nardin, there are some political theorists who have understood even the state as a 'purposive association', but he is critical of this view, preferring to consider the state as essentially a 'practical association' (1983, 4, 16–18).

Those who consider international society as a 'practical association' are said to have a 'practical conception' of international society; and, correspondingly, those who think of it as a 'purposive association' are said to have a 'purposive conception'. Nardin shows that the 'practical conception' of international society was dominant in the eighteenth and nineteenth centuries, but claims that in the present century the 'purposive conception' is gaining momentum. His evidence for this claim includes the establishment of the ILO and the United Nations, both of which are committed to the improvement of economic and social conditions within its member-states; a relative lack of stress on the need for a strict adherence to international law in the wording of the Charter; a recent tendency in the practice of the UN to regard the organization as a means for the economic development of poorer states; and the concern shown by eminent writers on world order, for example, the WOMP contributors, for a global transformation in pursuit of certain postulated values which go far beyond the minimum goal of the coexistence of sovereign states (1983, 23, 106, 107, 109).

Nardin is critical of the ascendance of the 'purposive conception' at the global level since, in his view, the degree of disagreement among states is such that institutions based on this conception are likely to be a source, not of unity, but of further division (1983, 110). However, he appears not to be opposed to international law and institutions based on the 'purposive conception' insofar as they operate among those states among which there is a sufficient degree of solidarity and consensus (1983, 5, 18). Translated into the language of welfarist writers,

Nardin's argument is that international society at the global level should concentrate on the 'law of coexistence', and that, although among some states united in the pursuit of some common goals the 'law of co-operation' may be effective and useful, this type of law and institution is unsuitable at the global level.

It is interesting to note that Nardin's argument for the 'practical conception' of international society is advanced in parallel with his endorsement of the conception of the state as essentially a 'practical association'. Indeed, what he is defending is the idea of international society gradually developed by classical writers on the law of nations who came by the eighteenth century to conceptualize international society and its relation to its constituent units, sovereign states, on the analogy of the state and its relation to its citizens (1983, 16–22, pt 1). Needless to say, those thinkers had advanced such a conception of international society long before it came to be considered as a proper function of the state to protect and enhance the social and economic welfare of its citizens. Thus, Nardin might be considered as relying on the domestic analogy, but, using a model, which, from the welfarist standpoint, is an outdated one.

However, it is a mistake to consider Nardin as using the domestic analogy at all. The contention that just as citizens are united in their subjection to the law of their state, so sovereign states, citizens of international society, are governed by the law of nations in fact goes against the domestic analogy inasmuch as it suggests that international society is already state-like when, in terms of its institutional structure, it clearly is not. Since, according to this view, international society is already state-like in being able to accord rights and obligations to its constituent units, it follows that there is no, or little, need for the institutions of international society to emulate those of domestic society any further. This is in fact the negation of the domestic analogy. It is no coincidence therefore that much of Nardin's argument about the bases of order in international society is very similar to that of Bull, a determined opponent of the domestic analogy, and that Nardin's conception of international law, which he presents in detail, emphasizes its 'specific character' and its capacity to function in its own distinctive ways in a decentralized world (Nardin 1983, chap. 2, pt 2).

It is worth pointing out here that it is 'international society as such' that in Nardin's view is a 'practical association' (1983, 18–19). By 'international society as such' he means the society of states organized by 'general international law'. As a matter of historical fact, general international law has been concerned primarily with the coexistence of states, and therefore 'international society as such', abstracted from the totality of international relations, has historically been a 'practical association'. However, such an abstraction tends to ignore the important development of the 'purposive' international law and institutions at the subsystemic level. Moreover, the historical fact that 'general international law' has been based on the 'practical conception' does not make it impossible for 'purposive general international law' to develop in future. The view, which Nardin appears to hold, that 'international society as such' is, by conceptual necessity, bound to be a 'practical association' is a reformulation of the older doctrine of the specific character of international law, which insisted that certain principles, such as compulsory jurisdiction, based on domestic analogues, were not only undesirable, but also logically incompatible with the very concept of international law.

Contemporary diplomatic school

The discussion so far tends to show that, contrary to the impression one might have of contemporary international thought, the domestic analogy, of various types, survives in the postwar debate about world order. Indeed, despite some important modifications and innovations, the various types of argument advanced in the postwar period about the conditions of world order are to a considerable degree a continuation of those positions which were formulated in the period of the League of Nations and its eventual demise, in which, as we noted, three of the four major patterns of thought we identified embodied the domestic analogy of some kind. However, it would be a mistake to suggest that the support for the domestic analogy is a preponderant force in contemporary international thought. A fourth line of argument, exemplified in the previous period by the writings of Edwin Borchard, has found influential adherents among the writers on international relations. The leading figure of this school, which is opposed to the domestic analogy, and might be labelled the 'contemporary diplomatic school' after Oppenheim's designation, is undoubtedly Hedly Bull. The outline of his argument has already been presented in the early part of this book.

Bull is critical of the twentieth-century trend of international law, exemplified by the League of Nations, the Kellogg–Briand Pact and the United Nations, to attempt to control the use of force by states on the basis of a criminal-law analogy. Bull's position here is identical to that of Borchard, who continued to express his strong preference for the nineteenth-century system well into the postwar period. Although not going so far as to argue that the nineteenth-century system is superior to the twentieth-century system with respect to the control of force, Julius Stone (1959) has also stressed the continuing relevance of the laws of war and neutrality in the present period (see also Stone 1958, 17, 145–6; 1968; 1977, 158).

Bull's preference for the nineteenth-century system of international law with respect to the control of force is based on what he calls the 'pluralist', as opposed to 'solidarist', view of international society. The former is distinguished from the latter by a relatively negative estimation of the degree of consensus that exists among the constituent units of international society, and in particular by the view that, in respect of law enforcement, there is not enough solidarity among them to make operative the type of international law based on the criminal-law analogy. Moreover, in Bull's view, this type of international law may even be positively harmful to the maintenance of international order. To the extent that it influences the course of events, Bull thinks, this type of law tends to interfere with those institutions with which international society had equipped itself for the limitation of war, such as the laws of war and neutrality, the balance of power and the principle of non-intervention (1966b, esp. 69ff.). Nardin's 'practical conception' of international society, explained above, is in line with Bull's 'pluralist conception' although Nardin does not argue specifically against the criminal-law analogy in twentieth-century international law. Since Bull is critical of this analogy, it is clear that he is opposed to any attempts, for example, that of Clark and Sohn, to develop the United Nations into an even more centralized international organization.

Indeed, Bull's opposition to the domestic analogy goes beyond the rejection of a criminal-law analogy. He is critical also of the cosmopolitanist form of the domestic analogy which leads to an advocacy of a world government. His opposition is based on the belief that such a body may interfere with the liberty of each nation to pursue its own mode of life, will deprive individuals of the right to pursue freedom from tyranny through foreign asylum, and by attempting to contain mutually hostile communities under one government, rather than according them sovereign independence, it may intensify conflict among them rather than contribute to its resolution (1966a, esp. 50). The view that the division of the world into sovereign states is a condition of national liberty is supported also by F. S. Northedge, whose ideas about international relations are in fundamental respects similar to those of Bull (Northedge 1976, 322–3; Suganami 1983). Nardin, through his adherence to the 'practical conception' of international society, also values its capacity for pluralistic permissiveness.

As for welfare internationalism, Bull's position is somewhat negative. He acknowledges that the expansion of the scope of international law to encompass economic, social and other matters represents a strengthening of the contribution of international law to international order. However, the expanding scope of international law is seen by him not as evidence of community-building, but as a way of controlling or preventing conflict which has also expanded its scope in accordance with increased international intercourse (1977, 153). Moreover, Bull expresses a degree of anxiety about a movement towards an international protection of human rights. According to him, 'carried to its logical extreme, the doctrine of human rights and duties under international law is subversive of the whole principle that mankind should be organised as a society of sovereign states', the principle which he endorses (1977, 152, 318). Bull, however, cannot consistently be regarded as being in opposition to welfare internationalism since he is also in favour of developing a cosmopolitan outlook within the sovereign states system (1977, 289, 316). The cultivation of such an outlook within the present system would necessitate support for welfare internationalism, and, in particular, an international protection of human rights.

Bull's view of contemporary world politics is characterized by the following three factors: his relatively positive assessment of the degree of order which can be achieved within the sovereign states system; his belief that global economic and social injustices and ecological problems have deeper causes than the institutional structure of the world; and his judgement that the present system, when reinforced by a more cosmopolitan outlook, will be able to cope tolerably well with the multifarious problems facing mankind without altering its fundamental structure (1977, chaps. 12, 13). These ideas place Bull in direct opposition to the advocates of global centralization, such as Richard Falk. Although in *The anarchical society* Bull concedes that Falk's views are 'one of the most significant points of departure in the study of world politics today', the former is severely critical of the latter's vision (1977, ix, 302ff.). There is in fact an important similarity between the two writers in that they both stress the necessity for a cosmopolitan outlook, but the difference between them is more conspicuous. Whereas Falk is determined to stress the dysfunctional aspects of the present system, Bull remains firmly in favour of a decentralized world structure.

Concluding remarks

This chapter has examined in some detail a variety of proposals and ideas about world order formulated in the postwar period by a number of writers well-known to students of International Relations in the English-speaking world. The proposals and ideas were presented in the light of the four prototypes identified in chapter 6: (1) a reformed-UN idea, most notably of Clark and Sohn, which follows the legalistic pattern of the reformed-League proposals of the previous period; (2) a variety of positions which in principle accept a world state as an ideal, upheld by those, like Schwarzenberger, Schuman and Morgenthau, who continued to adhere to the views they expressed in the previous period, as well as by those who formulated their views in the postwar era; (3) welfare internationalism, most notably of Jenks, Friedmann and Röling, also seen in the writings of McDougal and embodied in WOMP contributions; (4) the 'diplomatic school' approach, championed by Bull, and in certain essential respects supported by Nardin.

In discussing the second set of positions, we examined the striking case of Meyer, a world state advocate who became a CIA agent, and analysed the structure of Waltz's argument regarding the 'permissive cause' of war. We also investigated the role of the domestic analogy in ideas about regional integration, taking one eminent practitioner, Monnet, and one prominent theorist, Haas, as examples. In connection with welfare internationalism, we analysed the place of the domestic analogy in the works of two contemporary international theorists of a cosmopolitan outlook, Beitz and Linklater, and showed that the structure of their argument was in fact non-analogical.

The works examined in this chapter fall into three, partially overlapping, historical phases within the postwar era. The first is from the early postwar years to about the middle of the 1960s, in which the three successive editions of Clark and Sohn's *World peace through world law* appeared. This is a phase in which 'realism' reigned in the writings on international relations, but at the same time there was a serious interest in the idea of a world state, perhaps as a reaction to the inability of the United Nations to transcend Cold War rivalry. Schuman's *The commonwealth of man*, defending a world government as an ideal, Schiffer's *The legal community of mankind*, criticizing the attempt to secure peace within the framework of the sovereign states system, and Waltz's *Man, the state and war*, attaching special importance to the structure of the sovereign states system itself as the 'permissive cause' of war, all appeared in the middle of the first period.

163

The second phase is the 1960s and 1970s in which writings along the welfare internationalist lines increased and flourished. This was probably stimulated by the perceived decline of the Cold War tensions, and was clearly a reflection of an increased interest in the economic and social problems of the world which resulted partly from the growth in the number of newly independent and poor states. The WOMP proposals were written in this period.

The third phase is from the late 1970s to the present, which, on the one hand, saw a well-articulated attack by Bull and others on contemporary institutions and proposals embodying various forms of domestic analogy, and which, on the other hand, witnessed a serious defence of cosmopolitanism by Beitz and Linklater neither of whose argument, as we noted, involves the domestic analogy as an essential feature. This, however, does not mean that Beitz or Linklater would necessarily be opposed to institutional proposals which make a selective use of domestic analogues, for example, some proposals advanced by welfare internationalists, or contained in the WOMP volumes.

One important feature of the present phase of world order debate, therefore, is the opposition between a well-articulated attack on various domestic analogy positions, and a well-argued case for cosmopolitanism not unsympathetic to some form of domestic analogy. In addition, we may observe diversification in the use of the domestic analogy resulting partly from the rise of welfare internationalism and partly from the innovations made by some of the WOMP writers. Given this background, we are now faced with one vital question: what types of domestic analogy might be regarded as fruitful? This forms the central concern of the next chapter.

9 THE DOMESTIC ANALOGY AND WORLD ORDER PROPOSALS: TYPOLOGY AND APPRAISAL

A comparative analysis of a wide variety of ideas about world order which have emerged since the early part of the nineteenth century reveals that they are clustered around five basic positions. First, there is the legal school, advocating the internationalist, as opposed to the cosmopolitanist, form of domestic analogy. Second is the diplomatic school, critical of the ways in which and the extent to which the domestic analogy is employed by the legal school.

Both the legal and diplomatic schools support the idea that the sovereign states system should remain intact. They are concerned primarily with the problem of creating order in the external relations of sovereign states. And they both accept the principle that the official intercourse between states be conducted by diplomats, who act under instruction from the executive branches of their respective governments. The difference between the two schools is that while the legal school argues in favour of the legalistic use of the domestic analogy, the diplomatic school is opposed to it. The legal school advances the idea of 'peace through law' and, in its fullest form, advocates the creation of an international organization equipped with judicial, legislative and executive bodies for the management of international relations. By contrast, the diplomatic school prescribes the maintenance of international order through the operation of those practices, such as diplomacy, war and neutrality, which are claimed to be indigenous institutions of international society. The supporters of this approach consider international society as capable of sustaining order without a government derived from the domestic model.

Despite the opposition between the two schools, Oppenheim, who stood at the diplomatist end of the legalists, and Nippold, who was apparently at the legalist end of the diplomatists, were very close in their views about the desirable content of international law. Their difference was clearly a matter of degree. This example demonstrates that the legal and diplomatic schools should be treated as forming a continuum rather than separate circles, so to speak. For the

165

convenience of discussion, we shall call this continuum the legal–diplomatic (L–D) spectrum. Towards the legal end of this spectrum, we find, for example, the reformed-League idea of Leonard Woolf, and towards the diplomatic end is placed, for example, Edwin Borchard's persistent support of the laws of war and neutrality.

There are three other basic positions around which ideas about world order are clustered. They are democratic confederalism, federalism and welfare internationalism. Each of these approaches attempts to overcome in its own way what it sees as the major weakness of those proposals which are placed along the L–D spectrum, and each of them employs the domestic analogy in its distinctive form.

Democratic confederalism, exemplified earlier by the works of Lorimer and Bluntschli, subscribes to the confederal alternative, and might therefore be seen as a more radical form of legalism. The difference, however, is not just a matter of degree. The supporters of democratic confederalism stress that their proposed confederations are designed to reflect the wishes of the peoples divided into separate states which, in their view, ordinary confederations and international organizations fail to do.

Here it should be noted that even the more far-reaching schemes along the L–D spectrum accept that a law-making assembly should consist of diplomats, and that a mechanism of law enforcement should operate in accordance with the views expressed by the executive branches of national governments. Also, with respect to the peaceful solution of international disputes, these schemes expect the executive branches to play a major role since only those disputes which *diplomacy* fails to solve are to be brought to a court.

The adherents of democratic confederalism consider such a tendency as contrary to democracy, which they wish to extend from the domestic to the international sphere. In their view, state executives are often autocratic, and reflect the popular will far less accurately than do (representative) legislatures. They therefore suggest that an international assembly should consist of those who are elected by the state legislatures (or even by a popular vote), and that they should act without instruction from their state executives. Democratic confederalists make a qualitative leap in the use of the domestic analogy beyond the L–D spectrum by advocating the substitution of the principle of popular representation for the traditional principle of representation by diplomatic agents in the management of international affairs.

Federalism embodies the cosmopolitanist form of the domestic analogy, and objects to the sovereign states system as such. In this, federalism goes beyond the L–D spectrum, and also beyond democratic confederalism. When applied to the global level, the cosmopolitanist mode of domestic analogy could lead to an argument for a unitary world state, but practically all proposals for a world state appear to envisage the transformation of the present system into a world federation. Federalism may also be applied to the regional level either as a first step towards a wider federation, or simply as a means of regional integration. Among our nineteenth-century examples, Saint-Simon's project embodied the cosmopolitanist mode of the domestic analogy although, writing in the early part of the century, he was not concerned with structural transformation beyond Europe. More recently, some notable critics of the League of Nations accepted a world state as the ideal solution to the problem of world peace, Schwarzenberger and Schuman among them.

Welfare internationalism is critical of the tendency of the proposals along the L–D spectrum to be concerned primarily with the narrow objective of securing orderly relationships between states. It also objects to the idea common to legalism, democratic confederalism and federalism that the requisite transformation of the world could be expressed in a single institutional blueprint. It argues instead for multiplying and reinforcing international institutions which are concerned with the welfare of individuals located in separate states, gradually and pragmatically in accordance with the rising needs. It may be thought appropriate to give the label of 'functionalism' to this approach, since David Mitrany, who adopted it, is associated with that term. However, unlike functionalism, welfare internationalism is not necessarily committed to the view that the satisfaction of welfare needs by multifarious international institutions is bound by itself to enhance transnational solidarity and thereby contribute towards international integration (Friedmann 1970, 8–9 n. 14).

In this chapter, we shall first examine the degree of concession that can fruitfully be made to the domestic analogy along the L–D spectrum, and move on to assess the merits of democratic confederalism, federalism and welfare internationalism in turn as an approach to world order.

The L–D spectrum

Proposals along the L–D spectrum suggest the creation of at least one of three types of international institution: machinery for the peaceful solution of international disputes; a mechanism of law enforcement; and a law-making assembly. Somewhere in the middle of the spectrum, William Ladd proposed the establishment of the first and third types of institution, and Oppenheim, after the experience of the Great War, added the second. Many plans of the Great War period stressed the vital necessity of the first two types, while in the period of the League of Nations writers often debated on whether the problem of peaceful change should be solved by the third type. Towards the diplomatic end of the spectrum are ideas of Nippold, Baty and Stengel, and, more recently, those of Borchard and Bull. These diplomatist writers, however, either themselves proposed or at least did not object to having *some* form of machinery for the peaceful settlement of international disputes.

The argument in favour of setting up such machinery, especially when the proposal is of a more far-reaching kind, often takes the form that just as a court is indispensable for the peaceful solution of disputes between individuals, so a comparable body should be established in international society to settle disputes between states. This is among the commonest forms of domestic analogy, and if it is not stated so explicitly, it is at least assumed implicity by those who stand close to the legal end of the spectrum. At the other extreme, we find Karl von Stengel's conservative position that states should preserve the legal freedom to go to war, when diplomacy failed, to settle their differences. At this end of the L–D spectrum states can resolve their disputes by diplomacy, war or perhaps by voluntary arbitration. The problem is how far beyond this base-line the legal freedom of states to resort to war should be restricted. Those who favour the nineteenth-century system of international law, such as Borchard and Bull, do not go very much further than Stengel in this respect. Borchard was not opposed to an international court of justice, but did not support the view that compulsory jurisdiction could contribute to the peaceful settlement of international disputes. Lauterpacht, whose views we touched on briefly in chapter 1, was at the other extreme, and argued strongly in favour of the compulsory arbitration or adjudication of all disputes unresolved by other peaceful means, and wished to see international law take the same resolute attitude to violence as would any municipal legal system. Such a line of thought was criticized by Carr as utopian, but Brierly, himself sceptical of the value of compulsory jurisdiction by an international court, nevertheless insisted that there should be a legal ban on the use of force by states.

The central question here is, therefore, whether or not an international court of arbitration or justice should, and could profitably, be equipped with compulsory jurisdiction, and whether there should be a legal prohibition on the use of force by states other than as a means of law enforcement and self-defence. Stengel, Carr and Borchard replied negatively, Brierly positively in part, and Lauterpacht emphatically in the affirmative. How might we choose between these different opinions, and what degree of concession to the domestic analogy ought we to make on these issues?

One thing that is clear is that whether international law should incorporate compulsory jurisdiction and whether it should prohibit the use of force by states cannot be answered dogmatically with reference to the supposed 'nature' of international law. Those who see international law as a unique kind of law, having a 'specific character', tend to speak negatively of the domestic analogy, and are opposed to those who consider the anarchical structure of international law as merely a hitherto dominant historical condition, and the gradual approximation of international law to municipal law as constituting progress. But the question of whether the decentralized state of international law is unique and commendable, or primitive and deplorable, cannot be answered *a priori* in terms of some preconception about the essence of international legal order. Recently, Terry Nardin has criticized certain international lawyers, such as Lauterpacht, who at times confuse the conceptual question of what principles international law ought to embody in order to satisfy the definition of law, and the empirical question of what principles it should contain in order to contribute effectively to world order. It is important to note that this error is committed not only by some of those, like Lauterpacht, who insist that international law, in order to satisfy the definition of law, must emulate the standards of municipal law, but also by some of those, like Nippold (and perhaps even Nardin himself), who insist on the uniqueness of the international legal system (Nippold 1907, 148ff.).

The kind of question we are asking here, moreover, cannot be answered by merely repeating or rejecting the argument from analogy. The domestic analogy, it will be recalled, is presumptive reasoning about international relations based on the assumption that since domestic and international phenomena are similar in a number of respects, a given proposition which holds true domestically, but whose validity is as yet uncertain internationally, will also hold true internationally. What we are asking is whether an argument guided by such presumptive reasoning can be shown to be valid at the international level, and this cannot be answered by merely saying that presumptive reasoning will hold true, or that it will not because it is only presumptive. Clearly, what we must do is to examine the quality of presumptive reasoning case by case, and test the argument, if possible, in the light of international experience that has been gained.

1 *Compulsory jurisdiction*

As regards the incorporation of the principle of compulsory jurisdiction into international law, there are at least three grounds for criticism.

In the first place, while it may be true that all international disputes are justiciable, they are not necessarily profitably so from the viewpoint of their resolution. They are justiciable in the sense in which Lauterpacht insisted them to be so, namely that there is nothing in the nature of any international dispute which makes it intrinsically non-justiciable: an international court, just like any municipal court, can in principle either pronounce on the merits, or definitely dismiss a given claim on the ground that it is not entitled to protection and enforcement by the law (Lauterpacht 1933). However, while law can give *an* answer to every dispute, not all disputes can effectively be resolved thereby.

This point was clearly argued by Morgenthau (1973, 418ff.). According to him, international disputes are of three types: 'pure disputes'; 'disputes with the substance of a tension'; and 'disputes representing a tension'. As an illustration of 'pure disputes'; Morgenthau refers to a hypothetical case where the United States and the Soviet Union are in disagreement over the exchange rate between dollars and roubles for the diplomatic personnel of the two countries. It is conceivable that despite the existence of a tension between them, the two states treat the dispute as an issue which has no relation to the sources of their tension. In such circumstances, the dispute, according to Morgenthau's terminology, is a 'pure dispute'.

As an example of 'disputes with a substance of a tension', Morgenthau uses another hypothetical, but perhaps a little more realistic, case, namely a dispute over the interpretation of the Potsdam Agreement. He explains this as follows:

> One of the main issues of the tension between the United States and the Soviet Union is the distribution of power in Europe. The Potsdam Agreement is a legal document that endeavoured to settle the aspects of that issue connected with the occupation and administration of Germany by the Allies. The subject matter of the Potsdam Agreement, then, is identical with a segment of the issue that constitutes the subject matter of the tension between the United States and the Soviet Union. A dispute over the interpretation of the Potsdam Agreement has a direct bearing upon the over-all power relations between the United States and the Soviet Union. An interpretation favorable to one nation will add so much power to one side and

deduct that much power from the other side, since the issue is one upon which the power contest between the two countries has seized as one of its main stakes. (1973, 420)

As an illustration of 'disputes representing a tension', Morgenthau returns to the aforementioned case between the United States and the Soviet Union concerning the exchange rate of dollars and roubles for the diplomatic representatives of the two countries. While it is conceivable that such a dispute takes place without any relation to the tension between them, it is likely that the two states, keenly engaged in a contest of power, seize upon this dispute and make it the concrete issue by which to test their respective strengths. In such a case, the subject matter of the dispute has still no relation to the subject matter of the tension. Yet the dispute fulfils a symbolic and representative function in relation to the tension between the contestants.

Undoubtedly, it is only where a given dispute belongs to the first type, or closely approximates it, that a legal settlement can be of much use. In the second and third types, the contestants are not seriously interested in being offered a legal answer to the question involved. On the contrary, at least one of the contestants will be seriously interested in challenging what the law has to say. As Morgenthau puts it, a court is, in a sense, itself a party to such a dispute (1973, 420, 422). One of the weaknesses of the argument in favour of compulsory jurisdiction is that it depicts all international disputes as if they were analogous to a pure legal dispute between two citizens within a well-ordered state regarding some private property. Many cases of international dispute are so unlike this legalistic paradigm that an argument built upon it, even implicitly, is of doubtful value.

A second argument against compulsory jurisdiction is that it may not be effective unless backed by a system of sanctions, and may lead to unfair consequences unless accompanied by a system of peaceful change. According to this argument, compulsory jurisdiction on its own does not go far enough in the direction of a domestic model, and partial reliance on the domestic analogy is useless, or worse than useless.

Against this line of argument, Lauterpacht asserted in his work of 1933 that the absence of centralized sanctions would reduce, but not substantially impair the function of the judiciary, equipped with compulsory jurisdiction, as an instrument of peace (Lauterpacht 1933, 398). However, he did not show any empirical grounds for this problematic assertion. He was more seriously concerned to refute the other suggestion that, due to the absence of an international legislature, an international tribunal might perpetuate injustices by giving effect to

171

existing international legal rights. In the work of 1933, however, he argued that the judicial process was not as rigid as was suggested by this criticism, and that there were certain means of peaceful change already available within the existing system (Lauterpacht 1933, pt 4). He believed that the existing tendencies in the political integration of the community of states pointed to the future establishment of an effective international legislature. This would relieve obligatory judicial settlement of the strain imposed by the present imperfection of the legislative process. None the less, he wrote, 'it is improvident to reject a working minimum because the maximum cannot as yet be obtained': the rejection of obligatory arbitration or adjudication, in his view, would in the last resort amount to a sanction of the reign of force (Lauterpacht 1933, 346, 345).

Lauterpacht's argument that the absence of centralized sanctions would reduce, but not substantially impair, the function of the judiciary endowed with compulsory jurisdiction betrays his excessive confidence in the capacity of law to determine the behaviour of states even against their power and desire. Lauterpacht is much more persuasive when he argues that certain means of peaceful change already exists within the present system. But his argument that it would be improvident to reject a working minimum because the maximum could not yet be obtained presupposes that a judiciary endowed with compulsory jurisdiction would constitute a 'working minimum'. While his implicit assumption that the minimalist goal of the avoidance of the reign of force should precede the maximalist goal of the creation of a just peace might be accepted, there is still no good reason to suppose that a judiciary endowed with compulsory jurisdiction would, in the absence of organized sanctions, actually constitute a 'working' system at the global level characterized by the lack of social solidarity.

A third ground for criticism needs to be mentioned only briefly. It is that compulsory jurisdiction, when ineffective, may in fact make the situation worse. John Westlake argued long ago that between mutually hostile nations an arbitration treaty without reservation was undesirable since it would not only be ignored by one party, but also add a charge of bad faith to the original source of difference (Westlake 1904, 344). Clearly, we should not exaggerate the impact of this undesirable side-effect since it is difficult to establish its magnitude. None the less, we should at least bear this point in mind when assessing the overall value of compulsory jurisdiction in international relations.

These considerations lead us to the view that the transfer of the principle of compulsory jurisdiction from the domestic to the international sphere, by itself, is not likely to be desirable unless some drastic change can be made to the political conditions of the world at the same time. Most fundamentally, the idea of compulsory jurisdiction in international relations involves a mistaken use of the domestic analogy, according to which international disputes and pure legal disputes between individuals within the state are amenable to the same kind of legal control and management. Clearly, what is needed at present at the international level is not an increase in the formal powers of an international court, but a shift in the attitude of governments towards international adjudication and arbitration. Specialists in International Law and International Relations might make a small contribution to encouraging an attitudinal change on the part of governments by revealing some of their prejudices regarding the workings of the court, and this appears to be a more worthwhile task for those specialists than the drafting of any more blueprints for the creation of the fully empowered judiciary.[1]

2 A legal ban on the use of force by states

As regards the legal prohibition on the use of force by states, at least three lines of argument have been advanced against it by those who stand close to the diplomatic end of the L–D spectrum.

In the first place, a legal ban on the use of force is said inescapably to be ineffective in a world of states where there is only a limited amount of trust, and an abundance of military capability. Moreover, the argument runs, we need to be concerned with the undesirable side-effects of having such a ban. One of the side-effects is said to be that under the system of international law based on a prohibition of the use of force, each contestant will tend to see the other as the violator of this prohibition, and as a result the conflict will intensify because both sides assume themselves to be legally in the right, and become more uncompromising (Bull 1966b, 71). Secondly, the system of international law based on a ban on the use of force is assumed to be at least hostile to, if not necessarily logically incompatible with, the institution of neutrality, and to encourage states to adopt the policy of 'qualified neutrality' in favour of what they consider as the victim state. However, the argument runs, this tends to expand the conflict either because the belligerents may retaliate against those 'neutral states' who discriminate against them, or perhaps because the 'neutral states' in their support of the victim state may be made to feel it desirable to join in the war to suppress the delinquent state. Because there is no assurance that 'neutral states' would agree on which of the belligerents is legally in the right, the conflict can expand into a confrontation between two camps supporting the original belligerents. This is said to be another negative side-effect of the ban (Borchard and Lage 1937, pt 3, 1; Bull 1966b, 71). Thirdly, it is suggested that a legal ban on the use of force will deprive states of the traditional methods of maintaining international order and achieving a degree of justice (Bull 1977, 143–5, 189). These considerations, however, require a careful re-examination.

As regards the first of the three criticisms noted here, while it is clear that a legal ban on the use of force is bound to be violated in some cases, it will be a little unrealistic to suggest that it has absolutely no impact on the behaviour of states. If it is admitted that it will have some impact on their behaviour, the question then is whether the positive impact of cutting down the frequency of the use of force is outweighed by the negative side-effect of making the contestants more uncompromising. Self-righteousness can be expected of any state in a dispute, whatever its international legal commitments, and it will be exceedingly difficult, if possible at all, to determine how far this tendency is attributable to the particular content of the law under which states live. Those who insist that a legal prohibition on the use of force will inevitably make the contestants more intense and entrenched in their hostility argue without sufficient empirical evidence, and may therefore be criticized for dogmatism (see further Suganami 1983, 2370, 2377–8).

The second criticism noted above is a standard defence of the nineteenth-century system of the law of neutrality, and is used by various writers, such as Borchard, and, more recently, Hedley Bull. Morgenthau has used a similar line of argument in his criticism of the collective security system (Borchard and Lage 1937, pt 3, 1; Bull 1966b, 71; Morgenthau 1973, 408–10). The argument appears reasonably persuasive, but exaggerates the firmness with which neutrality is established as an institution of international society. It will be recalled that Borchard exalted this institution as one which 400 years of history had cultivated in the international system, and which was eminently more suitable to the international environment than was a League-type institution based on the domestic analogy. Brierly, however, was critical of those who considered neutrality as a well-established and well-adapted international institution.

According to Brierly's analysis, the institution of neutrality does not possess the kind of inevitable permanency in the international system which writers like Borchard attributed to it. Brierly argued that neutrality was very much a product of the circumstances of the nineteenth century. These circumstances included: the existence and growing influence of a power which favoured neutrality, namely the United States; the relatively peaceful character of the nineteenth century in

174

which most states were inclined to regard themselves as more likely to be neutrals than belligerents if war should break out; and what Brierly called a temporary balance between the political division of Europe and the means of warfare, which had made respect for neutrality and the efficient prosecution of war consistent with each other (1944, 26ff.). However, the institution of neutrality was already precarious when it was supposed to have reached its high-water mark at the turn of the century. Brierly wrote:

> In the nineteenth century . . . would-be neutral states did enjoy a fair degree of security against the risk of being drawn into war against their will and merely to suit the interests of a more powerful neighbour, and it was easy to attribute to the laws of neutrality a security which they really owed to contemporary, and as we can now see also temporary, conditions. When the process of building up these laws had culminated in the Hague Conferences of 1899 and 1907, they doubtless looked to the casual observer a solid and imposing structure. Yet for all its impressive façade the cracks in the edifice had begun to appear even before the turn of the century. In the practice of nations at war neutrality had never been quite so strictly applied as the books said that it ought to be and were inclined to assume that it was; it was often not truly impartial, but 'qualified' or 'benevolent', much as it had been in the eighteenth century and as it is again to-day . . . [Moreover,] the right of a state to be neutral in the wars of other states, if it so chose, had again become insecure. The German General Staff is believed to have adopted the Schlieffen Plan in or about 1897, and by that plan German armies were to pass through Belgian territory in the event of a war with France; so that even while the lawyers were talking at The Hague it seems likely that the Chancelleries of Europe knew that in the next war Germany, if it suited her, would violate the neutrality of a little state which she had herself guaranteed.   (1944, 29–30)

Because of these considerations, and because of the experience of two world wars in one generation, Brierly, writing in the middle of the twentieth century, saw neutrality as having been a transient and obsolete institution. It is open to debate whether his perception was in turn a short-sighted one. Yet his argument does point us to the important fact that those who support the institution of neutrality as against those institutions based on the domestic analogy must argue their case in the light of the particular historical conditions of international society rather than treat neutrality as if it were a permanently best-adjusted, unique institution of that society. If, in future, the rules in the United Nations Charter concerning the use of force continue to work reasonably effectively, states may tend to adopt a policy of 'qualified neutrality'. On the other hand, the danger of escalation into a nuclear holocaust may increase the number of states who wish to stay out of an ongoing war, and this may result in growth in the power and influence of neutral states – something which Brierly, writing in 1944, did not envisage.

A third argument against a legal ban on the use of force by states was that such a ban would deprive them of the traditional means of maintaining international order and achieving justice. This cannot be entirely true since even under the system of international law embodying a ban on the use of force it will still be legitimate to resort to force in self-defence or as a means of law enforcement against the violator of the ban itself. However, to the extent that a legal ban encompasses preventive war, anticipatory self-defence, intervention for the maintenance of the balance of power, use of force for just change, and humanitarian intervention, it may be suggested that the ban interferes with the mechanism of the balance of power, or rules out one effective means of achieving justice.

Indeed, circumstances are conceivable where a reasonably persuasive case can be made to the effect that, despite its illegitimacy from the viewpoint of the United Nations Charter, force was used in a manner of anticipatory self-defence, producing thereby a satisfactory outcome from the viewpoint of the balance of power and international order. Circumstances are also conceivable where the use of force by one state against another might have been defended on the grounds of justice. The American naval blockade of Cuba in the Missiles Crisis may be counted as an instance of the former, and India's use of force against Goa, or Tanzania's intervention in Amin's Uganda are possible instances of the latter. However, even if such interpretations of these three cases were accepted, it would still be open to question whether these and other possible exceptions were significant enough to make it advisable to do away with a general ban on the use of force altogether.

The foregoing discussion shows that none of the three lines of argument against a legal prohibition on the use of force is overwhelming. However, it will have to be conceded that international society will not necessarily turn into chaos simply because a legal ban on the use of force is lifted, or exceptions are made in the case of anticipatory self-defence and so on. It may seem difficult not to suppose that a legal prohibition on the use of force contributes to the sustenance of the climate of opinion which sees peace as the normal condition of international life and the use of force as an exception. But even in the nineteenth century, when states enjoyed *legal* freedom to resort to force, war was not thought to be the normal, let alone permanent, state of affairs in the life of states.[2]

Since we cannot show conclusively that we should prefer the nine-teenth-century system of international law to what has developed in this century in the area of the control of force, there is a clear case for continuing with what we now have. At any rate, it is unrealistic to assume that we can go back to where we were in 1914, since the idea that states do not have unrestricted legal freedom to resort to force has become part of the orthodox diplomatic assumptions of our century (see Franck 1970; Henkin 1971).

3 A mechanism of law enforcement

A mechanism of law enforcement is the second of the three types of institution we set out to consider. An international police force and a collective security system are two institutions of this kind pro-posed by those who stand close to the legal end of the L–D spectrum. It is doubtful whether those at the diplomatic end of the spectrum have a coherent conception of law enforcement in international relations since, according to their view, states are to be legally free to resort to war for purposes other than law enforcement. However, arguments against reliance on an international police force or collective security appear considerable.

As for an international police force, it presupposes such a high degree of trust among states that it is difficult to imagine how it can be created in the present circumstances. The failure of the United Nations to implement Article 43 of the Charter, requiring member-states to conclude special agreements with the Security Council regarding the formation of the United Nations Force, can be considered as firm evidence indicating the unrealizability in the foreseeable future of a police force at the international level (Nicholas 1975, 81–3). The UN has been engaged in various peace-keeping operations since 1956 when the United Nations Emergency Force was established in connection with the Suez War. However, the stationing of these peace-keeping forces requires the consent of the states in which they operate, and, with the notable exception of the United Nations force in the Congo, they have not been authorized to use force beyond self-defence. The UN peace-keeping forces have fulfilled an important role in the control of international conflict, but clearly they cannot be regarded as a means of law enforcement (James, 1969).

Even if, in a very distant future, an international police force were to be established, its effectiveness as a means of maintaining inter-national order would be in grave doubt unless comprehensive dis-armament had also been achieved. Even then an international police

177

force would have to cope with large-scale violence committed by an organized group which would probably have ignored disarmament provisions. Therefore, unless the police were equipped with considerable military strength, its effectiveness would be in doubt, but the more formidable its strength, the more difficult it would be to keep it under political control to secure its impartiality. Clark and Sohn's project takes note of these difficulties inherent in the idea of an international police force, and envisages not only comprehensive disarmament, but also a very strict control of the proposed police force by the organs of the reformed United Nations (see Clark and Sohn 1966, xviiff.). However, an intricate blueprint is no guarantee against the abuse of power, and more importantly, against the very likely charge of impartiality which would undermine the authority of the proposed institution.

Although collective security is treated here under the rubric of law enforcement, it is not envisaged as a means of enforcing the whole body of international law. Rather it is aimed specifically at forestalling or countering an unlawful use of force, as under the League system. It can, as under the UN system, also be used as a means of maintaining or restoring international peace and security against any threat to the peace, breach of the peace or act of aggression, and these might be defined without strict reference to legal criteria. Collective security assumes that the heart of the problem of world order is to restrain an aggressor by the concerted effort of the rest of the international community.[3]

The Covenant and the Charter are two documents which embody the idea of collective security, but, as Morgenthau puts it, 'the actual practice of the members of these two organizations has fallen far short of the collective measures authorized by these two documents' (1973, 293). If an international police force is unlikely to be realizable for a foreseeable future and its desirability itself is in doubt, a collective security system, even if desirable in many cases, appears as a general rule to be unworkable.

For collective security to work, the system must be near-universal in its membership. Every member must be ready to act swiftly, through diplomatic, economic or military means, even against its perceived short-term interests, to defend fundamental community values, such as international peace and security, against any other member who attempts to violate them. Moreover, for such a system to work, there must not be a sharp disparity in the economic and military capabilities among the member-states. Nor must there be any special historical enmity or friendship between particular states. The mode of aggression prevalent in the system must be such that it is relatively easy to determine whether or not violation has taken place, and who the violator is in each case. Furthermore, the state of military technology and the level of armament must be such that it is possible for a violator to be met by a quick, overwhelming response. In fact, the level of armament in the system would probably have to be reasonably low so that those states acting in pursuit of collective security would not find the prospect of joining in military sanctions too hazardous and costly. These conditions, which encompass attitudinal as well as objective factors, are virtually impossible to obtain or endure in the real world (Claude 1971, 249ff.). It is not surprising therefore that the League of Nations' collective security failed (though economic sanctions, if fully mobilized, could have worked against Italy), and that under the United Nations, the system functioned (if it can be said to have done so at all from the strict legal viewpoint) only in the exceptional and irregular circumstances of Korea (Akehurst 1984, 185ff.).

If the idea of communal law-enforcement at the international level appears so obviously inappropriate, how is it that so many thinkers have supported it even up until the post-1945 period? Blind reliance on the domestic analogy seems to be the answer. This form of domestic analogy was influential during the period of the Great War and its aftermath because, as we saw, the war was interpreted as having resulted from, among other things, the lack of organized coercion in international law. The shock of the First World War was particularly pronounced precisely because of the pre-1914 confidence in the power of the old-style international law to maintain world order. There is therefore some truth in Borchard's scathing remark that the peace-makers of the Great War period acted in hysteria. When international experience had been gained through the failure of the League of Nations, writers like Borchard saw their view reaffirmed. However, some League supporters, like Woolf, insisted that one instance of failure was insufficient to prove any approach intrinsically wrong. His conviction was based on the belief in the correctness of the domestic analogy, which he claimed was derived from 4,000 years of experience. The following passage from his *The war for peace* explains the idea underlying collective security or international police so well that it may be quoted at length:

> To prevent war is a problem of politics and government, not essen-
> tially different from the problem of preventing duelling or cock-
> fighting or of regulating the relations between the inhabitants of
> Middlesex and those of Surrey. It may be easier to prevent cock-
> fighting than war or to regulate the relations between Middlesex and

Surrey or England and Scotland than those between France and Germany. But there is nothing in the last problem which makes it essentially different from the others. To alter the international system so as to prevent war is simply a problem of human government; if the object is attainable, it can only be attained, like the objects of Bismarck, by applying reason to experience.

The idea that experience is not available from which we may learn what we shall have to do in Europe if the existing state of affairs is to be altered and wars prevented is ridiculous. It was mentioned above that a Civil Servant in Asia, as an officer of the British Government watching to see that a murderer was hanged by the neck until he was dead in accordance with the law, might be conscious that 3,800 years ago the officers of the Government of Sumer and Akkad were doing exactly the same thing not so very far away. That means that for 4,000 years, at least, human beings have had experience of communal government. All that time they have been posing themselves problems of government, and solving them or failing to solve them. What are these problems of government? They are simply questions of how the relations between individuals and groups shall be ordered and controlled – relations between individual and individual, between classes, nations, and races, between groups living in villages, towns, districts, states, or continents. This experience is so ancient and so catholic that there is nothing which we cannot learn from it about human government if we wish to do so. And among the things which we could most certainly learn from all this experience is what we must do in the year 1940 if we wish to prevent another European war.

(1940, 79–80)

Woolf's argument is noteworthy since it eloquently discloses the problematic assumptions of his type of approach, which, as we saw, contributed to the formation of the United Nations and continue to underlie more recent projects for world order, such as Clark and Sohn's. In the first place, the punishment of a murderer is treated as if it were a central problem of government. And secondly, the problem of maintaining order between two individuals is seen to be identical to the problem of maintaining order between two large, organized groups of individuals.

The weakness of the first assumption is revealed by Inis Claude, who characterizes it as a 'schoolboyish' view (Claude 1962, 259–60). The error of the second assumption has been noted by many, including Claude, Carr and Brierly (Claude 1962, 243ff.; Carr 1939, 269ff.; Brierly 1944, 46ff.). As these writers have pointed out, individuals, when united, acquire strength qualitatively different from what they each possess, and the central task of a government is to cope, not with individual robbers, but with the demands, often illegal, made by various strong groups within the state. If 4,000 years of domestic

experience can tell us anything about how to create order in international society, in these writers' view, it is how some states were more
successful than others in avoiding a civil war, rather than how they
have dealt with murderers.

The foregoing discussion shows that even if there is a case for a legal
prohibition on the use of force in international society, we cannot
expect this as a general rule to be backed by a mechanism of communal
law-enforcement, such as collective security. Woolf, taking note of the
failure of the League, therefore suggested that law enforcement should
be organized on a regional basis. The regional principle was also
strongly supported by Winston Churchill. Needless to say, this principle is based on the assumption that the world can be divided into
regional subsystems in each of which we can expect a degree of
solidarity comparable to that which obtains within the domestic
sphere, and sufficient to make collective enforcement of law operative.
This appears a somewhat less unrealistic assumption to make than the
idea that all nations of the world have an equal interest in fighting
against aggression in any part of the world. Even then, it is difficult to
find a region of the world in which collective security is workable,
given the conditions spelled out earlier for its effective functioning.
There are some regions, North America or Scandinavia, for example,
where social cohesion between states is very strong. But in these areas,
sometimes called 'security communities', a collective security system is
not likely to be necessary (for the idea of 'security community' see
Deutsch *et al.* 1957).

4 A law-making assembly

There remain proposals for a law-making assembly yet to be
discussed. As in the case of Ladd's Congress of Nations, the proposed
law-making assembly may be no more than a regularized form of
diplomatic conference, one which writers at the turn of the century,
such as Oppenheim and Schücking, wished to see the Hague Conference develop into. There will be little harm in such an arrangement,
though the fixity of procedures and membership might be thought
undesirable. In fact, so long as the idea of having a conference to
conclude treaties of general interest is accepted and practised by international society, there may be little need to insist on having a single
legislative assembly. Borchard, for example, did not see the absence of
an international legislature as a major defect of international law, for he
believed that states learned to co-operate by treaty in hundreds of

fields when the need arose. This is the line adopted by those who stand close to the diplomatic end of the L–D spectrum. Without a doubt, a periodic meeting of the representatives of states is valuable, and the United Nations General Assembly has become a quasi-legislature, in some writers' judgement (Falk 1970, 174–84; Bull 1977, 149). It may therefore be asked whether a full-fledged legislature, comparable to a parliament within the domestic sphere, capable of enacting international law periodically without the unanimous consent of the member-states is still to be desired.

It is interesting to note that whereas, within the limitations of the veto system, the founders of the United Nations took the idea of collective security seriously and attempted to create an institution approximating to an international police force, they were not so keen on the idea of an international legislature. In 1945, at the San Francisco Conference, the Philippines Delegation made the following proposal to endow the General Assembly with legislative authority:

> The General Assembly should be vested with the legislative authority to enact rules of international law which should become effective and binding upon the members of the Organization after such rules have been approved by a majority vote of the Security Council. Should the Security Council fail to act on any of such rules within a period of thirty (30) days after submission thereof to the Security Council, the same should become effective and binding as if approved by the Security Council.   (cited in Falk 1970, 175)

Such a proposal, if it had been accepted, would have endowed the United Nations with a legislative competence in its true sense. However, not surprisingly, the proposal was defeated by a vote of 26–1 at a drafting session (Falk 1970, 37). The reason why states are not willing to endow a global organization, such as the UN, with a full legislative competence is obvious: they do not want to commit themselves to upholding an institution which can make binding decisions against their will. Given the marked reluctance of states to accept the optional clause of the ICJ, with respect to compulsory jurisdiction, it is not surprising that they are not willing to set up a legislative body above themselves.

The absence of a legislature at the global level, however, is not necessarily a weakness of international law. Given the relatively small number of the units in the system, requisite regulative principles could be formulated by negotiation, bilateral and multilateral, and universal principles could develop through custom. Moreover, legislatures can be oppressive, as Thomas Baty so outspokenly pointed out, and more recently, Michael Akehurst has made a similar remark. According to him,

> all legal systems correspond to some extent to the prevailing climate of opinion in the society in which they operate, but in national legal systems the concentration of legislative power in the hands of a small number of individuals may result in the enactment of rules which most people do not want and are reluctant to obey. In international law the absence of a legislature means that states very largely create law for themselves, and it is unlikely that they will create law which is not in their interests or which they will be tempted to break. Of course, it is possible that a state may be forced to agree to a rule under duress, or that the interests of states may change, or that a change of circumstances may render a rule burdensome; but international law provides at least a partial solution to these problems.   (1984, 8)

Indeed, Brierly, among others, has stressed that the idea of making or amending the law by a majority vote is a relatively recent innovation even within the domestic sphere, and that even there the idea cannot usefully be applied to all cases. In particular, a legislative method is not likely to be helpful when there is a sizable minority strongly committed to pursuing its own goals. Given the marked lack of consensus among nations at the global level, the idea of an international legislature appears clearly to be unsuitable or very premature as a means of maintaining world order (Brierly 1958b).

However, a somewhat more limited conception of international legislature has been formulated by some writers. According to this idea, advanced, for example, by Lauterpacht, the main concern of an international legislature is not a periodic enactment of international law by a majority vote, but to make particular states abandon their existing legal rights when their continued enjoyment of these rights is seen by an overwhelming majority of states to be unjust or particularly inexpedient. According to Lauterpacht, the vested rights of states should be made to yield 'only to such an overwhelming impact of justice and expediency as [would be] expressed by a practically unanimous vote of the other members of the community' (1937, 160). Lauterpacht also considered that such a method of change would be precarious and unreal unless it formed part of a system of collective security, and perhaps even part of a 'comprehensive political organisation of mankind' (1937, 164).

As we saw, collective security seems as a general rule to be unworkable, and therefore an institution whose operation requires the effective functioning of a collective security system is, generally speaking, of rather doubtful value. However, in some exceptional circumstances, the kind of method Lauterpacht envisaged may work, and an institution capable of employing such a method cannot be dismissed as useless. The degree of success which the United Nations has achieved so far through the activities of the General Assembly, Security Council and the ICJ in shifting South Africa's attitude towards Namibia is a particularly striking example of this line of approach in operation. Even with respect to Rhodesia, the United Nations played a not insignificant role in delegitimizing the white minority rule and undermining its confidence and power (Doxey 1980). These are, of course, exceptional circumstances, and the limited degree of success the United Nations has achieved is due mainly to the overwhelming consensus among its members against colonialism and a particular form of racial discrimination. It is somewhat doubtful at the moment that the UN could operate in a similar way with regard to other contentious issues arising in the international arena, such as serious human rights violations in other parts of the world.

Nevertheless, whereas an international legislature periodically enacting a body of international law by a majority vote seems unrealizable, probably unnecessary and perhaps even undesirable, there would be little objection to an international organization having an authority to put pressure on its members to abandon their rights when these rights are seen by an overwhelming majority to be against the community norms. Such a function of an international organization, however, is perhaps more akin to excommunication or ostracism than to legislation in the usual sense of the term.

Having examined the merits of various proposals along the L–D spectrum, we shall now turn to the remaining three approaches to world order: democratic confederalism, federalism and welfare internationalism.

Democratic confederalism

Democratic confederalism is exemplified well by James Lorimer's project. It will be recalled that his proposed international parliament was bicameral, and its two Houses were to consist of those who were sent by the legislatures of the member-states. Unlike, for example, Ladd's Congress of Nations, which is placed along the L–D spectrum, the members of Lorimer's international parliament were to act without instructions from the state executives. Lorimer's critic, Bluntschli also allowed the principle of popular representation to guide him in his own proposal, but, we noted, to a lesser extent than did Lorimer. At the beginning of the twentieth century, Schücking, inspired by the German experience, and Bluntschli's example, suggested that at a later stage in the development of his 'Hague Union', a second chamber might be added to the periodic Hague Conferences. This was to be composed of delegates from the parliaments of the contracting parties, and they were to vote without instructions from home, though they were expected as a rule to represent the presumed will of their respective national parliaments (Schücking [1912] 1918, 304ff.). A more radical suggestion that a periodic congress of delegates sent by the parliaments of states should take over the role of the Hague Conferences was contained in Robert Cecil's Draft Sketch of a League of Nations.

Democratic confederalism is very much an outcome of the rise of parliamentary democracy in the domestic sphere and of the desire of the progressive thinkers of the late nineteenth and early twentieth century to expand the realm of democratic control. However, the approach continues to attract substantial support in the latter part of the twentieth century. Thus, for example, the idea that the representatives in the world legislative assembly should be elected by a popular vote, and that they should act as individuals, not as government delegates, was incorporated in Clark and Sohn's project for a revised United Nations. Among the WOMP writers, Kothari suggests the establishment of a World Parliamentary Assembly, consisting of representatives from various national legislatures. Another WOMP contributor, Galtung, is critical of those who see a panacea in a strong inter-governmental world organization. In his view, such an organization will capture only some of the world's problems and conflicts, namely those which governments will be prepared to place on the agenda of international politics. This, according to Galtung, must be remedied by allowing non-governmental entities to participate more actively in the process of world politics, and for this purpose he suggests the creation of various organs, including, most notably, the House of Transnational Associations, which he hopes will develop into a House of World Parties. A similar mistrust of governments is manifest in Richard Falk, who endorses the view that non-governmental groups and individuals should actively participate in the articulation of the international normative standards (Falk 1981, esp. chaps. 7–9; 1975a, 152–3).

To the extent that democratic confederalism envisages a very close union of states within a constitutional framework, arguments against those proposals which are located towards the legal end of the L–D spectrum apply equally well (and perhaps with a stronger force) to those which embody democratic confederalism. However, there remains a question specific to this type. It is whether, in setting up an international organization, states should introduce the idea of popular representation at all rather than base it solely on the orthodox international principle of representation by diplomatic agents.

In considering this question, we should bear in mind that the idea underlying democratic confederalism is not quite as utopian as it might seem. It is, albeit in a diluted form, embodied in the European Parliament. The idea that those other than the official representatives of the state executives should participate in the decision-making process of an international organization is incorporated in the International Labour Organization, and underlies the consultative status accorded by the United Nations to various non-governmental organizations.[4]

The crucial point, however, is that the democratic principle which underlies democratic confederalism is appropriate only where there is a strong sense of transnational unity among the peoples concerned. Where, as in the European Community, there is a sufficient degree of unity among the peoples of a given region to make a supranational institution operative, there is a case for accommodating the democratic principle in its organization. Indeed, given the supranational legislative competence of the European Community, it may be necessary that Community policies be scrutinized by a Parliament elected in such a way as to reflect the wishes of the peoples closely.

However, where the sense of transnational unity is relatively weak, an institution embracing different peoples must be correspondingly more decentralized in its organization. If within a decentralized structure a mechanism were to be established through which non-governmental voices could be heard, it would still not be very meaningful to accord much formal power to them since the member governments would have enough strength not to yield even to the majority opinions expressed transnationally. In such a situation, it is doubtful whether a mechanism for expressing non-governmental opinions could usefully be given much more than a subsidiary role. Presumably, it was this line of thinking that led Lagos and Godoy, who on the whole follow Galtung's line, to suggest that only a consultative status should be accorded to transnational organizations within their proposed institution. Thus, at the global level, the utility of the democratic confederal principle is an extremely limited one. The approach, applied to this level, commits the error of attempting to transfer a domestic political principle to the domain where the conditions are either unsuitable or as yet not ripe enough. This error the democratic confederal approach shares with those proposals based on the domestic analogy standing close to the legal end of the L–D spectrum.

Galtung is right in his criticism of inter-governmental organizations that they will capture only those world problems which the governments are willing to place on the agenda of international politics. Yet his idea of a House of Transnational Associations, let alone a House of World Parties, remains outside the realm of practicability. Falk's global populism, which leads him to argue for the articulation of international normative standards by non-governmental groups and individuals, goes too far in the direction of ignoring the existing power structure of the world. This criticism can be extended to Jenks and McDougal who, as we saw, wish to enhance the role of international lawyers as a progressive force in international society on the analogy of the progressive role lawyers have fulfilled in some domestic systems. Lawyers' progressive potential should not be underestimated particularly within a relatively centralized set-up backed by a high degree of value consensus, for example, in the European Community. Yet, the role which international lawyers can play collectively for the progress of international society as a whole is severely restricted because of its decentralized structure and the degree of discordance within it.

Federalism

It is a common characteristic of those who see in federalism the best approach to the political organization of mankind that they are extremely pessimistic about the degree of co-operation realizable within the system of sovereign states: they see this system, regionally or globally, as unstable, destructive and incapable of realizing true harmony. In a passage which epitomizes such a view Saint-Simon stated as follows:

> A congress is now assembled at Vienna . . . The aim of this congress is to re-establish peace between the powers of Europe, by adjusting the claims of each and conciliating the interests of all. Can one hope that this aim will be achieved? I do not think so, and my reasons for so predicting are as follows. None of the members of the congress will have the function of considering questions from a general point of view; none of them will be even authorized to do so. Each of them, delegate of a king or a people . . . will come prepared to present the particular policy of the power which he represents, and to shew that this plan coincides with the interest of all. On all sides, the particular interest will be put forward as a matter of common interest. Austria will try to argue that it is important for the repose of Europe that she

187

should have a preponderance in Italy, that she should keep Galicia and the Illyrian provinces, that her supremacy in the whole of Germany should be restored; Sweden will demonstrate, map in hand, that it is a law of nature that Norway should be her dependency; France will demand the Rhine and the Alps as natural frontiers; England will claim that she is, by nature, responsible for policing the seas, and will insist that the despotism which she exercises there should be regarded as the unalterable basis of the political system.

These claims, presented with confidence, perhaps in good faith, in the guise of means to ensure the peace of Europe, and sustained with all the skill of the Talleyrands, Metternichs, and Castlereaghs, will not, however, convince anybody. Each proposition will be rejected because nobody, apart from the mover, will see in it the common interest since he cannot see in it his own interest. They will part on bad terms, blaming on each other the lack of success of the assembly: no agreement, no compromise, no peace. Sectional leagues, rival alliances of interests, will throw Europe back into this melancholy state of war from which vain efforts will have been made to secure her . . . Assemble congress after congress, multiply treaties, conventions, compromises, everything you do will lead only to war; you will not abolish it, the most you can do is to shift the scene of it.

([1814] 1952, 34–5)

With such a pessimistic prognosis of the degree of co-operation attainable within the system of sovereign states, it is not surprising that Saint-Simon should have suggested its radical transformation.

Such a pessimistic characterization of the states system, however, may be said to exaggerate its defects. 'Le Congrès ne marche pas, il danse' is indeed a well-known description of the Congress of Vienna, yet most of the demands which Saint-Simon had attributed to Austria, Sweden, France and England in the above passage were in the end conceded to them through diplomatic bargaining (Mowat 1922, 8, chap. 2). Saint-Simon seems not to have seen that between sovereign states there could be such a thing as 'reciprocal' interest in contradistinction to 'common' interest. Besides, if sovereign states were so incapable of co-ordinating their actions as is suggested by the above passage, it is difficult to see how such a radical departure as is recommended by Saint-Simon could even begin to take place.

One observation which may be entered here is that those supporters of the federal approach who are pessimistic about the degree to which co-operation can take place between states because of their 'sovereignty' may be resorting to what in chapter 2 we termed an international application of a domestic definition. In the present case, it is the idea that the word 'sovereignty' means the same thing when transferred from the sphere of domestic politics to the international realm. Inside the state, 'sovereignty' may be taken to mean 'supreme political authority'; but, when the same word is used in the external relations of states, the word is interchangeable with 'constitutional independence' (James 1986). It may be partly because they ignore this point, and assume the word to have identical meaning domestically and internationally that those supporters of the federal approach are pessimistic about the degree of co-operation realizable between sovereign states: among those entities which one characterizes as 'supreme political authorities' one might be inclined to expect irreconcilability and the dominance of conflict; among 'constitutionally independent' entities, not necessarily so.

Frederick Schuman's pessimistic prognosis of the states system appears partly due to his failure to distinguish the internationally relevant sense of the word 'sovereignty' from its domestic sense (Schuman 1945, 22–4). At any rate, in his judgement, all states systems of the past had collapsed, and the Western states system was destined in the near future to destroy itself with or without nuclear weapons unless a radical change could be achieved through the political unification of the world under one government.

Of course, it cannot be denied that Schuman's prognosis may in the end turn out to have been accurate. There is little doubt that in the latter part of the twentieth century mankind lives under the constant threat of its own annihilation. The point, however, is whether the situation would be improved, and annihilation avoided, if the world were to be united under one government. In considering this question, we must make sure to avoid circularity: by the phrase 'united under one government' we cannot mean 'united so effectively under one government as to rule out the real likelihood of any major disturbance'. And there are many countries in the world which are not so effectively governed. This reveals the real weakness of the world federal approach, its arbitrary selection of a domestic model: only a well-ordered state is taken as a relevant analogue. However, if, for example, India at the time of the British withdrawal, Pakistan at the time of the secession of Bangladesh, and Cyprus before the Turkish invasion are taken as a domestic analogue, the case for a world state becomes quite unconvincing. Indeed, one cannot expect from the world as a whole a higher degree of social cohesion than one expects from a relatively poorly governed community where civil war is a real threat. It seems that the most we can hope for from the viewpoint of federalism is the regional integration of mutually friendly national communities under a supranational regime. But even this, contrary to the optimism of some of the neo-functionalist writers at one stage (which, in the case of Haas, we

189

noted, was based on analogy from the American experience), has only had a limited degree of success among the member-states of the European Community.

There is another line of argument against a world federal approach. It is that a world state endangers individual and national liberty. As Schiffer put it: 'Single persons who have to fear their rulers have an opportunity to save themselves by leaving their countries; a world state would eliminate this opportunity' (1954, 104). And F. S. Northedge, among others, has remarked that the present international system, for all its failings, has produced the least unsatisfactory combination yet discovered of order in the whole and freedom for the subordinate parts (1976, 31, 321–3). By 'freedom for the subordinate parts', he means 'the liberty to lead our national lives as we think best' (1976, 323).

The potential tyranny of the central government is a problem which the supporters of the world federal approach would have to consider seriously. Yet it can be said against Northedge's defence of the states system that perhaps it is too sanguine. His is a view which only those who are satisfied with their national regimes can fully endorse. It is oblivious of the fact that in many parts of the world people do not have the liberty to lead their lives as they think best. It also pays insufficient attention to the extent to which the division of mankind into separate political communities institutionalizes such a sanguine outlook on human conditions.

It was noted earlier that those who in principle accept the cosmopolitanist mode of the domestic analogy do not necessarily concentrate their attention on advocating the establishment of a world state. Morgenthau and Waltz fall into this category. While their positions seem more defensible than a straight world federalist stance, their arguments are not flawless.

Morgenthau realized the immense difficulty of achieving what he regarded as an ideal solution to the problem of world order, namely the creation of 'a state coextensive with the confines of the political world' (1973, 487), and suggested that, as a practical first step, what statesmen must do is to lessen international tension by recourse to skilful diplomacy divested of the spirit of ideological crusade. Morgenthau's view that a world community must precede a world state is clearly more acceptable than the possibly self-contradictory idea of some world federalists that, since there is a serious limit to the degree of co-operation obtainable among sovereign states, they must therefore co-operate and create a world state. Yet if a world community has come into existence, as Morgenthau envisaged, through the lessening of an international tension by skilful diplomacy and increased international co-operation along the functionalist lines, it remains unclear why, in addition to such fortunate circumstances, anything so formidable as a world state is still to be required. Morgenthau did not address this question. It may be recalled here that Oppenheim, impressed by the degree of co-operation which he witnessed before the Great War, particularly among liberal states, saw no real need for a radical transformation of the international system at that time.

Waltz, as we noted, stopped at the level of diagnosis, but his view of the sovereign division of the world as the most fundamental cause of the recurrence of war betrays his implicit endorsement of the cosmopolitanist mode of domestic analogy. The weakness of Waltz's argument is clear from our detailed exposition in the previous chapter. While the division of the world into sovereign states (Waltz's third image) is among the necessary conditions of war, these conditions are found in the other images also, in the nature of man and in the nature of the state. Moreover, here 'necessity' is not a matter of degree, and all necessary conditions are absolutely, and hence equally, necessary for the type of event in question, in this case, the phenomenon of war. As Waltz remarks, the structure of the states system, besides being a necessary condition of war, may turn itself into an 'efficient cause' of war in the sense that it tempts or prompts mutually hostile states in a crisis to resort to a preventive war rather than resolve the conflict by diplomacy. This, however, is only one of the several ways in which wars have come about, and not the only way. Therefore, Waltz's stress on the sovereign division of the world not only as the most fundamental 'permissive cause' (or 'necessary condition') of all wars, but also as an 'efficient cause' of some, may be said to put an undue emphasis on the third image at the expense of the other images in his tripartite scheme. This bias, as we argued, was due to Waltz's implicit acceptance of the central tenet of the domestic analogy: that the primary responsibility for the disorderly features of the international system lies with the fundamental characteristic of the system itself.

Welfare internationalism

It will be recalled that the primary concern of the proposals along the L–D spectrum is to create a framework in which sovereign states can coexist in an orderly manner. Welfare internationalism, to which we now turn, is strongly critical of this, and argues for strengthening those institutions which are designed to promote the welfare of individuals located in separate states. Moreover, it will be noted, the institutions envisaged by the legal, democratic confederal and world federal approaches are systematic entities expressed in single blueprints or well-defined schemes. Welfare internationalism does not adhere to the idea that the desirable goals of mankind can be obtained by a systematic, all-embracing constitutional project. Instead of suggesting a unified scheme, therefore, the supporters of this approach stress that all forms of institution should be created to cope with multifarious problems requiring international co-operation. The degree of centralization, membership, representation, decision-making procedure and other structural or procedural aspects of the institutions are to be worked out case by case. In clear contrast to federalism, welfare internationalism does not involve the contradiction of assuming on the one hand that there is a serious limit to the degree of co-operation attainable within the states system and suggesting on the other hand that states must co-operate to establish a federation. In fact, welfare internationalism assumes the possibility of a great deal of co-operation within the states system with respect to multifarious problems facing mankind.

It is not suggested here that what might be termed 'welfare issues' are not included in other types of proposal. Thus, Saint-Simon's European Parliament, which was associated with the federal approach, was to direct 'all undertakings of common advantage to the European community', including linking of the Danube to the Rhine, and the Rhine to the Baltic, by canals. State education in the whole of Europe was to be under the direction and supervision of the great parliament, which was also to draw up a code of ethics (Saint-Simon [1814] 1952, 49). Even Ladd's Congress of Nations, which we located along the L–D spectrum, was to settle principles of a 'civil and pacific nature affecting the intercourse of the world and the happiness of mankind' (Ladd [1840] 1916, chap. 6). The issues to be treated by the Congress were to include, among other things, diplomatic immunity, extradition, the treatment of refugees, the slave trade, piracy, the use of railroads and canals, free navigation of bays and rivers, maritime safety and salvage, copyrights, postal service, weights, measures and coinage, the right of discovery and colonization, and disarmament. Many of these issues overlap with the concern of welfare internationalists.

However, what distinguishes welfare internationalism is that instead of setting up one supreme legislative authority to make laws for all purposes, it suggests a pluralistic approach. Those states who have a common set of problems are to create their own institution specifically adjusted to their needs. The membership and shape of each institution are to be determined in accordance with the purposes which it is required to serve. The absence of an overriding authority above these separate institutions is thought to be even advantageous since they can modify their shape in response to changing circumstances without involving a cumbrous process of decision-making at the universal level. Only the members of each institution need to agree to its modification in accordance with its own provisions (Mitrany 1943, 32ff.).

As we noted, welfare internationalism can be interpreted as containing the domestic analogy in that its emphasis on the need to increase the role of international law and institutions with regard to welfare issues has been inspired by the rising role of municipal law and institutions in dealing with such issues. It is with respect to those welfare issues which cannot be treated effectively without the co-operation of states that welfare internationalists argue in favour of international institutional control, and this line of argument is advanced at least implicitly in parallel with their endorsement of an institutional control of welfare issues within the state. Welfare internationalism originates in the welfare state idea, as can be seen clearly from the examples of Carr, Brierly and Mitrany. After the Second World War an international law of welfare itself began to show signs of growth, and writers such as Jenks and Friedmann argued strongly in favour of its further expansion. Their idea, too, was essentially one of applying the notion of the welfare state to the international level.

Unlike the more common form of the domestic analogy, however, the type of domestic analogy contained in welfare internationalism does not involve the personification of states. This form of domestic analogy therefore is immune to the standard criticism against the analogy that states are, after all, not like natural persons. None the less, it has to be conceded that the welfare internationalist approach as such does not clearly state in which specific areas states need to co-operate or can do so without engendering counterproductive frictions of the kind Terry Nardin is concerned to stress. Nor does it clarify what form of institutional arrangement is best suited to a given need. There is, therefore, no guarantee that an institution designed by an adherent of this approach will succeed in enabling the member-states to satisfy the needs of their citizens. 'Trial and error' is the price of pragmatism.

This, however, does not mean that there is no way of judging the likelihood of success on the part of particular international institutions inspired by welfare internationalism. The more radically ambitious ones, such as those contained in some of the WOMP proposals, have little chance of being accepted by governments for the foreseeable future.[5] Among them are Galtung's idea of 'globalization', and the corresponding notion of international 'socialization' advanced by Lagos and Godoy; the idea of radically enhancing the role of UNESCO (contained in Mazrui's project), and of transforming ECOSOC into the central organ of the UN (advanced by Kothari); and the idea of taxation by the UN with the view to social engineering at the global level (contained in Mazrui's project).

These are valuable ideas in terms of their ability to direct the grass-roots supporters of world order movements. Furthermore, there is a potentiality of success in the case of 'globalization' especially with respect to sea-bed resources. The idea of international taxation, too, can be said to exist in an embryonic form, for example, as a key element of the New International Economic Order: that the richer nations should set aside a specified portion of their GNPs in aid, rather than making their decisions for aid on an *ad hoc* basis from year to year (Armstrong 1982, 137). However, the ideas listed above, unless they are diluted considerably, remain on the whole too ambitious to be taken seriously by governments as realizable projects in the present circumstances.

Conclusion

The domestic analogy debate, contrary to the impression we might form by a cursory survey, turns out to be a multilateral debate. The opposition between the legal school and the diplomatic school is central to this debate, yet these two schools are not disparate circles, so to speak, but form a continuum along which varying degrees of concession are made to the internationalist form of the domestic analogy. In addition, three other positions have been identified, which all participate in the debate: democratic confederalism, federalism and welfare internationalism, each employing a distinctive form of domestic analogy.

As regards the proposals along the L–D spectrum, the foregoing examination leads us to the following conclusion. The transfer of the principle of compulsory jurisdiction from the domestic to the international sphere is not desirable in the present circumstances. None the less, a legal ban on the use of force may continue to operate with some positive consequences. Those who reject the domestic analogy and favour the institution of neutrality exaggerate the firmness with which that institution had been established in international society. The collective enforcement of order through an international police force or a system of collective security, however, is based on a misguided use of the domestic analogy. At the global level, a full-fledged international legislature is unrealizable for the foreseeable future, probably unnecessary and perhaps even undesirable. An international organization authorized to put pressure on states to abandon their rights, however, might have some limited effectiveness when backed by an overwhelming majority.

Overall, the degree of concession to the domestic analogy which can profitably be made along the L–D spectrum is rather limited, and the optimum point at present might be said to be closer to the diplomatic end. This does not, however, mean that the domestic analogy along the L–D spectrum is entirely unsound. For example, a system of arbitration and adjudication, voluntary for all states and compulsory for those who, in their mutual relations, are willing to accept the principle in advance is undoubtedly profitable, and such a system can be said to contain a modest degree of concession to the domestic analogy. Also fruitful at the international level is a system of regular conferences for consultative and quasi-legislative purposes, and this also embodies a degree of concession to the analogy. Above all, the principle that states do not have unrestricted legal freedom to resort to force, derived by analogy from one of the most fundamental principles of domestic society, appears defensible despite the criticisms voiced by the members of the diplomatic school.

It must be added here, however, that the degree of concession that can fruitfully be made to the domestic analogy along the L–D spectrum *appears* limited not only because it actually *is*, but also because international society has already moved considerably away from its nineteenth-century structure in the direction of legalism. This is the result of the collaboration of leading governments and politicians particularly in this century. But it is also partly due to the persistence of the idea that international society must be made to approximate to the standards of domestic society a little further. Many of the authors we have examined can claim to have kept such an idea alive, though some of them may have gone a little too far in the direction of legalism, forgetting the existing characteristics of international society and of its members.

As for democratic confederalism, federalism and welfare internationalism, our conclusions are as follows. The democratic confederal approach may have considerable merits when applied to the relations of those nations among whom transnational solidarity is exceptionally strong. But as an approach to *world* order it is ineffective. It commits the error of attempting to transfer a domestic political principle to the international sphere where the conditions are unsuitable or not yet ripe. A similar line of argument can be advanced against Falk's global populism, and Jenks' and McDougal's idea of enhancing the progressive role of international lawyers at the *world* level, although these approaches may have some desired effects within a community of nations located within a relatively centralized framework and sharing fundamental values.

The federal approach also involves the mistake of assuming that those institutions operative at the national level will necessarily be workable at the global level. Its use of a domestic analogue is arbitrary, and counter-examples can easily be identified indicating the futility of attempting to embrace mutually hostile communities under one regime. Moreover, federalism underestimates the extent to which international co-operation can take place among sovereign states. It has been suggested that this underestimation may stem from the tendency of the adherents of this approach to assume that the word 'sovereignty' means 'supreme political authority', internationally as well as domestically. However, the defenders of the states system, such as Northedge, may exaggerate the virtues of the present system.

Welfare internationalism remains relatively unscathed, and this is partly because the type of domestic analogy it employs is not of the standard form. However, while its pragmatism can be praised, it fails to state clearly what form of institution is required, and for which specific area of welfare needs. In addition, it was noted that some of the WOMP proposals, inspired by welfare internationalism, may turn out to be beneficial in their ability to direct grassroots movements for world order, but that they are likely to be too ambitious to be taken seriously by governments for the foreseeable future.

CONCLUSION

In chapter 1 we outlined the debate about the domestic analogy in the history of ideas about world order by indicating who appear to be among its critics, and who among its supporters. In chapter 2, however, we noted that the domestic analogy in fact encompasses a wide variety of ideas, and that there are some cases which require careful consideration in order to establish whether or not the analogy can be said to be involved in the argument concerned. The implication was that the debate about the analogy might not be understood accurately if we considered it simply as one between its 'supporters' and 'critics'. The *type* of domestic analogy employed, and the *extent* to which it is accepted need to be analysed.

Bearing this in mind, we examined in chapters 3–8 proposals for world order in six historical periods, mainly with respect to Anglo-American sources. These chapters revealed a variety of attitudes towards the domestic analogy. In chapter 9, we suggested five basic positions around which ideas about world order are clustered, each embodying a distinctive attitude towards the analogy. The domestic analogy debate has been shown not to be a bilateral, but a multilateral one.

One important feature of the debate about the domestic analogy is the extent to which writers' attitudes towards the analogy are influenced by the events and circumstances in the domestic and international spheres against the background of which their ideas about world order are formulated. There are, however, also some writers whose views are relatively insulated from the changing domestic and international conditions.

In the nineteenth century, constitutionalism and liberalism made marked advances within the domestic sphere and interest grew in the democratization of legislatures, while internationally the system remained relatively unorganized in formal terms despite a number of *ad hoc* conferences under the Concert of Europe. In addition, it was felt necessary to fill existing gaps in international law. Given these

197

circumstances, it is not surprising that the proposals by Saint-Simon, Ladd, Lorimer and Bluntschli took the shape they did. These writers all saw principles of good government at work within the domestic sphere, noted the primitive state of affairs in the international domain, found it imperative to transplant those principles to the uncultivated field of international relations and took for granted the need for an international legislative assembly.

What is perhaps surprising is the extent to which these writers took their own indigenous constitutions as their models. Thus, we argued, Saint-Simon's model for a reorganized Europe is likely to have been the *Charte Constitutionnelle* of 1814, and in the case of Ladd, there is little doubt that the principle of the separation of powers, which he saw as a distinctive feature of his plan, was a product of the constitutional history of the United States. Likewise, Lorimer's scheme for an international government incorporated the basic structure of the English Parliament, and Bluntschli appears to have modelled his project for a unified Europe on the German Imperial Constitution of 1871.

It is interesting to note, however, that these writers appear to have been less than fully candid about their real models. Saint-Simon said his model was the English constitution, and there is no mention in his essay of the French Charter. Ladd said of his Court and Congress of Nations that they found their closest working models in the Court and the Diet of the Helvetic Union presumably, as we indicated, in order to stress the viability of his project. Lorimer's characterization of his international government that it was to fulfil functions similar to those of the Delegations system of the Austro-Hungarian Empire was inaccurate, and was perhaps meant to play down the ambitiousness of his scheme. Bluntschli's suggestion that the German Imperial Constitution was unsuitable as a model for European unification may have been due to his concern to protect the scheme from the charge of parochialism.

The legal character of the bodies proposed by these authors varied from Saint-Simon's federation (based on the cosmopolitanist mode of the domestic analogy) to Ladd's relatively decentralized form of international organization (embodying the internationalist mode of the analogy). The projects of Lorimer and Bluntschli were an intermediate type, and their democratic confederalism embodied a distinctive type of domestic analogy, which in turn reflected the development of democratic legislatures in the late nineteenth century.

For the writers of the next historical period, the domestic circumstances remained essentially the same, so that, for example, Schücking repeated Bluntschli's line in incorporating democratic confederalism in his project. However, the international circumstances were markedly different from the somewhat stagnant conditions of the nineteenth century. The Hague Peace Conferences symbolized to the writers at the turn of the century the coming of the new era in which, internationally also, the rule of law would gradually but steadily make advances. Given this new international background, what we called the graduated use of the domestic analogy, exemplified well by Schücking, is unsurprising. Unlike his nineteenth-century predecessors, Schücking did not concentrate on working out the constitutional details of a perfectly organized world society, to be transplanted all at once from the domestic to the international field, but instead tried to show how new institutions could be built gradually on the foundations which had come into existence in the international system.

However, as was exemplified by Oppenheim, some writers considered it as unnecessary to develop international law beyond a certain limit in its gradual approximation to municipal law. In the case of Oppenheim, this threshold lay at the level of introducing organized sanctions into international law. This was because he considered the growth of liberalism within the domestic sphere as having made states so law-abiding as to render unnecessary an international mechanism of law enforcement. Oppenheim took into consideration not only contemporary international developments, but also international implications of the domestic conditions of his time, and this resulted in his graduated and limited use of the domestic analogy. As Oppenheim observed, there were those who insisted that the threshold beyond which international law need not or should not approximate to municipal law lay at an even lower level. These constituted Oppenheim's diplomatic school, and expressed their conservative views against what they saw as the excesses of the legalists, and of the legalistic trend in international society at that time. Thus, the critical attitude of the diplomatic school towards the domestic analogy can in turn be said partly to reflect the international circumstances of the period.

If the perception of international peace and progress at the turn of the century produced confidence in the relatively anarchical system of international law, and in the power of international law, without radically altering its structure, to contribute to world order, the Great War brought about a sudden revision of this attitude. The examples of Oppenheim, Nippold and Liszt are particularly striking. Before their experience of the war they were all opposed to the idea of organized sanctions in international law. But both Oppenheim and Nippold openly admitted that the experience of the war had made them abandon their pre-war confidence in the law of nations without organized sanctions. Liszt changed his attitude in the same way. The idea that the freedom of states to resort to war would have to be legally restricted, and that coercive measures were as necessary in international law as in municipal law became the guiding principle of the period. This convergence of opinion as regards the degree of concession which international law must make to the domestic analogy could not be understood without reference to the Great War itself, which was commonly interpreted as having resulted from, among other things, the weakness of legal constraints under the nineteenth-century system. As we saw in some detail, the League of Nations, established in reaction to the war, embodied several ideas derived primarily from domestic sources. It is interesting to observe, however, that there were some writers whose views on world order were relatively unaffected even by the experience of the Great War. For example, Thomas Baty, a possible member of Oppenheim's diplomatic school, continued to stress the decentralized nature of traditional international law as being not only its unique, but also commendable, feature.

The interpretations of domestic and international backgrounds on the basis of which ideas about world order are formulated can be diverse. This was clearly the case with various opinions expressed in the next historical period, in the face of the failure of the League of Nations. All those whom we examined with respect to this period acknowledged that the League had failed in its primary purpose. Yet some, like Leonard Woolf, insisted that one instance of failure was insufficient to prove any approach intrinsically wrong, and argued in favour of the type of domestic analogy which underlay the League of Nations. Some, like Schuman, thought that the League failed because it did not go far enough, while others, like Borchard, argued that it was bound to fail because it had gone too far in the direction of municipal legal order. Yet others, like Mitrany, saw in the League's failure the reaffirmation of the bankruptcy of *laissez-faire* liberalism, and put forward welfare internationalism, which contained a distinctive mode of domestic analogy. Welfare internationalism reflected a shift in the conception of good government within the domestic sphere.

The approach most influential in the creation of the United Nations, however, was the reformed-League idea, although welfare internationalism also played a substantial part. Just as the shock of the Great War had produced the view that international law must be equipped with some form of coercive machinery, so the experience of the Second World War provided the leading politicians and government officials with a further confirmation of the idea that international society must be organized in such a way as to respond effectively to any aggressive behaviour by its members. The police analogy was at the centre of the United Nations thinking. It is, however, to be noted that while the drafters of the Covenant put a great deal of stress on the idea of 'cooling off', those of the Charter were more concerned with the creation of machinery which could respond in a forthright manner to an act of aggression. This is no doubt a reflection of the fact that while there was a strong impression particularly in Britain, that the July 1914 crisis could have been defused and the Great War averted, had the Great Powers been able to confer on the issues of the day, a predominant opinion during the Second World War blamed for what had developed the lack of an early and decisive response to the aggressive policies of the Axis Powers. However, the attempt to bring the constitutional structure of international society a little closer to the domestic system with respect to law enforcement than had been achieved by the Covenant was to a great extent counterbalanced by the institution of the veto. As we noted, Brierly, for example, saw in this the return of the nineteenth-century principle of the Concert of Europe.

From the time of the Hague Peace Conferences to the establishment of the United Nations, the tendency to use specific (and this often meant one's own indigenous) constitution as a model for one's project existed to some extent. Thus, at the beginning of the present century, Schücking used as his models for what he proposed to call the 'Union des Etats de la Haye' various constitutional instruments of Germany, such as the German Act of Confederation of 1815, the Vienna Final Act of 1820 and the German Imperial Constitution of 1871. As we noted, former President Taft, who headed the League to Enforce Peace, argued for the creation of a world court on the model of the United States Supreme Court. President Wilson and Colonel House incorporated in their pan-American project a provision which they most certainly copied from the United States Constitution. A similar provision was included in their League plan, and this later became the basis of the tenth article of the Covenant. Robert Cecil referred to English legal history in support of his proposal for an international court, and the Conference system of the British Empire inspired Alfred Zimmern and General Smuts in their respective League proposals. The Committee of Imperial Defence was mentioned as a potential model for an international institution for the maintenance of law and order even by David Mitrany. And President Roosevelt, in explaining to the Soviet Ambassador at the Dumbarton Oaks Conference the idea that a party to a dispute can be heard, but not vote, characterized it as a principle 'imbedded by our forefathers in American law'.

However, these examples are more in the nature of exceptions rather than the rule. The tendency to present a detailed blueprint for an ideally organized world along the lines of a specific constitution declined altogether in the twentieth century. This was partly due to the rise of gradualism at the turn of the century. Moreover, the growth of international law and institutions since the turn of the century meant that the need to add to the existing system became less strongly felt. In addition, even where the need to add to the existing system was felt, a planner could formulate his project on the basis of what already came to exist in the international sphere rather than, as in the nineteenth century, borrow institutions ready-made from the domestic sphere. Furthermore, constitutionalism itself has become less fashionable in the twentieth century among writers on international relations. Thus, the setting up of constitutional machinery at the international level, unlike in the case of a number of well-known nineteenth-century writers, was no longer treated as a panacea for, or even a necessary condition of, world order. A constitutional approach was considered by Mitrany, for example, as inadequate and misguided. Moreover, Carr's influential critique of utopianism intensified the opposition to a legalistic approach to international relations, and with it any attempt to draw up a constitutional blueprint of a future world. The welfare internationalist approach, which Mitrany advocated in opposition to old-style constitutionalism, and which Carr and Brierly supported in their writings, underlay the creation of various international institutions in the mid- to late 1940s. Among them are FAO, ICAO, and UNESCO.

Despite the decline in the tendency to use a specific domestic constitution as a blueprint, however, it is of great interest to note that political theories which underlay some of the proposals from the early nineteenth century to the mid-twentieth century continued to reflect the domestic political concerns of the day. Accordingly, political theories underlying such proposals show a historical transition from the theory of the mixed state (in the case of Saint-Simon), through the theory of the separation of powers and representative government (Ladd, Lorimer and Bluntschli), to the idea of the planned economy and the welfare state (Carr, Brierly and Mitrany). It is tempting to suggest here that the proposals of these writers reveal that, as domestic society has become more democratized, and the idea of bourgeois democracy has been challenged or superseded by the idea of mass democracy, international ideas themselves have shown a parallel transition.

Two qualifications are necessary, however. First, there are expected to be many proposals which will not fit this pattern. Thus the parallelism of the two realms of thought cannot be advanced as a general proposition in a statistical sense. What we can say about those writers' proposals is that together they form a set of important historical signposts. However, secondly, it will be objected that it is illegitimate to string together the history of one nation in a particular period (say, post-Napoleonic France) and the history of another nation in another period (say, mid-nineteenth-century America), and to construe a universal history out of such manipulation. This is an important qualification to bear in mind. It will be meaningful to argue that parallelism obtains in the two realms of thought with respect to the writers noted here, and others like them, only to the extent that a degree of crossnational unity can be assumed in the history of Western political thought, encompassing that of France, America, Britain and Germany since the early decades of the nineteenth century. These qualifications, however, do not undermine the power of the examples discussed to illustrate the ways in which domestic political ideas exert influence upon proposals for world order.

Ideas about world order formulated in the post-1945 period are wide-ranging, but they are to a considerable degree continuations of those ideas which were advanced in the period of the League of Nations. The reformed-League idea along the old legalistic lines now became the reformed-UN idea of Clark and Sohn, though their project also embodied democratic confederalism. Those who were critical of the sovereign states system itself, such as Schwarzenberger and Schuman, continued to express their views into the post-1945 period. But seeing the unrealizability of a world state in the near future, many who in principle accepted the cosmopolitanist form of domestic analogy argued in favour of making practical first steps which fell far short of a structural reformation of international society. Waltz, while not advocating the creation of a world state, concurred with those who in principle accept the cosmopolitanist form of the domestic analogy, by insisting that the states system itself is the most fundamental cause of the recurrence of war. At the regional level, opposition to the sovereign division of Western Europe was clearly expressed by Jean Monnet, and Haas advanced the idea of regional integration on the analogy of the American experience.

The coexistence of 'realist' thinking and a considerable interest in the idea of a world state and of a reformed-UN was characteristic of the first phase of the period after 1945, up to about the middle of the 1960s. The interest in a world state and in a radically reformed-UN was undoubtedly a reaction to the inability of the United Nations to transcend Cold

War rivalry, while 'realism' was a reaction to the apparent unrealizability of the ideal itself.

In the second phase of the postwar era, encompassing the 1960s and 1970s, the welfare internationalist line of thought gained ascendancy. This was probably due to the perceived decline of Cold War tensions, and was clearly a reflection of an increased interest in the economic and social problems of the world. This in turn resulted partly from the intensification of international economic activities and partly also from the pressures exerted by the increased number of newly independent, poor nations. Most of the WOMP proposals appeared in this phase of the postwar period. These proposals made selective use of domestic models, and there is a strong undercurrent of welfare internationalist thought in the WOMP contributors' general outlook.

The third phase, from the late 1970s to the present, has seen a well-articulated attack by Bull and others against contemporary international institutions and proposals which embody various forms of the domestic analogy. It is possible to see a parallel between this and the rise of the diplomatic school at the turn of the century when its members argued against what they regarded as the excesses of the legalists and the legalistic trend at the international level. Indeed, Nardin's conception of international law and international society is highly reminiscent of the older doctrine of the specific character of international law. So, too, are the views of Bull and Manning. Against these conservative opinions, the present phase has also seen progressive views expressed by Beitz and Linklater. It is noteworthy, however, that these two writers' structure of thought is not in fact analogical, and that they cannot be said to make use of the domestic analogy. However, neither of these writers would necessarily be opposed to institutions and institutional proposals which make selective use of domestic analogues. In chapter 9, an attempt was made to delineate what this selection should be: what degree of concession to the domestic analogy might be fruitful at the present stage, and what type of domestic analogy might be accepted?

The degree of concession that can fruitfully be made along what we called the legal–diplomatic (L–D) spectrum turned out to be somewhat limited. The optimum point at present may be said to lie closer to the diplomatic end of the spectrum. However, the diplomatic approach is not entirely flawless. Especially when advanced with exaggerated confidence, this approach produces unwarranted conclusions. Thus the argument against a legal ban on the use of force by states advanced by the supporters of this approach is alarmist inasmuch as it is based on the fear that the negative side-effect of the ban would outweigh the intended effect of lessening the frequency of war. The supporters of the diplomatic approach also exaggerate the value of the institution of neutrality and the firmness with which it had been established in international society. Moreover, Northedge's evaluation of the states system seems too sanguine about the extent to which it enables its constituent units to live as they think best. The strength of the diplomatic approach lies in its critical attitude towards the domestic analogy, but this can in turn harden into a dogmatic premise similar to the doctrine of the specific character of international law influential at the turn of the century. The parallel between this legal doctrine and the diplomatic approach should warn us that a puritanical concern to preserve the unique realm of international relations from contamination through reliance on the domestic analogy may itself turn into futile dogmatism devoid of empirical substantiation.

In addition to the legal restriction on the freedom of states to use force, a number of institutions, making a modest degree of concession to the domestic analogy, are found to be defensible. Among them are a system of adjudication and arbitration, voluntary for all states and compulsory for those who, in their mutual relations, are willing to accept the principle of compulsory jurisdiction in advance; and a system of regular conference for consultative and quasi-legislative purposes.

Beyond the L–D spectrum, democratic confederalism (and some of its variants) were criticized, when applied to the global level, for paying insufficient attention to the strengths of existing governments within the decentralized international system, and to the absence of transnational solidarity. Federalism, too, when applied to the global level, was rejected on the grounds, among others, that its use of a domestic model is arbitrary. It also contains an inner contradiction of assuming on the one hand that there is a serious limit to the degree of co-operation attainable within the states system, and suggesting on the other hand that states must co-operate to establish a federation. Welfare internationalism remains relatively unscathed, but, it was suggested, the approach itself does not guarantee the success of those institutions designed by its adherents for the achievement of given welfare needs. In particular, some of the WOMP proposals, inspired by welfare internationalism, cannot be taken seriously as projects within the realm of realizability for the foreseeable future although these proposals are effective in their ability to alert us to the deficiencies of the present system, and perhaps to those ideas and institutions which already exist in an embryonic form, but need to be developed further.

Since welfare internationalism rejects the world state alternative, one important question which arises is how far the former can contribute to social and economic well-being in the life of mankind divided into separate states. Does this objective in fact require the transcendence of the states system? The question is important since, if welfare internationalism is shown fully to produce desired effects only through the abolition of the states system, the value of the approach is seriously undermined.

Clearly, however, the 'transcendence of the states system' in the sense of the structural alteration of the present system would not solve the problem of human welfare unless the new arrangements were to be accompanied by the sense of community among mankind. It must, however, be noted that the growth in the sense of community among mankind is itself to some extent hindered by the division of mankind into sovereign states which tends to reinforce national parochialism.

Some of the measures recommended along the L–D spectrum may encourage mankind to move towards a higher sense of unity. Among them, for example, are the enshrinement in the law of the idea that states do not have unrestricted freedom to use force against one another, the institution of voluntary arbitration and adjudication, and the regular assembly of states to discuss issues of common interest and to articulate the standards of international conduct. Between those nations which already share an exceptionally high sense of solidarity, as well as democratic values, the democratic confederal approach might help enhance these values and bring the nations closer together. Welfare institutions might also protect or strengthen unity, or act as a symbol of progress towards unity, in a divided world. However, none of these approaches are by themselves sufficient to bring about the change in the outlook of mankind from particularism to universalism without which institutions based on the domestic analogy of any form are likely to remain limited in their scope and effectiveness.

It is important to note, however, that even within the present system there are some elements of universalism. Without this, the human rights ideology, for example, would not exist, nor perhaps the very notion of the society of states.[1] Yet the area in which the citizens of another country are held to be of equal worth to those of one's own country is severely restricted under the present regime as the North–South problem amply illustrates. The gradual expansion of this area is what constitutes the transition from particularism to universalism.[2]

The community of mankind, in which universalism prevails over national parochialism, is therefore one where the area in which the citizens of another state are treated in the same way as those of one's own state has expanded to the full. The last phrase, 'to the full', taken literally, suggests that in the ultimate world community the citizens of separate states should be treated totally without prejudice to their nationality. If such a community were to continue to be organized as a system of states, its constituent units would not have the character of those which constitute the present system. This is because the conception of the state underlying the system would have altered radically from what it is now. States would no longer exercise their legal independence selfishly, but accept it as their principle to act as though they were bound by a supreme legislative authority enacting laws for the common good of mankind. Even in such a situation, the laws would still have to be made rather than left to the spontaneous concurrence of national wills. Thus a law-making assembly of some form would be required, probably together with certain other elements of an international government.

Whether this new global arrangement can be classified as a world state, in contradistinction to the sovereign states system, in terms of its constitutional characteristics, is an elusive question. This can only be answered if we can work out the requisite degree of centralization for the global system, which it is difficult to do in the abstract. Moreover, it is perhaps possible to envisage a decentralized and pluralistic global association in which the division between citizens and non-citizens is not institutionalized in the same way as it is in the present sovereign states system.[3]

Whatever the ultimate institutional structure, it seems clear that in the initial stages of the transitional process towards the ultimate goal, the legal freedom of action enjoyed by each state *vis-à-vis* other states will diminish progressively since each state will share an increasing amount of responsibility for the common good of mankind. Even those currently poor countries, which will be placed at the receiving end of the globally redistributed wealth, will be subject to the curtailment of their legal freedom inasmuch as the issue of domestic distribution of wealth will in turn be under the surveillance of the international community.

In fact, the knowledge of the ultimate structure matters far less than the awareness of the general direction in which international society must progress. Just as it would be absurd to try to envisage the ultimate state of our knowledge, so it would be unwise to concentrate on the speculation of the ultimate institutional structure of the world. It might, of course, be objected that this analogy is imperfect: whereas the ultimate state of our knowledge, if there could be such a thing at all, could be known only when we got there, the knowledge of what the ultimate institutional structure should be could contribute to our getting there. This objection, however, ignores the point that the knowledge of the ultimate structure of the world is itself part of the ultimate knowledge. James Lorimer's claim to solve the ultimate problem of international jurisprudence through the transfer to the international sphere of certain domestic institutions of the nineteenth-century liberal type ignores the historical limitations of the answer being given.

The idea of the expansion of the area in which the citizens of another state are treated in the same way as those of one's own state was supported by E. H. Carr, although what he had in mind was regional, rather than universal, international co-operation. He wrote, in a striking passage which should be noted as well as his critique of idealism: 'British policy may have to take into account the welfare of Lille or Düsseldorf or Lodz as well as the welfare of Oldham or Jarrow' (1939, 306). He wrote of his own vision as itself a utopia, although he was hopeful that 'a direct appeal to the motive of sacrifice would [not] always fail' (1939, 307). In a world in which a direct appeal even to the motive of enlightened self-interest would not always succeed, the vision of separate nations sharing an increasing amount of responsibility for the common good of mankind would remain realized only to a very limited degree.

None the less, it seems clear that the move towards the universalist goal is more likely to come from among those national communities which share liberal values and concern for welfare. In this respect, it is of considerable importance to note Michael Doyle's recent observation that no liberal states have ever been engaged in war among themselves (Doyle 1983). He considers that three factors have contributed to peace among liberal states: a degree of democratic control of foreign policy; the sharing of liberal values, and mutual trust on the grounds of ideological unity; and a vested interest in peace as a result of commercial interdependence.[4] These circumstances and the expectation of peace may contribute to the gradual overcoming of national parochialism among some liberal states, which may in turn strengthen the chances of co-operation among them for the cross-national enhancement of the social and economic well-being of their citizens.[5] The achievement of the goals of welfare internationalism, therefore, may not in fact presuppose the abolition of the states system, but requires the closer co-operation of those states which are committed to the values of liberty and welfare within their borders.

NOTES

1 The domestic analogy debate: a preliminary outline

1 This important point in his argument can be inferred from his statement that by 'world order' or 'order in the great society of all mankind' he means 'those patterns or dispositions of human activity that sustain the elementary or primary goals of social life among mankind as a whole' (1977, 20). By 'the elementary or primary goals of social life' he means 'the common goals of all social life', namely the limitation of violence, the keeping of promises and the stability of possession (1977, 19).

2 Although the 'Germanic Body' is repeatedly mentioned as his model by Saint-Pierre in his Project ([1712] 1714), it is somewhat unlikely that he used it more than as a very general guideline. His scheme is extremely detailed in comparison to a rather brief sketch he gives of the institutional structure of the German Empire, and there are many features of his Project which cannot have been borrowed from the empire.

3 Kant finds an example of such a congress in the Assembly of States-General at The Hague in the first half of the eighteenth century. It is curious that Kant should have thought that 'to this assembly, the ministers of most European courts and even of the smallest republics brought their complaints about the hostilities carried out by one against another', and that 'thus, all of Europe thought of itself as a single federated state, which was supposed to fulfil the function of judicial arbitrator in these public disputes' (Forsyth, Keens-Soper and Savigear 1970, 253–4).

4 It must be stressed that Kant, unlike many writers examined in this book, was not engaged in producing a blueprint for peace with the view to its adoption in the near future. See Hinsley 1967, chap. 4; Gallie 1978, chap. 2; Forsyth 1981, 103; Linklater 1982, chap. 6.

2 The range and types of the domestic analogy

1 Correspondingly, Manning argues that international society is not really a society, but a *quasi*-Gemeinschaft (1972a, 176–7).

2 See Bull 1977, chaps. 1, 4. Elsewhere, however, Bull does not draw a sharp distinction between 'peace' and 'orderly social life' (1966a, 35).

3 See Ehrenberg 1960, chap. 3. Also, there were a hundred cases of Papal arbitration in Italy alone in the 13th century (Thomson, Meyer and Briggs 1945, 129).

4 For 'sovereignty' as 'constitutional independence', see James 1986.

3 Some nineteenth-century examples

1 The following summary of this doctrine is based on Ionescu 1976, in which various relevant remarks by Saint-Simon are scattered.

2 Ladd's main source of information is Rees *et al*. 1819. None of the three agreements mentioned there – the Treaty of Sempach (1393), the Convention of Stantz (1481) and the Treaty of Peace at Arrau (1712) – refers to the existence of 'the court of judges or arbitrators' empowered to settle disputes 'arising between any two or more members of the Union', although the Treaty of Sempach stipulates regulations concerning trials and punishment in each canton of deserters and criminals, and the Convention of Stantz contains rules concerning treatment of the instigators of separatist activity. See Dumont 1726–31, vol. 2, pt 1, 235–6; Oechsli 1886, 203–6; Parry 1969, 305–13. The process for the peaceful settlement of disputes which to some extent resembles an inter-cantonal court is stipulated by the treaty of perpetual league of 1 August 1291 among the three forest communities of Switzerland (see Newton 1923, 42–3), but Ladd's sources do not refer to this treaty. According to Forsyth, the Diet, which was not explicitly provided for in the basic treaties of the Helvetic Union, 'exercised undefined powers of a legislative, judicial, and executive nature' (1981, 24). Forsyth warns that we must not read into the old Swiss Confederation 'the structures and concepts of later times' (1981, 19). This is precisely what Ladd appears to have done.

3 See Ladd [1840] 1916, 42–3. Ladd's source is an unnamed article from the *Christian Spectator* of 1832, and the picture of the Swiss Diet Ladd obtains from this source is mostly accurate. See Oechsli 1922, 21–2, 249ff.; Codding 1961, 21ff.; Hughes 1962, 3ff.

4 Ladd had earlier proposed, in his petition to the US Congress, a compulsory adjudication of international disputes by a Court of Nations, and it appears to be a tactical consideration that led him to advance a less demanding scheme in his 1840 essay. See Ladd [1840] 1916, 113, 130; Schwarzenberger 1936a, 20.

5 See Bluntschli 1879–81, 2:279–312. Bluntschli consistently spelled 'Staat' as 'Stat'. Hence 'Statenverein', etc.

6 On 'Delegations', see Wheare 1963, 5. The text of the Constitution of 21 December 1867 is in Bernazik 1911, 439–52. See also May 1951, 38–41.

7 Lorimer's project is found in Lorimer 1884, 2:279–87. For the likely domestic models, the following items have been consulted: Newton 1923, 270ff.; Schwartz 1955, esp. 59, 99; Codding 1961, 69ff.; Hughes 1962, xiii; Phillips 1967, esp. 101–2.

8 Lorimer in fact believed that the process of democratization was a universal trend. He remarked, 'even in non-constitutional countries – Russia, I believe, being no exception – the monarch no longer carries the national

will in his pocket' (1884, 2:242). However, it was particularly in the light of the rise of parliamentary democracy in Britain, it appears, that Lorimer was prompted to argue for establishing a link between national legislatures and his proposed international government. See Lorimer 1884, 2:240ff.

9 See Bluntschli 1879–81, 2:305. See also Articles V, VII and XXVIII of the German Constitution in Newton 1923, 239ff.

10 See Article LXXVI of the German Constitution in Newton 1923, 239ff., and Bluntschli 1879–81, 2:305ff.

11 See Saint-Simon [1814] 1952, 28–9, 40; Ladd [1840] 1916, chap. 11. Saint-Simon stressed the intellectual and scientific progress of mankind while Ladd considered moral improvement as the great mobilizing force of human history.

4 Contending doctrines of the Hague Peace Conferences period

1 However, the failure of the Declaration of London to secure ratification was regarded as fatal to the proposal for an International Prize Court, and accordingly Hague Convention XII, proposing to establish such a court, remained unratified (Oppenheim 1952, 2:876).

2 See Schücking [1912] 1918, chaps. 2–3. Fenwick, the translator of Schücking's work, ignores the important distinction between *Staatenbund* (confederation) and *Bundesstaat* (federation), and translates 'Staatenbund' consistently as 'federation', which obscures Schücking's gradualist argument.

3 Vollenhoven's plan involved the establishment of an international navy, to be composed of national contingents and directed by an international body. The navy was to act as an executive organ to enforce an award of an international court and to suppress violations of neutrality by belligerent states (Schücking [1912] 1918, 300ff.).

4 For example, Max Waechter, a German naturalized in Britain, who appears to have spent much of his time and wealth for the promotion of public welfare and world peace, took up in 1909 the idea of the United States of Europe on the model of the USA, and founded in 1913 a European Unity League (Waechter 1912, 4–5; Waechter no date).

5 By a 'High Court of Arbitral Justice' was meant at that time an international court of justice rather than a court of arbitration (Scott 1909, 1:423ff.; Wehberg [1912] 1918, 125–7).

6 Oppenheim himself never stated so clearly that this was his position. However, this can be inferred from his writings (1905–6, 2:55–6; [1911] 1921, 21–2). Lauterpacht agrees that this was Oppenheim's view of international law (1933, 404).

7 The metaphor of 'machinery', which Oppenheim used to refer to a legal institution is perhaps indicative of the belief in progress of his time which was backed by rapid technological developments. The word 'machinery' has come to be used to refer to legal institutions so commonly that it is now a 'dead' metaphor.

8 Stengel, however, was in favour of developments in the laws of war (1909, 44–5, 71).

9 See, for example, Wehberg [1912] 1918 on the particular significance at that time of the question regarding the desirability of an international court. The sociologist Georg Simmel once observed that the more closely contestants resemble each other, the more intense is a conflict between them (1955, 43ff.). This seems precisely to have been the case with Oppenheim's attitude towards someone like Nippold.

5 The impact of the Great War

1 See Miller 1928, 1:386 for a newspaper comment which asserted that the Covenant attempted to create a world state in which the United States would become a junior partner; and Miller 1928, 1:387 for a suggestion that the word 'constitution' be avoided in the Preamble of the Covenant as that word connoted to American students of law and history the formation of a world state. Similarly, the 'Executive Council' was reduced to 'Council', the 'Body of Delegates' became 'Assembly', the term 'League' was preferred to 'Union', and the 'Chancellor' became 'Secretary-General' (Miller 1928, 1:363-4, 403, 142, 220–1). It may be added here that a similar consideration led the United States at the Dumbarton Oaks Conference, which met in 1944 to prepare a proposal for the United Nations Charter, to oppose the Soviet suggestion that the new organization be named 'World Union' (Russell 1958, 419).
2 The Bryce group proposal was not merely an attempt to generalize the Bryan treaties, but an element of coercion was to be added to the idea of a 'cooling-off' period. Moreover, while the group never explicitly based their proposal on the domestic analogy, they nevertheless utilized a set of concepts borrowed from domestic organization, such as 'executive authority' and 'legislative body' in their discussion (Bryce *et al.* 1917, 16, 17, 28). It is noteworthy that G. L. Dickinson, a member of the group, said of his own proposal, which was virtually identical to the group's proposal, that it constituted a preliminary step towards the ultimate federal goal (1915, 34).
3 In this connection it may also be noted that the term 'Covenant', which Wilson liked and used to refer to a new set of obligations which states were to accept after the war, probably came from Scottish history rather than Hobbes, for example (Baker 1922, 1:213; Seymour 1926, 4:27).
4 Wilson is reported to have said that what he wanted to do for the world was what he unsuccessfully attempted to do for the American continent a year or two before (Rappard 1925, 103).
5 Sir Walter Phillimore had been appointed the chairman of the Committee on the League of Nations by the foreign secretary, and the Committee's Draft Convention was submitted to the British Government in March 1918. The Committee saw in some contemporary proposals for a loose association of states a feasible approach to the problem of postwar international organization, and extracted from these proposals the elements which they saw as practicable and expedient. Their draft, therefore, reflected the leading ideas of the time (Zimmern 1939, 180ff.; Miller 1928, 1:4).
6 Cecil also argued for the necessity of coercion in international law on the

analogy of the institution of the Star Chamber by Henry VII (Seymour 1926, 4:40–1).

7 Thus, in 'Class B' mandates, the mandatory was to secure equal opportunities for the trade and commerce of other members of the League (The Covenant of the League of Nations, Art. 22, para. 5).

8 Paragraph 1 refers to 'peoples not yet able to stand by themselves under the strenuous conditions of the modern world' and attempts to secure 'the well-being and development of such peoples'. Paragraph 2 uses the word 'tutelage', and, it is to be noted, 'tutla' in Roman law meant 'guardianship' (Lauterpacht 1927, 192 no. 3). Paragraph 3 refers to 'the stage of the development of the people', and paragraph 4 uses the expression 'until such time as they are able to stand alone'.

6 The effect of the failure of the League on attitudes towards the domestic analogy

1 Schwarzenberger's concern for blueprints can be seen in his *Power politics* (1941), chaps. 25, 32, 378–9. It is interesting to note that those writers who are often classified as 'realist' (T.Taylor 1978a, 122) turn out to be in principle in favour of a world government.

2 Mitrany was also interested in the transition taking place within the domestic sphere from the phase of traditional democratic institutions to the phase where technocratic organizations play an increasing role, and was in favour of applying the same principle to international integration (Taylor and Groom 1975, 3–5).

3 Kant's primary concern was to reduce the 'uncontrolled freedom' of states in their external relations, and, as regards the cosmopolitical rights of men, he is well known for having stated that 'the Rights of men as Citizens of the world in a cosmopolitical system, shall be restricted to conditions of universal Hospitality' (Forsyth, Keens-Soper and Savigear 1970, 214). Carr, by contrast, attributed to the states system a much broader, and more positive, role of enhancing the economic and social well-being of individuals living in separate states. The fact that in the passage quoted in the text, Kant had formulated his argument in terms of the state, while, in the comparable passage, Carr focussed on the individual is consonant with this shift of concern. It is not suggested here, however, that Kant's political and moral philosophy was not based on individualism.

4 See *Law Quarterly Review*, vol. 54 (July 1938), 438–9. The copy of *Neutrality for the United States* available in the Keele University Library shows that that was the very copy which the reviewer had used for the article in this journal. The copy bears a signature 'J. F. W.', presumably that of John Fischer Williams.

7 The domestic analogy in the establishment of the United Nations

1 Paul Taylor notes that in 1939 Curry's *The case for federal union* (1939) was a best-seller in Britain (P. Taylor 1971, 98). See also Lipgens 1982, 44ff. for the idea of European federation supported by the Resistance fighters.

2 See Kelsen 1967, 13–15 for the relationship between 'self-help' and 'self-defence'.

3 In a letter to the opening session of the Food and Agriculture Conference held in 1943, Roosevelt wrote: 'In this and other United Nations conferences we shall be extending our collaboration from war problems into important new fields. Only by working together can we learn to work together, and work together we must and will' (Russell 1958, 66, n. 11).

4 Thus, according to Penrose, negotiators at the Food and Agriculture Conference learned a great deal from 'the masterly work of the British Ministry of Food, Ministry of Health, and Advisory Committee on Nutrition, in the distribution of scarce supplies to the best advantage among the different groups of the population' (1953, 123). One striking use of the domestic analogy, not involving the personification of states, is found in Keynes' famous plan for an International Clearing Union. This body was to keep banking accounts in exactly the same way as central banks in each country kept accounts for commercial banks, and to create international purchasing power by allowing member-states overdraft facilities. Horsefield remarks that the Clearing Union was conceived 'along the lines of the British banking system'. Unlike any ordinary banking system, however, the Union was to charge a rate of interest on both credit and debit balances (Penrose 1953, 42; Horsefield 1969, 18–19). The original plan of Keynes was much whittled down in the process of negotiation which eventually led to the creation of the Bretton Woods system (Harrod 1951, chap. 13).

5 However, the chart which Roosevelt drew in the course of the Teheran Conference shows that the ILO, Health, Agriculture and Food were to come under the Assembly (Sherwood 1948, 789–90).

6 Any hint of the UN's connection with the League was suppressed in line with the American tactic of emphasizing the novelty of the new organization (Brierly 1958a, 315; Nicholas 1975, 14).

7 The following discussion closely follows Brierly 1958a and Kelsen 1967, 16–176.

8 The domestic analogy in contemporary international thought

1 The following summary is based on 'Main features of the whole plan' provided in the Introduction of Clark and Sohn 1966, xviiff. The actual plan is much more comprehensive than can be summarized in these three paragraphs.

2 This is similar to Schücking's proposal that in order to heighten the sense of solidarity among the participants of the future Hague Conferences, the name 'Union des Etats de la Haye' should be given to the emerging world confederation.

3 Schuman 1945 clearly demonstrates how thin the divide is between world federalism and 'realism'.

4 The summary here is based on Waltz 1959, 230ff. In Waltz 1979 the first two images are labelled a unit-level 'reductionist' theory, and the third image becomes a system-level 'structural' theory.

5 It is possible that the domestic analogy implicit in Waltz's diagnosis is of the 'internationalist', rather than 'cosmopolitanist' variety. However, to the extent that Waltz considers the states system as such as the most fundamental 'permissive cause' of all wars, he can be said implicitly to endorse the analogy in its 'cosmopolitanist' mode.

6 Monnet was an Assistant-General of the League of Nations, and after the Second World War headed a French governmental body responsible for industrial planning, the Commissariat Général du Plan. After the presidency of the ECSC's High Authority between 1952 and 1955, he gathered together a group of leading political, industrial and trade union figures to form the Action Committee for a United States of Europe, which played a major role in the establishment of the European Atomic Energy Community and the European Economic Community (Henderson 1962, 139; Arbuthnott and Edwards 1979, 193).

7 Jenks was Director-General of the International Labour Office from 1970 until his death in 1973, having joined its Legal Section in 1931. For the functions of the International Labour Office within the International Labour Organization (ILO), see Oppenheim 1955, 722–3.

8 As part of the training, Jenks recommends the study of comparative law so that the international lawyer may make full use of the 'general principles of law recognized by civilized nations', and therefore of 'the municipal law analogies bearing on any problem with which he may be confronted' (1958, 417). For a similar view, see Friedmann 1964, chap. 12.

9 It must, however, be pointed out that until the entire system of international law has been replaced by a world federal law with a substantial degree of supranationalism embodied in it, the traditional system of 'international' law must be said to remain, however much it may begin to deal with issues relating to the welfare of individuals.

10 Cosmopolitanism in Beitz (and Linklater) must therefore be clearly distinguished from what we have called the cosmopolitanist mode of the domestic analogy, which leads to an argument for a world state.

11 Among the many works of Falk similar to his *A study of future worlds* are: Falk and Mendlovitz 1964; Falk 1971; 1975b. According to Falk, 'the World Order Models Project can be understood as an unwitting attempt to develop the New Haven [McDougalite] approach so that it better satisfies the needs for a global reform movement' (1975b, 1013). Falk's reliance on Kuhn's idea of a 'paradigm shift' is explicit (Falk 1975b, 976–7). See, however, Watson 1980.

12 Each of the four volumes of Falk and Mendlovitz 1966 contains an identical Prefatory Note in which it is stated that Clark and Sohn's *World peace through world law* serves as a model of the kind of world order that is needed if the prospect of major warfare is to be eliminated from international life. Mendlovitz continues explicitly to support Clark and Sohn's work as a general editor of the WOMP volumes (Falk 1975a, xxv).

13 In this regard, it is instructive to note that Clark and Sohn's proposed Bill of Rights is not designed to guarantee the rights of citizens against their respective national governments, and that their World Development Authority was proposed not because (as with Beitz, for example) the North–

215

South gap is unjust in itself, but because they consider economic disparity as a major source of international tension (Clark and Sohn 1966, xxxvii).

14 Galtung writes: 'The argument is in favor of an entirely new, different type of nomadic existence where nobody is forced to move because the territorial units are not sufficiently self-reliant, but where the identification with the territorial unit is not so blind and parochial that it degenerates into local, national, or regional chauvinism' (1980, 330). Compare Mitrany 1943; 1975a, 168–70.

15 Vincent has, however, moved away from this position in the direction of welfare internationalism (Vincent 1986, esp. chap. 7).

9 The domestic analogy and world order proposals: typology and appraisal

1 To be fair to Lauterpacht, the main aim of his work of 1933 was not to advance a blueprint, but to combat government policies indirectly. For this purpose, he found it imperative at the least to prevent his fellow international lawyers from continuing to supply governments with a legal doctrine that in international relations certain classes of disputes were inherently non-justiciable. Lauterpacht considered this doctrine as pernicious in that in his view it legitimized governments' reluctance to recognize the beneficial role a judiciary could play in international relations. See Lauterpacht 1933, 434ff.; see also Kelsen 1934, 20.

2 It is true that some, particularly German, writers of the nineteenth century wrote in praise of war. See, for example, Moltke's letter of 11 December 1880 to Bluntschli, reprinted in Bluntschli 1879–81, 2:271–4. See also Stengel 1909, chap. 6. However, by the late nineteenth century, the belief in the moral unacceptability of an aggressive use of force appears to have become prevalent in Europe though this did not apply to colonial expansion (Ceadel 1987, 12).

3 By 'collective security' here is meant precisely that, and not 'collective defence'. See Wolfers 1962, 181–204; Claude 1971, 245–8.

4 The ILO's General Conference has a tripartite composition. Each member government nominates four persons to the Conference, of whom two are the delegates of the government, and the other two represent the employer and the workers respectively, being chosen by the government in consultation with the more representative industrial organizations. The Conference is authorized to adopt ILO conventions by two-thirds of the votes cast. However, these conventions bind only those states which ratify them. See Oppenheim 1955, 721–4. For the consultative status of non-governmental organizations at the UN, see Willetts 1982, Appendixes.

5 'Welfare internationalism', as defined earlier, is distinguished by, among other things, its rejection of the view that the desirable goals of mankind can be obtained by a single, systematic, all-embracing constitutional project. Instead of suggesting a unified scheme, the supporters of this approach stress that all forms of institution should be created to cope with multifarious problems requiring international co-operation. To the extent that most WOMP proposals envisage an all-embracing constitutional entity

at the global level, they contradict 'welfare internationalism' as defined here. None the less, they are inspired by this approach inasmuch as many of the institutions envisaged by the WOMP contributors are designed to enhance the welfare of individuals located in separate national communities.

Conclusion

1 On the one hand, it may be argued, in order for the notion of the society of states to exist it is sufficient that there prevails among those who act and talk in the name of states the assumption that states are persons forming a society under its rules. See Manning 1972. On the other hand, it may be thought, the prevalence of such an assumption is precarious unless supported by the conviction that the members of separate states form a community of a kind. See Bull 1977, 317.

2 A persuasive argument in favour of universalism is found in Linklater 1982. In the following the necessity of universalism defended by Linklater on the grounds of moral philosophy and philosophy of history is assumed.

3 This may take the form of what Bull calls 'a new mediaevalism' (1977, 254–5, 264–76, 285–6, 291–4).

4 Doyle's explanation is not entirely satisfactory since, clearly, not all pairs of liberal states have kept peace between them as a result of the operation of these factors. For example, peace between Latvia, listed as liberal between 1922 and 1934, and Chile, also counted as liberal between 1900 and 1924 and in 1932, is very unlikely to have been attributable to the factors noted by Doyle. Presumably, the geographical distance and the absence of a close relationship between them were decisive. See Doyle 1983, 210.

5 In this connection, the following comments by Linklater on Kant are of great interest: 'Republicanism [according to Kant] is a product of man's aspiration to have the freedom to which he is entitled as a rational being expressed in the practices of his community. But, when they established the republican regime men were doing more than gaining recognition of their own rational nature; they were creating a political society more able than any of its predecessors to be incorporated within an international political community. A republican constitution, in which men *qua* men are treated as ends in themselves, would by its very nature provide a core around which other states would gather to form a free federation of nations. A man who takes his place within a republican constitution can perceive himself as taking part in that historical process which will culminate in a political structure which treats all men, not merely those within the state, as ends in themselves' (1982, 115-16).

REFERENCES

Adams, H. B. 1884. *Bluntschli's life-work*. Presented to the seminary of historical and political science. Baltimore: Johns Hopkins University.

Adams, W. P. 1973. *The first American constitutions*. Translated by R. Kimber and R. Kimber. Chapel Hill: University of North Carolina Press.

Akehurst, M. 1984. *A modern introduction to international law*. 5th edn. London: Allen and Unwin.

Arbuthnott, H. and G. Edwards (eds.) 1979. *A common man's guide to the Common Market: the European Community*. London: Macmillan for the Federal Trust.

Armstrong, D. 1982. *The rise of the international organisation: a short history*. London: Macmillan.

Baker, R. S. 1922. *Woodrow Wilson and world settlement: written from his unpublished and personal material*. 2 vols. New York: Doubleday.

  1938 (ed.). *Woodrow Wilson, life and letters*. 8 vols. London: William Heinemann.

Baty, T. 1909. *International law*. London: John Murray.

  1930. *The canons of international law*. London: John Murray.

  1959. *Alone in Japan: the reminiscence of an international jurist resident in Japan 1916–1954*. Edited by M. Hasegawa. Tokyo: Maruzen.

Beals, A. C. F. 1931. *The history of peace*. London: Bell.

Beitz, C. 1979. *Political theory and international relations*. Princeton: Princeton University Press.

  1983. Cosmopolitan ideals and national sentiment. *The Journal of Philosophy* 80:591–600.

Bentwich, N. 1930. *The Mandates system*. London: Longmans, Green.

Bernazik, E. 1911. *Die Österreichischen Verfassungsgesetze*. 2nd edn. Vienna: Manzche.

Blackstone, W. 1773. *Commentaries on the laws of England in four books*. 5th edn. Oxford: Clarendon Press.

Bloom, S. 1948. *The autobiography of Sol Bloom*. New York: G. P. Putnum's Sons.

Bluntschli, J. C. 1878. *Das moderne Völkerrecht der zivilisierten Staten*. Nördingen: Beck.

  1879–81. *Gesammelte kleine Schriften*. 2 vols. Nördingen: Beck.

Borchard, E. 1934. Realism v. evangelism. *American Journal of International Law* 28: 108–17.

1938. Neutrality and unneutrality. *American Journal of International Law* 32:778–82.

1943. The place of law and courts in international relations. *American Journal of International Law* 37:46–57.

Borchard, E. and W. P. Lage 1937. *Neutrality for the United States.* London: Oxford University Press.

Bourgeois, L. 1919. *Le Pacte de 1919 et la Société des Nations.* Paris: Bibliothèque-Charpentier.

Bowett, D. W. 1958. *Self-defence in international law.* Manchester: Manchester University Press.

Brierly, J. L. 1944. *The outlook for international law.* Oxford: Clarendon Press.

1958a. The Covenant and the Charter. In Lauterpacht and Waldock 1958, 314–26.

1958b. The legislative function in international relations. In Lauterpacht and Waldock 1958, 212–29.

Briggs, H. W. 1951. In memoriam: Edwin M. Borchard, 1884–1951. *American Journal of International Law* 45: 708–9.

Bromberger, M. and S. Bromberger 1969. *Jean Monnet and the United States of Europe.* Translated by E. P. Halperin. New York: Coward-McCann.

Brown, P. M. 1916. International administration. In Moore *et al.* 1916, 312–22.

Bryan, W. J. and M. B. Bryan 1925. *The memoirs of William Jennings Bryan.* Philadelphia: United Publishers of America.

Bryce, J. 1928. *The Holy Roman Empire.* New edn. London: Macmillan.

Bryce, J. *et al.* 1917. *Proposals for the prevention of future wars.* London: Allen and Unwin.

Bull, H. 1966a. Society and anarchy in international relations. In Butterfield and Wight 1966, 35–50.

1966b. The Grotian conception of international society. In Butterfield and Wight 1966, 51–73.

1971. Order vs justice in international society. *Political Studies* 19: 269–83.

1977. *The anarchical society: a study of order in world politics.* London: Macmillan.

Bury, J. P. T. 1950. *France 1918–1940.* 2nd edn. London: Methuen.

Butterfield, H. and M. Wight (eds.) 1966. *Diplomatic investigations: essays in the theory of international politics.* London: Allen and Unwin.

Carnegie Endowment for International Peace, Division of International Law 1920. *Treaties for the advancement of peace between the United States and other powers negotiated by Honorable William Bryan, Secretary of State of the United States.* With an introduction by J. B. Scott. New York: Oxford University Press.

Carr, E. H. 1939. *The twenty years' crisis 1919–1939.* London: Macmillan.

1941. The future of international government. *Peace Aims Pamphlet* 4:1–9.

1942. *Conditions of peace.* London: Macmillan.

1945. *Nationalism and after.* London: Macmillan.

Ceadel, M. 1987. *Thinking about peace and war.* Oxford: Oxford University Press.

Churchill, W. S. 1948–54. *The Second World War.* 6 vols. London: Cassell.

Clark, G. 1940. *A memorandum with regard to a new effort to organize peace and containing a proposal for a 'federation of free peoples' in the form of a draft (with explanatory notes) of a constitution for a proposed federation.* New York: privately printed.

1950. *A plan for peace.* New York: Harper.

Clark G. and L. B. Sohn 1958. *World peace through world law.* Cambridge, Mass.: Harvard University Press.

1960. *World peace through world law.* 2nd edn. (revised). Cambridge, Mass.: Harvard University Press.

1966. *World peace through world law: two alternative plans.* 3rd edn. Cambridge, Mass.: Harvard University Press.

Clark, I. 1980. *Reform and resistance in the international order.* Cambridge: Cambridge University Press.

Claude, I. L., Jr 1962. *Power and international relations.* New York: Random House.

1971. *Swords into plowshares: the problems and progress of international organization.* 4th edn. New York: Random House.

Cobban, A. 1970. *France since the revolution, and other aspects of modern history.* London: Jonathan Cape.

Codding, A. G., Jr 1961. *The federal government of Switzerland.* London: Allen and Unwin.

Cohen, R. 1981. *International politics: the rules of the game.* London: Longman.

Coudenhove Kalergi, Count 1926. *Pan-Europa.* Vienna: Paneuropa-Verlag.

Cousins, N. and J. G. Clifford (eds.) 1975. *Memoirs of a man: Grenville Clark.* Collected by M. C. Dimond. New York: Norton.

Curry, W. B. 1939. *The case for federal union.* Harmondsworth: Penguin.

Dalfen, C. M. 1968. The world court: reform or re-appraisal. *The Canadian Yearbook of International Law.* 6:212–25.

de Smith, S. A. 1973. *Constitutional and administrative law.* 2nd edn. Harmondsworth: Penguin Education.

Deutsch, K. W. *et al.* 1957. *Political community and the North Atlantic area: international organization in the light of historical experience.* Princeton: Princeton University Press.

Dickinson, E. D. 1916–17. The analogy between natural persons and international persons in the law of nations. *The Yale Law Journal* 26:564–91.

Dickinson, G. L. 1915. *After the war.* London: Fifield.

Dodge, D. L. [1815] 1905. *War inconsistent with the religion of Jesus Christ.* With an introduction by E. D. Mead. Boston: Ginn.

Donelan, M. 1983. Grotius and the image of war. *Millennium* 12:233–43.

Doxey, M. P. 1980. *Economic sanctions and international enforcement.* 2nd edn. London: Macmillan for the Royal Institute of International Affairs.

Doyle, M. W. 1983. Kant, liberal legacies, and foreign affairs. *Philosophy and Public Affairs* 12:205–34, 323–52.

Dumont, J. (ed.) 1726–31. *Corps universel diplomatique du droit des gens.* 8 vols. Amsterdam: Brunel.

Durkheim, E. 1959. *Socialism and Saint-Simon.* Edited with an introduction by A. W. Gouldener. Translated by C. Sattler. London: Routledge and Kegan Paul.

Eherenberg, V. 1960. *The Greek state*. Oxford: Blackwell.

Engel, S. and R. A. Métall (eds.) 1964. *Law, state and international legal order*. Knoxville: University of Tennessee Press.

Falk, R. A. 1968. *Legal order in a violent world*. Princeton: Princeton University Press.

1970. *The status of law in international society*. Princeton: Princeton University Press.

1971. *This endangered planet: prospects and proposals for human survival*. New York: Vintage Books.

1975a. *A study of future worlds*. New York: Free Press.

1975b. A new paradigm for international legal studies: prospects and proposals. *The Yale Law Journal* 84:969–1021.

1981. *Human rights and state sovereignty*. New York: Holmes and Meier.

Falk, R. A. and C. E. Black (eds.) 1970. *The future of international legal order*. Vol. 2. Princeton: Princeton University Press.

Falk, R. A. and S. H. Mendlovitz 1964. Towards a warless world: one legal formula to achieve transition. *The Yale Law Journal* 73: 399–424.

1966 (eds.). *The strategy for world order*. 4 vols. New York: World Law Fund.

Forsyth, M. G. 1981. *Unions of states: the theory and practice of confederation*. Leicester: Leicester University Press.

Forsyth, M. G., M. Keens-Soper and P. Savigear 1970. *The theory of international relations: selected texts from Gentili to Treitschke*. London: Allen and Unwin.

Franck, T. M. 1970. Who killed Article 2(4)? Or: changing norms governing the use of force by states. *American Journal of International Law* 64:809–37.

Friedmann, W. 1941. *What's wrong with international law?* London: Watts.

1964. *The changing structure of international law*. London: Stevens.

1970. The relevance of international law to the processes of economic and social development. In Falk and Black 1970, 3–35.

Fromkin, D. 1981. *The independence of nations*. New York: Praeger.

Gallie, W. B. 1978. *Philosophers of peace and war*. Cambridge: Cambridge University Press.

Galtung, J. 1980. *The true worlds*. New York: Free Press.

Gideonse, H. D., R. B. Fosdick, W. F. Ogburn and F. L. Schuman 1946. *The politics of atomic energy*. New York: Woodrow Wilson Foundation.

Gladwyn, Lord 1972. *The memoirs of Lord Gladwyn*. London: Weidenfeld and Nicolson.

Greer, T. 1965. *What Roosevelt thought: the social and political ideas of Franklin D. Roosevelt*. East Lansing, Michigan: Michigan State University Press.

Grey of Fallodon, Viscount 1928. *Twenty-five years, 1892–1916*. 3 vols. London: Hodder and Stoughton.

Groom, A. J. R. and P. Taylor (eds.) 1975. *Functionalism: theory and practice in international relations*. London: University of London Press.

Grotius, H. [1646] 1925. *De jure belli ac pacis*. Translated by F. W. Kelsey. Oxford: Clarendon Press.

Haas, E. B. 1958. *The uniting of Europe: political, social and economical forces 1950–57*. London: Stevens.

1961. International integration: the European and the universal process. *International Organization* 15:366–92.

1964. *Beyond the nation-state: functionalism and international organization*. Stanford, Calif.: Stanford University Press.

1968. Technocracy, pluralism and the New Europe. Reprinted in Nye 1968, 149–76.

1970. The study of regional integration: reflections on the joy and anguish of pretheorizing. *International Organization* 24:607–46.

1976. Turbulent fields and the theory of regional integration. *International Organization* 30:173–212.

Halévy, E. 1937. *A history of the English people in 1815*. 2 vols. London: Penguin Books.

Hall, W. E. 1895. *A treatise on international law*. 4th edn. Oxford: Clarendon Press.

1904. *A treatise on international law*. 5th edn. by J. B. Atlay. Oxford: Clarendon Press.

1909. *A treatise on international law*. 6th edn. by J. B. Atlay. Oxford: Clarendon Press.

Hankey, M. 1921. Diplomacy by conference. *The Round Table*. 42:287–311.

Harrod, R. F. 1951. *The life of John Maynard Keynes*. London: Macmillan.

Hemleben, S. J. 1943. *Plans for world peace through six centuries*. Chicago: University of Chicago Press.

Henderson, W. O. 1962. *The genesis of the common market*. London: Cass.

Henkin, L. 1971. The reports of the death of Article 2(4) are greatly exaggerated. *American Journal of International Law*. 65:544–8.

Higgins, R. 1969. Policy and impartiality: the uneasy relationship in international law. *International Organization* 23:914–31.

Hinsley, F. H. 1967. *Power and the pursuit of peace: theory and practice in the history of relations between states*. Cambridge: Cambridge University Press.

Hobbes, T. [1651] 1962. *Leviathan*. Edited and abridged with an introduction by J. Plamenatz. London: Collins.

Holbraad, C. 1970. *The Concert of Europe: a study in German and British international theory 1815–1914*. London: Longman.

Holland, T. E. 1898. *Studies in international law*. Oxford: Clarendon Press.

Horsefield, J. K. 1969. *The International Monetary Fund 1945–1965*. Washington, DC: International Monetary Fund.

Hughes, C. J. 1962. *The parliament of Switzerland*. London: Cassell.

Hull, C. 1948. *The memoirs of Cordell Hull*. 2 vols. London: Hodder and Stoughton.

Ionescu, G. (ed.) 1976. *The political thought of Saint-Simon*. London: Oxford University Press.

Jacobs, F. G. and L. N. Brown, 1983. *The Court of Justice of the European Communities*. 2nd edn. London: Sweet and Maxwell.

James, A. M. 1969. *The politics of peace-keeping*. London: Chatto and Windus for the International Institute for Strategic Studies.

1973 (ed.). *The bases of international order*. London: Oxford University Press.

1986. *Sovereign statehood: the basis of international society*. London: Allen and Unwin.

Jay, W. [1842] 1919. *War and peace: the evils of the first and a plan for preserving the last*. With an introduction by J. B. Scott. New York: Oxford University Press.

Jellinek, G. 1922. *Allgemeine Staatslehre*. 3rd edn by W. Jellinek. Berlin: Springer.

Jenks, C. W. 1958. *The common law of mankind*. London: Stevens.

1963. *Law, freedom and welfare*. London: Stevens.

1969. *A new world of law? A study of the creative imagination in international law*. London: Longman.

1970. *Social justice in the law of nations: the ILO impact after fifty years*. London: Oxford University Press.

Johnsen, J. E. (compiler) 1948. *Federal world government*. The reference shelf 20.

Joynt, C. B. and P. E. Corbett 1978. *Theory and reality in world politics*. London: Macmillan.

Keal, P. 1983. *Unspoken rules and superpower dominance*. London: Macmillan.

Keeton, G. 1939. *National sovereignty and international order*. London: Peace Book Company.

Kelsen, H. 1934. The legal progress and international order. *The New Commonwealth Research Bureau Publications*, series A. no. 1.

1967. *Principles of international law*. 2nd edn. Revised and edited by R. W. Tucker. New York: Holt, Rinehart and Winston.

Kothari, R. 1974. *Footsteps into the future: diagnosis of the present world and a design for an alternative*. Amsterdam: North-Holland Publishing.

Kuhn, T. 1962. *The structure of scientific revolutions*. Chicago: University of Chicago Press.

Kunz, J. L. 1968. *The changing law of nations*. Ohio State University Press.

Ladd, W. [1840] 1916. *An essay on a congress of nations for the adjustment of international disputes without resort to arms*. Reprinted from the original of 1840 with an introduction by J. B. Scott. New York: Oxford University Press.

La Fontaine, H. 1911. The existing elements of a constitution of the United States of the World. *International Conciliation* 47:3–13.

Lagos, G. and H. H. Godoy 1977. *Revolution of being: a Latin American view of the future*. New York: Free Press.

Latané, J. H. (ed.) 1932. *Development of the League of Nations idea: documents and correspondence of Theodore Marburg*. 2 vols. New York: Macmillan.

Lauterpacht, H. 1927. *Private law sources and analogies of international law (with special reference to international arbitration)*. London: Longmans, Green.

1933. *The function of law in the international community*. Oxford: Clarendon Press.

1937. The legal aspect. In Manning [1937] 1972, 135–69.

Lauterpacht, H. and C. H. M . Waldock (eds.) 1958. *The basis of obligation in international law and other papers by the late James Leslie Brierly*. Oxford: Clarendon Press.

Lawrence, T. J. 1895. *The principles of international law*. Boston: D. C. Heath.

1899. *The principles of international law*. 2nd edn. Boston: D. C. Heath.

1900. *The principles of international law*. 3rd edn. Boston: D. C. Heath.

1910. *The principles of international law*. 4th edn. Boston: D. C. Heath.

1913. *The principles of international law*. 5th edn. Boston: D. C. Heath.

League to Enforce Peace 1916. *Enforced peace: proceedings of the first annual national assemblage of the League to Enforce Peace, Washington, May 26–27, 1916*.

Lees, J. D., R. M. Maidment and M. Tappin 1982. *American politics today*. Manchester: Manchester University Press.

Leuchtenburg, W. E. 1963. *Franklin D. Roosevelt and the New Deal 1932–1940*. New York: Harper and Row.

Linklater, A. 1982. *Men and citizens in the theory of international relations*. London: Macmillan/London School of Economics and Political Science.

Lipgens, W. 1982. *A history of European integration*. Vol. 1, *1945–1947: The formation of the European unity movement*, with contributions by Wilfried Loth and Alan Milward. Translated from German by P. S. Falla and A. J. Ryder. Oxford: Clarendon Press.

Liszt, F. von 1915. *Das Völkerrecht*, 10th edn. Berlin: Springer.

1918. *Das Völkerrecht*, 11th edn. Berlin: Springer.

Lorimer, J. 1877. Le problème final du droit international. *Revue de droit international* 9:161–206.

1884. *The institutes of the law of nations*. 2 vols. Edinburgh: Blackwood.

Lough, J. and M. Lough 1978. *An introduction to nineteenth century France*. London: Longman.

Luard, E. 1982. *A history of the United Nations*. Vol. 1. London: Macmillan.

Manning, C. A. W. 1936. The future of the collective system. *Problems of peace*, 10th series, *Anarchy or world order*. London: Allen and Unwin. 152–77.

1937. Some suggested conclusions. In Manning [1937] 1972, 169–90.

[1937] 1972 (ed.). *Peaceful change: an international problem*. Reprint of the 1937 edn with a new introduction for the Garland edition by C. Marzani. New York: Garland Publishing.

1972a. *The nature of international society*. Re-issue. London: Macmillan.

1972b. The legal framework in a world of change. In Porter 1972, 301–35.

Markham, F. M. H. (ed. and tr.) 1952. *Henri Comte de Saint-Simon (1760–1825): selected writings*. Oxford: Blackwell.

May, A. J. 1951. *The Hapsburg monarchy: 1867–1914*. Cambridge, Mass.: Harvard University Press.

Mayall, J. 1975. Functionalism and international economic relations. In Groom and Taylor 1975, 250–77.

Mazrui, A. A. 1976. *A world federation of cultures: an African perspective*. New York: Free Press.

McDougal, M. S. and associates 1960. *Studies in world public order*. New Haven: Yale University Press.

McWhinney, E. 1964. *Peaceful coexistence and Soviet–Western international law*. Leyden: A. W. Sijthoff.

Meyer, C., Jr 1948. The United Nations lack authority and power. Reprinted in Johnsen 1948, 85–94.

1980. *Facing reality: from world federalism to the CIA.* New York: Harper and Row.

Miller, D. H. 1928. *The drafting of the Covenant.* 2 vols. New York: G. P. Putnum's Sons.

Mitrany, D. 1943. *A working peace system, an argument for the functional development of international organization.* London: Oxford University Press for the Royal Institute of International Affairs.

1966. *A working peace system.* Published in co-operation with the Society for a World Service Federation. Chicago: Quadrangle Books.

1975a. *The functional theory of politics.* Introduction by Paul Taylor. London: Martin Robertson/London School of Economics and Political Science.

1975b. The prospect of integration: federal or functional? Reprinted in Groom and Taylor 1975, 53–78.

Monnet, J. 1978. *Memoirs.* Translated by R. Mayne. Foreword by R. Jenkins. London: Collins.

Moore, J. B. 1933. An appeal to reason. *Foreign Affairs* 11:547–88.

Moore, J. B., C. Tower, G. G. Wilson, P. M. Brown and D. J. Hill 1916. *Symposium on international law: its origin, obligation, and future.* Reprinted from *American Philosophical Society Proceedings* 55:291–329.

Morgenthau, H. J. 1929. *Die internationale Rechtspflege, ihr Wesen und ihre Grenzen.* Leipzig: Robert Noske.

1946. *Scientific man versus power politics.* Chicago: University of Chicago Press.

1948. *Politics among nations.* New York: Alfred A. Knopf.

1964. The impartiality of the international police. In Engel and Métall 1964, 210–23.

1973. *Politics among nations.* 5th edn. New York: Knopf.

1977. Fragment of an intellectual autobiography: 1904–1932. In Thompson and Meyers 1977, 1–17.

Mowat, R. B. 1922. *A history of European diplomacy 1815–1914.* London: Edward Arnold.

Nardin, T. 1983. *Law, morality and the relations of states.* Princeton: Princeton University Press.

Newton, A. P. 1923. *Federal and unified constitutions.* London: Longmans.

Nicholas, H. G. 1975. *The United Nations as a political institution.* 5th edn. London: Oxford University Press.

Nijhoff, M (ed.) 1915. *War obviated by an international police: a series of essays written in various countries.* The Hague: Nijhoff.

Nippold, O. 1907. *Die Fortbildung des Verfahrens in völkerrechtlichen Streitigkeiten.* Leipzig: Duncker and Humblot.

1908. *Die zweite Haager Friedenskonferenz.* 2 vols. Leipzig: Duncker and Humblot.

[1917] 1923. *The development of international law after the war.* Translation by A. S. Hershey of *Die Gestaltung des Völkerrechts nach dem Weltkriege* (1917). Oxford: Clarendon Press.

Northedge, F. S. 1976. *The international political system.* London: Faber and Faber.

Nye, J. S., Jr 1968 (ed.). *International regionalism*. Boston: Little, Brown.
1971. *Peace in parts*. Boston: Little, Brown.

Oechsli, W. 1886. *Quellenbuch zur Schweizergeschichte*. Zürich: F. Schulthers.
1922. *History of Switzerland 1499–1914*. Translated from German by E. Paul and C. Paul. Cambridge: Cambridge University Press.

Oppenheim, L. 1905–6. *International law*. 2 vols. London: Longmans, Green.
[1911] 1921. *The future of international law*. Translation by J. P. Pate of *Die Zukunft des Völkerrechts* (1911). Oxford: Clarendon Press.
1912. *International law*. 2 vols. 2nd edn. London: Longmans, Green.
1914 (ed.). *The collected papers of John Westlake on public international law*. Cambridge: Cambridge University Press.
1920–1. *International law*. 2 vols. 3rd edn by R. F. Roxburgh. London: Longmans, Green.
1952. *International law*. 2 vols. 7th edn by H. Lauterpacht. London: Longman.
1955. *International law*. Vol. 1, 8th edn by H. Lauterpacht. London: Longman.

Palmer, G. E. H. (compiler) 1934. *Consultation in the British Commonwealth: a handbook of the methods and practice of communication and consultation between the members of the British Commonwealth of Nations*. With an introduction by Professor A. Berriedale Keith on the constitutional development of the British Empire in regard to the Dominions and India from 1887 to 1933. London: Oxford University Press.

Parry, C. (ed.) 1969. *The consolidated treaty series*. Vol. 27. Dobbs Ferry, New York: Oceana.

Penrose, E. F. 1953. *Economic planning for the peace*. Princeton: Princeton University Press.

Pentland, C. 1973. *International theory and European integration*. London: Faber and Faber.

Phillimore, W. 1920. *Schemes for maintaining general peace*. Foreign Office handbooks, no. 160. London: HM Stationery Office.

Phillips, O. Hood. 1967. *Constitutional and administrative law*. 4th edn. London: Sweet and Maxwell.

Porter, B. (ed.) 1972. *The Aberystwyth papers: international politics 1919–1969*. London: Oxford University Press.

Pritchett, C. H. 1977. *The American constitution*. 3rd edn. New York: McGraw-Hill.

Pufendorf, S. [1688] 1935. *De jure naturae et gentium*. Translated by C. H. Oldfather and W. A. Oldfather. Oxford: Clarendon Press.

Rappard, W. E. 1925. *International relations as viewed from Geneva*. New Haven: Yale University Press.

Rees, A. *et al.* 1819. *The cyclopaedia: or universal dictionary of arts, science, and literature*. 39 vols. London: Longman.

Renouvin, R. 1949. *L'Idée de fédération Européenne dans la pénsee politique du XIXe siècle*. Oxford: Clarendon Press.

Reves, E. 1946. *The anatomy of peace*. London: Allen and Unwin.

Reynolds, P. A. and E. J. Hughes 1976. *The historian as diplomat. Charles Kingsley Webster and the United Nations 1939–1946*. London: Martin Robertson.

Röling, B. V. A. 1960. *International law in an expanded world*. Amsterdam: Djambatna.

Roosevelt, E. 1950. *This I remember*. London: Hutchinson.

Root, E. 1908. The sanction of international law. *American Journal of International Law* 2:451–7.

Russell, R. B. 1958. *A history of the United Nations Charter: the role of the United States 1940-1945*. Assisted by J. E. Muther. Washington, DC: The Brookings Institution.

Ryder, T. T. B. 1965. *Koine eirene: general peace and local independence in ancient Greece*. London: Oxford University Press for the University of Hull.

Sabine, G. H. 1963. *A history of political thought*. 3rd edn. London: Harrap.

Saint-Pierre, Abbot [1712] 1714. *A project for settling an everlasting peace in Europe*. London: printed for J. W.

Saint-Simon, C.-H. de [1814] 1952. *The reorganization of the European community*. In Markham 1952, 26–68.

Schiffer, W. 1954. *The legal community of mankind*. New York: Columbia University Press.

Schmitt, C. 1939. *Völkerrechtliche Grossraumordnung mit Interventionsverbot für raumfremde Mächte*. Berlin: Deutscher Rechtsverlag.

Schücking, W. [1912] 1918. *The international union of the Hague Conferences*. Translation by C. G. Fenwick of *Der Staatenverband der Haager Konferenzen* (1912). Oxford: Clarendon Press.

Schuman, F. L. 1933. *International politics*. New York: McGraw-Hill.

1945. The dilemma of the peace-seekers. *The American Political Science Review* 39:12–30.

1946. Toward the world state. In Gideonse *et al*. 1946, 35–55.

1954 *The commonwealth of man: an inquiry into power politics and world government*. London: Robert Hale.

1969. *International politics*. 7th edn. New York: McGraw-Hill.

Schwartz, B. 1955 *American constitutional law*. Cambridge. Cambridge University Press.

Schwarzenberger, G. 1936a. *William Ladd*. Preface by J. B. Scott. 2nd edn. London: Constable.

1936b. *The League of Nations and world order: a treatise on the principle of universality in the theory and practice of the League of Nations*. London: Constable.

1941. *Power politics: an introduction to the study of international relations and post-war planning*. London: Jonathan Cape.

1943. *International law and totalitarian lawlessness*. London: Jonathan Cape.

1964. *Power politics: a study of world society*. 3rd edn. London: Stevens.

Scott, J. B. 1909. *The Hague Peace Conferences of 1899 and 1907*. 2 vols. Baltimore: Johns Hopkins Press.

1920 (ed.). *The proceedings of the Hague Peace Conferences: translation of official texts, the conference of 1899*. New York: Oxford University Press.

Seymour, E. (ed.) 1926. *The intimate papers of Colonel House, arranged as a narrative*. 4 vols. London: Ernest Benn.

Shackleton, R. 1949. Montesquieu, Bolingbroke, and the separation of powers. *French Studies* 3:25–38.

Sherwood, R. E. 1948. *Roosevelt and Hopkins: an intimate history*. New York: Harper.

 1949. *The White House papers of Harry L. Hopkins*. 2 vols. London: Eyre and Spottiswoode.

Simmel, G. 1955. *Conflict*, translated by K. H. Wolff; and *The web of group-affiliations*, translated by R. Bendix, with a foreword by E. C. Hughes. New York: Free Press.

Smuts, J. C. 1918. *The League of Nations: a practical suggestion*. London: Hodder and Stoughton.

Snell, J. L. 1976. *The democratic movement in Germany 1789–1914*. Edited and completed by H. A. Schmitt. Chapel Hill: University of North Carolina Press.

Spinelli, A. 1966. *The Eurocrats: conflict and crisis in the European Community*. Translated by C. G. Haines. Baltimore: Johns Hopkins Press.

Spinoza, B. [1677] 1958. *The political works*. Edited and translated by A. G. Wernham. Oxford: Clarendon Press.

Stein, E. 1981. Lawyers, judges and the making of transnational constitution. *American Journal of International Law* 75:1–27.

Stengel, K. von 1909. *Weltstaat und Friedensproblem*. Berlin: Reichl.

Stone, J. 1958. *Aggression and world order: a critique of United Nations theories of aggression*. London: Stevens.

 1959. *Legal controls of international conflict: a treatise on the dynamics of disputes-and war-law*. 2nd impression, revised. London: Stevens.

 1968. De victoribus victis: the International Law Commission and imposed treaties of peace. *Virginia Journal of International Law* 8:356–73.

 1977. *Conflict through consensus: United Nations approaches to aggression*. Baltimore: Johns Hopkins University Press.

Suganami, H. 1983. The structure of institutionalism: an anatomy of British mainstream International Relations. *International Relations* 7:2363–81.

 1986. Reflections on the domestic analogy: the case of Bull, Beitz and Linklater. *Review of International Studies* 12: 145–68.

Taft, W. H. 1915. *United States Supreme Court the prototype of a world court*. Judicial settlement of international disputes, 21.

Taylor, P. 1971. *International co-operation today: the European and the universal pattern*. London: Elek.

Taylor, P. and A. J. R. Groom 1975. Introduction: functionalism and international relations. In Groom and Taylor 1975, 1–6.

Taylor, T. 1978a. Power politics. In T. Taylor 1978b, 122–40.

 1978b (ed.). *Approaches and theory in international relations*. London: Longman.

Thompson, K. and R. J. Meyers (eds.) 1977. *Truth and tragedy: a tribute to Hans Morgenthau*. Washington, DC: The New Republic Book Company.

Thomson, D., E. Meyer and A. Briggs 1945. *Patterns of peacemaking*. London: Kegan Paul, Trench, Trubner.

Treitschke, H. von [1897–98] 1963. *Politics*. Abridged, edited and with an introduction by Hans Kohn. New York: Harcourt, Brace and World.

Trevelyan, G. M. 1937. *Grey of Fallodon, being the life of Sir Edward Grey afterwards Viscount Grey of Fallodon*. London: Longmans, Green.

Vattel, E. de [1758] 1916. *Le droit des gens*. Translated by C. G. Fenwick. Washington, DC: Carnegie Institute of Washington.

Verdross, A. 1954. General international law and the United Nations Charter. *International Affairs* 30:342–8.

Vincent, R. J. 1974. *Nonintervention and international order*. Princeton: Princeton University Press.

1986. *Human rights and international relations*. Cambridge: Cambridge University Press in association with the Royal Institute of International Affairs.

Waechter, M. 1912. *How to make war impossible: the United States of Europe*. London: Twentieth Century Press.

No date. The European Unity League: an instrument for carrying out the greatest and most important social reform. London: European Unity League.

Walters, F. P. 1952. *A history of the League of Nations*. 2 vols. London: Oxford University Press.

Waltz, K. N. 1959. *Man, the state and war*. New York: Columbia University Press.

1979. *Theory of international politics*. Reading, Mass.: Addison-Wesley.

Walzer, M. 1978. *Just and unjust wars*. London: Allen Lane.

Watson, J. S. 1980. A realistic jurisprudence of international law. *The Yearbook of World Affairs* 34:265–85.

Wehberg, H. [1912] 1918. *The problem of an international court of justice*. Translation by C. G. Fenwick of *Das Problem eines internationalen Staatengerichtshofes* (1912). Oxford: Clarendon Press.

Westlake, J. 1904. *International law*. Part I, *Peace*. Cambridge: Cambridge University Press.

Wheare, K. C. 1963. *Federal government*. 4th edn. London: Oxford University Press.

Wight, M. 1973. The balance of power and international order. In James 1973, 85–115.

Willetts, P. (ed.) 1982. *Pressure groups in the global system: the transnational relations of issue-oriented non-governmental organizations*. London: Frances Pinter.

Wilson, E. 1960. *To the Finland Station*. London: Collins.

Wilson, W. 1899. *The state, elements of historical and practical politics*. Revised edn. London: D. C. Heath.

Wolfers, A. 1962. *Discord and collaboration: essays on international politics*. Baltimore: Johns Hopkins Press.

Wolff, C. [1764] 1934. *Jus gentium methodo scientifica pertractatum*. Translated by J. H. Drake. Oxford: Clarendon Press.

Woolf, L. S. [1916] 1971. *International government*. New York: Garland Publishing.

1940. *The war for peace*. London: Routledge.

Worcester, N. 1822. *A solemn review of the custom of war*. The Society for the Promotion of Permanent and Universal Peace. Tract 1. London.

Wright, M. 1984. Central but ambiguous: states and international theory. *Review of International Studies* 10:233–7.

York, E. 1919. *Leagues of nations, ancient, mediaeval, and modern.* London: Swarthmore.

Zimmern, A. 1939. *The League of Nations and the rule of law 1918–1935.* 2nd edn. London: Macmillan.

INDEX OF PERSONAL NAMES

SUBJECT INDEX

adjudication
    compulsory, 65, 168, *see also*
        arbitration, compulsory; compulsory
        jurisdiction
    international court of justice, 68–9,
        70–1, 80, 89–90, 168, 201
    International Court of Justice (ICJ),
        126, 131, 133, 182, 184
    Permanent Court of International
        Justice, 63, 80, 90, 92, 97, 126
    world court, 156
American Peace Society, 22, 49
analogy, definitions of, 24
appeasement, 96
arbitration
    in ancient Greece, 33
    compulsory, 105, 168, *see also*
        adjudication, compulsory;
        compulsory jurisdiction
    diplomatic school on, 17, 71, 72, 74–5,
        168
    domestic analogy in, 32–3, 76
    Hague system of, 35
    natural-law writers on, 20
    Permanent Court of Arbitration, 62–3
    treaty(-ies), 63, 172
    voluntary, 195, 205, 206
Atlantic Charter, 118
Austro-Hungarian Empire
    Delegations, 55, 198
    Ministry of War, 55

balance of power, 15, 16, 133, 161
    domestic analogy and, 30–1
Bangladesh, secession of, 189
bellum justum, 5
British Empire, 120
    Committee of Imperial Defence, 85,
        111, 201
    Conference system of, 84–5, 201
    Imperial Conference, 85
    War Council, 85
British parliamentary system, 130, *see
    also*, England, Parliament
Bruce Report, 119–20, 126

Bryan Treaties, 35, 83–4, 86
Bundesreich *v*. Staatenbund, 58
Bundesstaat *v*. Staatenbund, 34

central guidance mechanism, 149, 157
CIA, 134, 163
civil war, 181, 189
collective security, 106, 112, 117–18, 174,
    178–81, 182, 183–4, 194–5
    indivisibility of peace, 86, 88–9
    under the League and the UN, 178
    regional, 96, 181
    security guarantee, 86–9
    see also executive, international; law
        enforcement; police force; sanctions
community-building, 98–100, 111,
    139–41, 162
compulsory adjudication, *see under*
    adjudication
compulsory arbitration, *see under*
    arbitration
compulsory investigation
    of labour and international disputes,
        83, *see also* inquiry by commission
compulsory (obligatory) jurisdiction, 69,
    80, 112, 131, 168–73, 182, 194, 205,
    see also adjudiction, compulsory;
    arbitration, compulsory
Concert of Europe, 2, 61, 85–6, 118, 127,
    197, 201
confederaton(s), 34, 46, 64, 65, 85, 87,
    166
    confederal, 97, 116
    see also federation(s)
conference(s)
    ad hoc, 2, 61, 197
    diplomatic, 44, 48, 54, 64
    natural-law writers on, 20
    regular, 84–6, 195, 205
Congo, United Nations force in the, 177
Congress of Vienna, 21–2, 41, 187–8
constitutional independence, 36, 189, *see
    also* sovereignty
constitutionalism, 2, 197, 202
    international, 101

233